DATE DUE

Leadership in Continuing and Distance Education in Higher Education

Related Titles of Interest

Successful College Teaching: Problem-Solving Strategies of Distinguished Professors
Sharon A. Baiocco and Jamie N. DeWaters
ISBN: 0-205-26654-1

Faculty Work and Public Trust: Restoring the Value of Teaching and Public Service in American Academic Life
James S. Fairweather
ISBN: 0-205-17948-7

College Teaching Abroad: A Handbook of Strategies for Successful Cross-Cultural Exchanges
Pamela Gale George
ISBN: 0-205-15767-X

Emblems of Quality in Higher Education: Developing and Sustaining High-Quality Programs
Jennifer Grant Haworth and Clifton F. Conrad
ISBN: 0-205-19546-6

The Art of Writing for Publication
Kenneth T. Henson
ISBN: 0-205-15769-6

Revitalizing General Education in a Time of Scarcity: A Navigational Chart for Administrators and Faculty
Sandra L. Kanter, Zelda F. Gamson, and Howard B. London
ISBN: 0-205-26257-0

Multicultural Course Transformation in Higher Education: A Broader Truth
Ann Intili Morey and Margie K. Kitano (Editors)
ISBN: 0-205-16068-9

Sexual Harassment on Campus: A Guide for Administrators, Faculty, and Students
Bernice R. Sandler and Robert J. Shoop
ISBN: 0-205-16712-8

Shaping the College Curriculum: Academic Plans in Action
Joan S. Stark and Lisa R. Lattuca
ISBN: 0-205-16706-3

For more information or to purchase a book, please call 1-800-278-3525.

Leadership in Continuing and Distance Education in Higher Education

Cynthia C. Jones Shoemaker
The George Washington University

Allyn and Bacon
Boston • London • Toronto • Sydney • Tokyo • Singapore

Executive editor and associate publisher: Stephen D. Dragin
Series editorial assistant: Elizabeth McGuire
Manufacturing buyer: David Suspanic

Library of Congress Cataloging-in-Publication Data

Shoemaker, Cynthia
    Leadership in continuing and distance education in higher education/Cynthia C.
Jones Shoemaker.
      p. cm.
    includes bibliographical references and index.
    ISBN 0-205-26823-4
    1. Continuing education—United States. 2. Distance education—United States. 3.
Educational leadership—United States. 4. Continuing education—United States—
Finance. 5. Education, Higher—United States—Planning. I. Title.
LC5251.S52 1998   97-43211
374′.973—DC21   CIP

Printed in the United States of America
10 9 8 7 6 5 4 3 2 1   02 01 00 99 98

This book is dedicated to all who help adult students believe the following (from the words of Edward O. Wilson, two-time Pulitzer Prize winner and biologist): "You are capable of more than you know. Choose a goal that seems right for you and strive to be the best, however hard the path. Aim high. Behave honorably. Prepare to be alone at times, and endure failure. Persist! The world needs all you can give."

It is also dedicated to my husband, Douglas Shoemaker, and to our children, Roger, Michael, Steven, Allison, Peter, and Kate. May continuous learning enrich their lives as it has ours.

Contents

List of Figures

Preface

Adults across the land are continuing their education. Whether they do this in a traditional classroom or at a distance doesn't seem to matter to many of them. The desire for learning is strong and essential as the global society moves into the Information Age. The powerful demographic force of the "Baby Boom" population (those born between 1946 and 1964) deciding to go "back to school" is also fueling the growth of continuing and distance education. This group is being joined by their children and "Generation X," creating a second surge in education demographics. Adult students, ages 23 to 75+, may seek to enhance their current or new careers or to better understand the rapid changes in their world. How will institutions of higher learning respond to these demographic and societal trends? The answers will vary depending on their own unique strengths and special offerings.

Higher education has an important role to play in the development of knowledge workers. As Peter Drucker says in *The Age of Social Transformation* (p. 62):

> By the end of this century knowledge workers will make up a third or more of the work force in the United States—as large a proportion as manufacturing workers ever made up, except in wartime. The majority of them will be paid at least as well as, or better than, manufacturing workers ever were. And the new jobs offer much greater opportunities.
>
> But ... the great majority of the new jobs require qualifications the industrial worker does not possess and is poorly equipped to acquire. They require a great deal of formal education and the ability to acquire and apply theoretical knowledge. They require a dif-

ferent approach to work and a different mind-set. Above all, they require a habit of continuous learning.

Many institutions of higher education today have some form of a Division of Continuing Education to address the adult market, which is much larger than the 18- to 22-year-old traditional college youth market (which declined in enrollment in the 1990s due to birth trends). Some predictors see all universities and colleges as eventually offering three major services: Undergraduate Education, Graduate Education, and Continuing Education (for credit and noncredit), with a provost or chief administrator for each.

However, this eventuality will require thoughtful, informed guidance. There is little education for leadership in the field of continuing education, which calls for an understanding of the academic culture and mores, as well as excellent modern marketing and management skills. This combination of academic, marketing, and management expertise is vital to provide programs for a fast-changing market.

In my 23 years of administering and teaching in continuing education at four institutions of higher education and talking to thousands of adult students, I have seen countless good-hearted practitioners "reinvent the wheel" trying to respond appropriately and effectively to the changing needs in this area. There has been very little material for them to consult. I developed this book to fill that resource void. The book would be appropriate for use as a guide by practicing higher education professionals—administrators and program people and their staffs—who are launching or expanding and strengthening continuing education and distance learning at their universities and colleges. It could also be used as a text in master's degree programs in higher education administration and leadership.

The book provides a framework for leadership in the combined fields of higher education, management, and marketing. It is divided into three sections. Section I, Challenges and Changes in Continuing Education, has chapters reminding academia of how much students are helped by their efforts and listing some of the current challenges to doing so. Section II, Leadership for the 21st Century in Continuing Education, has chapters on participative management and encouraging creativity. Leadership, planning, decision making, team building and empowerment, motivation, and problem solving are addressed. The areas of noncredit programs and the wonderful expansions possible through distance education are also discussed. The third section, Marketing and Finances in Continuing Education, discusses some of the current realities and future educational needs in this fast-growing field. Each of the twelve chapters of the book concludes with a bibliography of both works that were consulted in the preparation of the text and additional related resources that may be of interest to the reader.

Much of this book can be related to the Malcolm Baldridge Awards criteria: Finding out what customers need; establishing a vision, mission, and strategy and interpreting it; planning that is not done in a vacuum but includes projections of future adult student/customers and adult student markets to develop key goals; plans that are based on data, carefully selected, managed and used; and adult student/customer satisfaction and relationship enhancement. There are more details on this in the section on "Evaluating the Institution's 'User-Friendliness'" in Chapter 11.

I would like to acknowledge the valuable assistance of Douglas Shoemaker and David Burt, who share my belief that educating adult students is a worthwhile line of work; and of Roger Whitaker, who read and commented on three of the chapters. My appreciation also goes to Thomas S. Gross, of Johns Hopkins, for his comments on the manuscript and to my other two reviewers (who remain anonymous).

A special word of thanks goes to the editorial and production staffs at Allyn and Bacon, especially to Stephen Dragin for his continuous encouragement and sense of the future.

CCJS

► Section I

Challenges and Changes in Continuing Education

There are many new challenges in education in the 1990s, and continuing adult education and lifelong learning are on the leading edge. People are living longer; they can expect to have a number of jobs and careers; and continual learning is a must for a long, productive and fulfilled life. Institutions of higher education are rethinking who they are and what they are about as it becomes more and more evident that there are more adults than young people ages 18 to 22 and that ever larger numbers of them want to, and need to, learn. Does the institution provide "education services" of many kinds or only traditional in-class instruction for one age group? This is a question many institutions are addressing. By 1980, 72% of the institutions of higher education had noncredit programs for adults, and in the 1990s this number was even higher.

There are two major changes occurring in society today that impact continuing education, and, indeed, all formal education. These changes are also evident in the workplace. The first is the on-going transition into the Information Age, which has resulted in technology not only being used to address problems but also being reviewed as an approach to enhancing the entire mission of an organization or enterprise. One example of this transition can be seen in federal agencies and corporations installing chief information officers (CIOs) who will sit at the highest levels and help to rethink the implementation of the organizations' missions and goals (Fose-Affirm Panel, 1996).

The second challenge is the rapidly expanding multicultural demo-

1

graphics on a national level. While cultural diversity in the classroom is not new, it may be new among the ranks of senior faculty and administrations in institutions of higher education and represents a trend. Awareness and insight into cultural expectations help to ensure that each student's needs will be met in a way that is meaningful and understandable for the student, regardless of cultural background. This includes having appropriate same-culture models among the faculty and administration. Some higher education senior administrators even report a challenge from the many strong, vocal, multicultural constituencies that are telling them how to conduct their mission–by calling them, writing them, and even suing them (Tracht-enberg, 1996). This can be seen as part of the varied chaos of daily events that Peter Vaill (1994, 1996) calls "managing in permanent white water."

As detailed in Chapter 1 and Chapter 2, a challenge in higher education lies in finding a framework for managing new units or divisions of continuing education. Definitions, a mission statement, faculty expectations and attitudes toward nonstandard scheduling, central university administration support and expectations, and budget objectives all merit careful consideration, as do the general goals, objectives, and learning opportunities planned for programs.

What kind of person is needed to lead this unit or division? There is very little education for the management of this field which brings a peculiar need for the understanding of academic culture and mores, together with a need for excellent modern management skills which encourage creativity, and marketing knowledge and skills. The three together create a framework from which to pursue these challenges, and are needed in order to keep pace with a fast changing market, and the programs for it. But this person is hard to find.

Distance learning is a challenge and a trend in continuing higher education. Planning for technology to support the entire institution in enhancing the general mission and its components is usually a needed first step. Surprisingly, this planning is often not connected to actual distance education classes, although implications for administration and distance classes affect each other. Models for classes, library support, administrative use, and other higher education support services using technological enhancement are becoming more abundant. Legal issues and evaluative research lag behind but as more "best practices" become available, especially via the Internet and through associations for distance learning, some of the mystery about how to implement and manage distance education, will subside. (Chapter 9 discusses these issues in more detail.)

The opportunities open to institutions of higher education as the global society moves into the Information Age are numerous. The educational problems and needs of adults in the workplace, for the leaders of the workplace, and for traditional college-age students, challenge institutions of higher education to rethink their purpose and their programs. Providing education services for students with longer lifetimes and changing careers and jobs, in a high quality, accredited framework, will continue to be an endeavor worthy of the highest commitment. Intelligence is not static, and the excitement of providing opportunities for the growth and intellectual development of all students will remain a leading goal of farsighted educators in higher education.

BIBLIOGRAPHY

Fose-Affirm Panel (1996). "The Federal Chief Information Officer: A Seat at the Table." Federal Office Systems Exposition Conference, April 2–4, Washington, DC.

Trachtenberg, S.J. (1996). "The Role of the CIO." Paper presented at the George Washington University Management Forum, February 14, Washington, DC.

U.S. Department of Labor, Bureau of Labor Statistics (1989). "New Labor Projections Spanning 1988–2000." *Monthly Labor Review, 112* (11), 3–11.

Vaill, Peter (1989). Managing as a Performing Art: New Ideas for a World of Chaotic Change. San Francisco: Jossey Bass.

Vaill, Peter (1996). "Managing a Changing Environment." Speech given at the George Washington University Management Forum, April 3, Washington, DC.

Wee, Eric L. (1996). "More College Students Live, Then Learn." *The Washington Post.*, March 5.

► 1

Higher Education Writes Futures in the Sky

"This college took my future as I had written it on the paper, and wrote it in the sky." These are the words of a former community college student who was accepted into the astronaut training program after overcoming low self-esteem and a lack of education. Education has been called the high-technology blueprint for a growing economy. The driving forces and impacts of social, intellectual, economic, political and technological changes as seen on global, national, regional, and local levels will be felt in the arena of higher education, also. The "umbrella challenge" to education to help individuals keep up with changes and reflect on them is a unifying force, but leadership is needed to accomplish this unification and synthesis..

Many (if not all) institutions of higher education have written futures "in the sky" for young people since the time the institutions were founded. Now with the advent of continuing and distance education this service of inspiration and learning can be extended to many more individuals—that is, to those past young adulthood who are changing their futures and improving their present lives. With a society that is living longer and with many jobs and several career changes predicted for working adults, "going back to school" is becoming a "must" and not an option.

How are institutions going to adapt to and serve a growing adult population, whether local or distant? The answers lie in the leadership knowledge, skills, and practices of those who administer these programs. Much has been written in the various fields of leadership, and the reader is invited to read further in all the disciplines bridged in this chapter and discussed in this book. The end-of-chapter bibliographies are a good starting place.

Leadership is defined in many ways. In Chapter 3 this writer and many others define it as planning for change, then implementing, putting into operation, and evaluating the changes. It further means facilitating group goal and group vision attainment. Yukl (1994) defines it as "observable behaviors that are exhibited while working with individuals and groups in an organization" (p. 256). Dejzoka (1983) defines leadership as the "proactive integration of an organization's people, materials, and ideas such that activities and efforts are directed toward the realization of institutional goals. The willingness of an organization's members to be led is regarded by many as a function of the leader's personal qualities" (p. 36).

An important first step in leading any continuing and/or distant education organization is creating a vision for the organization and conveying and translating it to the staff, to the faculty, and to the rest of the institution. Next comes setting the direction and goals of the organization. Does the dean or director understand and believe in high expectations for the students in the programs? Does he or she have a vision and communicate it? Does the dean take the time to be visible to staff and students in the various centers and programs? The commitment and vision must be visible.

The vision gains incredible strength and is most empowering when it is jointly arrived at with staff, perhaps at a yearly 1-day staff retreat. Altruistic words such as "educating more students to attain their full potential" are more inspiring than budget and finance goals such as "enrolling more students" or "making more money," as one university president said to a faculty meeting (sadly enough, a true story).

A mission statement can also be developed jointly during a staff retreat if needed, but many institutions already have one in place. A theme for the year can be adopted at this time in areas in which the staff wants to improve. Goals, objectives and activities to enable achieving the vision flow logically then, in alignment with the first steps of goal setting and creating a vision.

Staff development, often neglected or perfunctorily addressed if staff members are not enrolled in courses, is a mark of effective and growing organizations and is an important component of leadership in all education (Blase and Anderson, 1995). It begins with leaders knowing the value of reeducating themselves and their staffs. Maintaining and increasing their knowledge through participating in workshops, courses and conferences— and *talking* about this knowledge—is a first step. Reading useful literature (on marketing, management, demographics, or future trends) and sharing the content with staff is another important element. Staff meetings can be used for discussing some of this material in a seminar approach at regular intervals to heighten awareness of trends and future geographic areas for classes and students at various levels (graduate, undergraduate, and non-credit).

As with all levels of education, being aware of student needs and setting and clarifying expectations for staff are part of instructional leadership. Most leaders in academia know various educational and instructional approaches, but do they communicate this knowledge to staff? As more staff is hired that may or may not have higher academic degrees or degrees in education or learning, this communication is more needed. Maximizing the efforts made by individual staff members is also a part of instructional leadership at any level of education.

A leader's being aware of student needs in continuing and distance education may take the form of providing more and better resources to students. Such awareness might entail providing more audio-visual equipment to centers, perhaps several projection or LCD panels; providing library software disks with Internet access for all new students; making available career center services; or providing other resources for instruction and activities. This might even include providing maps and building floor plans on a Web site.

Maintaining and developing knowledge and skill in influencing internal and external political environments are additional vital functions of a leader in continuing and distance education. The internal political environment can be understood and influenced at two levels: (1) within the immediate organizational unit or building and (2) within the institution. Leaders should have the "know-how" about the politics within their own organization. They use their power within the organization to achieve their goals for the centers and programs. Understanding the empowerment that comes through participatory management leading to strength and creativity of programs, and the disempowerment that comes from autocratic management (although it is the norm for many institutions of higher education), is part of maintaining or building the internal political environment. Two-way communication with joint, friendly, interactive problem solving is a hallmark of effective internal organizations. Having knowledge of and providing motivator factors to staff (see Chapter 7), such as recognition, growth, autonomy, self-esteem, and emphasizing the worth of the work, costs almost nothing and yields much in helping an organization pull together and grow. Knowing the value of positively influencing the behavior and attitudes of staff is a key component of internal leadership. Influencing the external political environment, whether it is the larger institution of higher education or the external surrounding community or metropolitan area, requires additional leadership knowledge, skill, and behaviors. Being aware of national and international trends might even be part of this external environment knowledge for distance education.

Knowing the importance of reaching out to build liaisons with the community and to build resources and budget within the institution is part of essential connection building. Telling the staff about these efforts and how well they're working can further extend the utility of these external liaisons in achieving the goals of the centers and programs. Taking various staff members to important meetings builds their competence and "buy-in" of new processes or goals. Creating supportive coalitions and alliances within the academic community and with the external community helps to make things happen for centers and programs. Encouraging professional marketing staff to also build such liaisons and contacts helps to bolster contract course programs and to further improve public relations.

SUMMARY

The quote from the community college student about building her future in the sky is symbolic in the way it affirms and validates the work of many individuals in higher education. The leadership to accomplish the building of these "futures" and helping adults develop to their full potentials can be learned and can be taught. A natural ability to lead is valuable, but this process is so important that it cannot wait for the random appearance of charisma in deans and directors in continuing and/or distance education. Bridging the fields of knowledge in leadership and management, higher education, and marketing to adults requires ongoing (continuous) learning that is also discussed with staff.

Growth and development in spite of problems such as faculty power struggles and intrigues, faculty tenure and diversity issues, and budget and space issues requires leadership that sets a direction for the unit and functions effectively in internal and external political environments. The knowledge, skills, and behaviors leaders use to develop and enunciate a vision will create strength and empowerment for their programs. Maximizing and developing staff can mean the difference between just doing more of the same old things and doing things that will develop growth. A keen understanding of both the internal political environment and the external political environment enables innovative leaders to move their institutions of higher education proudly into the twenty-first century.

BIBLIOGRAPHY

Blase, J. J., and G. Anderson (1995). *The Micropolitics of Educational Leadership: From Control to Empowerment.* New York: Columbia University, Teachers College Press.

Dejzoka, E. L.(1983). *Educational Administration Glossary.* Westport, CT: Greenwood Press.

Yukl, G. (1994). *Leadership in Organizations.* Englewood Cliffs, NJ: Prentice Hall.

▶ 2

Challenges, Issues, and Trends in Continuing Education in Higher Education

The traditional mission of a university or college is teaching, research, and service. Part of the ability to achieve the mission of an institution of higher education can include extending its reputation and credibility for providing high-quality, relevant courses to reach out to and serve the surrounding population. By empowering the adult community and alumni through life-long learning opportunities, an institution extends the learning community and the intellectual capital of the region (and of further regions if they are reached by distance learning). Preparing people to meet changes, empowering them, and enhancing their lives gives the institution an additional link to the society and the community and provides a balance to other academic initiatives as a service to their community.

A university or college can be seen as not just a place with buildings only, with a distinction between the central campus and satellite or remote "outposts," but also as a resource that offers educational services at locations and at times that best match the needs and interests of able students. Educational services are indeed expanding in the "Knowledge Age." What would happen if academia thought about programs that adults want and need instead of merely extending (convenient) parts of what they are already doing to adult and evening classes? According to futurists, the greatest unrealized job market is in unsolved problems, and solutions to unsolved problems often lie in insights gained through education. However, as mentioned in the Preface, there is little education for the field of management of continuing education/distance education that addresses the peculiar needs for academic professionalism, creative management, and modern marketing skills. Continuing education provides an additional way to stay in the black financially, as this has been found to be a revenue-producing enterprise.

An editorial in a 1996 issue of *U.S. News and World Report* calls for the U.S. government to take the lead, with higher education and continual learning as a place to start, in correcting many of society's ills, including decay and anxiety. "Higher education is an investment in the greatest strength a country has, its people," it states and goes on to call for a GI bill type of funding for students who qualify for scholarships for higher education for the Information Age (Zuckerman, 1996).

The challenge of dealing with the demographic and technological changes that call for new approaches to higher education can cause leaders to feel they are "on a merry-go-round" or "the blind are leading the blind," or any number of similar phrases. The pace of change itself is changing, and linkages and implications between changes can snowball. One effect is lack of a sense of progress or of cumulative achievement; the accomplishments might well be impressive, but the achievements are rapidly overshadowed by other events. Some writers see leading as learning (Senge, 1990; Vaill, 1996), as the dynamic, rapidly changing situations require ad hoc thinking and the ability to face new challenges. Individuals in leadership roles thus are put in a learning mode. Control may have been the goal in the 1980s, but learning, continual learning, and new beginnings are likely to be the watchwords for the 1990s and into the next century (Vaill, 1996). Seeking perspective and leading "outside the box," or learning to adopt new paradigms, are some of the leadership behaviors that will be necessary in the next decade (Kantor, 1983, Naisbitt, 1990; Ackoff, 1970). "What can we do with our own enormous capacities to learn and think?" may be the necessary question for individuals as well as institutions. To gain perspective, looking at the history of continuing education is illuminating.

PAST VIEWS OF CONTINUING EDUCATION

The teaching of adults has been in evidence since the times of Plato and Socrates, and also goes back to the ancient Chinese and Hebrew cultures. But the concept that for teaching adults a different framework might be needed than the framework for teaching children (called pedagogy) was discussed in the 1920s and 1930s and re-enunciated by Malcolm Knowles in 1973 in his book *The Adult Learner: A Neglected Species*. Knowles proposed a framework for adult learners that included new methods of teaching as well as content that built on students' experiences. His approach, which he called *andragogy,* continues to inspire practitioners of adult education.

Educational goals that undermine the disposition to go on learning are miseducation in the opinion of many. For many years conventional or traditional classroom methods were thought to do just that. Linderman in 1926 in *The Meaning of Adult Education* wrote that the resource of highest value in adult education is the learner's experience. Authoritative teaching and examinations that leave no room for original thinking have no place in the Knowles vision of adult education. In the 1920s concepts of intelligence were static, conventional education had standardized limitations, and higher educational facilities were frequently limited to a certain socio-economic/intellectual class. It was thought that the majority of adults were not interested in continuing education, or that they could go to public agencies for free short courses. Alternatively, adult education was viewed as supporting the cultural interests of the leisured classes. The search for new methods and incentives for adult education was spurred on in part by the rigid, uncompromising, authoritative approach of the conventional institutions of learning (Knowles, 1973).

Knowles's writings and search for new methods and incentives gave a foundation to a training industry that has grown explosively. New methods for adult learning with an emphasis on self-direction and life-centered student experience began to be used with great benefit in training classes in business and industry. While it is not the purpose of this book to describe that industry, much that is good and helpful to ongoing continuing education in institutions of higher education can be found in these theories. Public school systems, county recreation departments, community colleges, labor unions, and state and local governments all offer training/education courses to good effect. In fact, ground rules may need to be established where topics or areas of different educational or social institutions might overlap.

In 1872 George Washington University in Washington, DC started offering civil servants late afternoon classes at what was then the Colombian College, an early example of adapting to the needs of adult students. The college sensed a demand and made scheduling adjustments to facilitate attendance. The president even extended the adaptation to include offering classes "where and when it would be convenient for the people who wanted it and were willing to pay for it" (Kayser, 1970, p.7) Other earlier higher education offerings came out of county extension efforts of land grant colleges such as Cornell University and most state institutions.

Lawrence Jacks in 1929 envisioned a kind of education based on continuity of the learning, possibly called "continuation school." The American Council of Education director saw business and industry as becoming educational institutions (Knowles, 1978). In 1930 a college president said that there was gradually emerging a concept of education as a lifelong process, "beginning at birth and ending at death," a process full of "reality and meaning to the learner" (Jacks, 1930, p. 123).

By 1940 most of the elements for a theory of adult learning had been discovered, but it was not until the 1950s that these elements were clarified and the knowledge explosion, which continues today, began to make continual learning a life requirement. In the 1950s, C. O. Houle found three types of adult learners: goal-oriented learners, activity-oriented learners, and the learning-oriented who sought knowledge and self-enhancement (Knowles, 1978).

Since the 1950s many institutions of higher education have developed some form of adult and continuing education, whether for credit, noncredit, or both. Futurists see higher education as eventually having three main segments: undergraduate education, traditional graduate education, and continuing education (Cosmos, 1984). Whatever the source of the initiative, many institutions have some sort of adult or evening division and it is the purpose of this book to facilitate the growth and development of such a division, especially for professionals new to this field. Some of the issues discussed in the next section affect all age groups in higher education, but the focus here will be on continuing education of adult students.

ISSUES IN CONTINUING EDUCATION

Up-to-date technology—for curriculum, for administration, and for reaching students at greater distances—will definitely continue to be an issue in higher education. As more universities require adult graduate students and younger students to own or have access to a computer for a variety of degree programs, this requirement will seem less novel and more routine. Access to libraries and the Internet can be handled in many ways including for example, the distributing of disks with the appropriate software for access to students at distant or off-campus sites. Software packages for financial management, personnel administration, and registration transactions are becoming more the norm than the exception (Abecassis, 1996), as is networking all the buildings of the institution, both local and distant. Groupware further enhances this capability, as do client/server technology and eventually "middleware" (Peters, 1996).

Distance Learning Issues

By February 1996 there were 24 million people on the Internet in the United States and Canada, with a 26% increase from October to December 1994 alone (*Chicago Tribune*, 1996). The exponential increase in cross-computer communication and information access has a number of implications for universities and colleges. First, institutions of higher education must accept that they do not *own* information. The Hubble telescope, for instance, produced a great deal of information that is not owned by an academic institution. Faculty may supplement, orient, refine, and annotate information, but not claim it as their exclusive property, which for some will be a new role. Some think that most faculty won't change their attitude toward technology until they have to. The day may come when it is as unacceptable for a university faculty member to say, "I don't use technology" as for a medical doctor to say, "I don't use X ray" (Whitaker, 1995).

The distance learning concept usually includes technology-enhanced offerings such as audio, video, or computer-based or -assisted instruction or instructional television (sometimes called ITV) via satellite, microwave, or cable network. Often a toll-free telephone number or other source of telephone interaction is added, either one-way or two-way. Two-way desktop video capability is also an option. Distance learning can also encompass audiotapes of lectures augmented by Internet discussion groups for credit opportunities that span several continents. Bringing more education to more people, wherever they are located, appears to be a meaningful service and goal in this era of global transition into the Information Age. The argument that ITV or distance learning leads to less meaningful personal contact than that which occurs in the classroom may be a myth—it assumes that students have meaningful contact now. With electronic mail contact, students have three or more contacts with the professor or teaching assistant *per week* in programs at some institutions (Lynch, 1994). However, institutions of higher education may need to implement faculty incentives to encourage willingness to teach courses with a distance technology component. These might include promotion, tenure, salary increase, course relief, or the assignment of a teaching or research assistant (a very popular option).

Institutions will need to be alert to critical legal issues such as intellectual property rights. A number of workable models have been developed by universities in the western United States with great distances to cover. The University of Wisconsin Extension's Instructional Communications System (ICS) is one of the largest. It may be that using client/server groupware, such as Lotus Notes™, that ensures the security of courses so they are only accessible to registered students will be a better alternative delivery vehicle than the less-than-private Internet. State-supported institutions will probably continue to lead in technological distance learning in order to provide equitable opportunity to all, as is their mandate.

A great need for careful, evaluative research on the outcomes of distance learning still exists. Highly technical or very distinctive degree programs that are not otherwise easily available seem to be the best early candidates for success (Lynch, 1994). Considerations of student satisfaction and tolerance, when placed against lack of access to education, become less of an issue for many students.

Distance learning can have a profound and positive impact on students with disabilities, allowing them learning opportunities that may have previously been inaccessible to them. Questions of access are still very much under discussion at the time of this writing for the "information infrastructure" in general. There are sociological implications around different access for age, social class, gender, and international citizenship and expectations (NII Conference, 1996). Some countries behind the "dollar curtain" that lack adequate telephone lines are using CD-ROMs for medical and other professional libraries. The day may come that college courses are available on interactive CD-ROM also (White, 1994).

Institutions of higher education must, however, guard against "vendor-dictated solutions" in purchasing information technology. Seeing technology as enhancing the entire mission of the institution and working back to solve particular problems with technology will produce a more integrated (and inter-operable) set of solutions than the reverse. "Stovepiping" with different systems in a university not connecting (such as the registrar's office and student accounts) can lead to expensive problems, as many government agencies have discovered.

An institution of higher education might address these problems with a task force such as an information management advisory group made up of heads of major departments and chaired by a chief information officer. Related steps might include choice of a standard methodology with pilot projects and training; involving more interdisciplinary teams; and involving department chairs, managers, and technical staff. Then technology acquisitions can support the framework. Information, orientation, and training can include institution-wide communication to reinforce the information management framework (CIO/IAC, 1997). An option is an adjunct professor training program for using technology in the classroom, with an extra pay incentive for those who participate; another option is administrative training.

Institutions of higher education may need to re-examine their understanding of their student base and be willing to form partnerships with other institutions that share the same base. For example, many federal agencies have field offices in cities where colleges and universities are located. Specialized training and degrees needed in an ever more sophisticated government workplace are sometimes available at these locations in tandem with the local educational institutions, but this possibility is not routinely being adequately addressed or being fully extended through distance learning to more remote locations.

Internal Issues

Some seemingly large challenges to continuing education exist within the internal environment of the institution of higher education in many institutions. One large issue is in the area of faculty expectations, power struggles, and intrigues. Faculty tenure and diversity issues further complicate these challenges. Further internal issues and challenges include budgets and resources and space and facilities. Of course, distance learning confronts space questions with new solutions (see Chapter 9), but it is expensive to launch. Historians note that these internal challenges and others are merely an extension of issues that have existed on the main campus or in residential programs over time. All of these challenges will be re-visited in various chapters of this book, as we consider the need for leadership to turn challenges into new opportunities for solutions.

CHALLENGES OF SETTING UP A NEW CONTINUING EDUCATION UNIT

Any innovation encounters difficulties and resistance, and starting a new off-campus or continuing education unit in an institution of higher education is certainly a demanding undertaking. Accessible higher education for youth and adult students is a worthwhile goal and a continuing challenge (Birnbaum, 1988). Even if there is an "implementation dip" (the feeling of two steps forward and one step back) as the program gets underway, steady perseverance usually carries the day. At least 6 years are required to judge a program that impacts a wide audience. Rensis Likert (1961) calls this time the "institutional lag" and describes the 6 years as divided into 2-year increments: 2 years of input, 2 years of attitude change, and 2 years of output (see Chapter 3 for more applications of this concept).

A dean involved in the process of setting up a new, off-campus learning center in an institution that had only had traditional programs, enunciated five challenges that might be universals:

- Definition of continuing education
- Faculty expectations
- Attitudes toward nontraditional scheduling
- Administration support and expectations
- Budget

His suggestions for dealing with these areas, presented in the following subsections, may be useful to those in a similar situation.

Definition of Continuing Education

Make sure both parties discussing "continuing education" are using the same definition early in the conversation. Does the phrase mean noncredit only? Credit only? Or both in a wider definition that includes all nontraditional education programs? Whole conversations have occurred with both parties talking about entirely different entities. This was seen as a crucial challenge in dealing with other deans and department chairs, especially if an institution is changing its approach to adult students and continuing education. A mission statement, such as the following sample, will help to attain the clarity needed. The mission statement can be printed in flyers, brochures, semester planning schedules, and wherever else it is appropriate.

> Off-Campus Programs seeks to provide graduate and undergraduate programs of excellence, further developing the strengths of the University, at locations and times that are convenient for adults. Currently, more than _x_ students are served per semester at more than _x_ locations. Off-Campus Programs offer the most extensive off-campus Master's degree programs in this metropolitan area. Expanding professional opportunities and developing student potential are the foundation stones of the Off-Campus Programs Mission.
>
> The University and the Off-Campus Programs Office continue to take pride in offering degree programs off-campus. These are identical in quality to those offered on campus in keeping with the Mission Statement of the University. (Jones, 1986)

(See Appendix A for an alternative sample off-campus programs mission statement.)

Faculty Expectations

Many faculty have had their earliest training with the 18- to 22-year-old age group and now find themselves at a more nontraditional institution with greater numbers of adult students. Faculty will have different expectations as to how students will behave or should be treated if their previous experience is largely with the younger age group. This can show in many surprising ways, such as the words used in a syllabus, the attendance policy, or the make-up policy.

Attitudes toward Nontraditional Scheduling

Formatting and scheduling of courses also can bring to the fore different expectations. Meeting once a week for several hours versus three times a week for 1 hour can require different teaching styles and a variety of curriculum components to keep the "rhythm" of the class going and students learning and involved. In a survey of comparable institutions it was found that faculty needed a period of transition to different semester starts and endings for weekend classes, different timing and pacing of classes, and to content appropriate for compressed formatting. Several institutional representatives said that discussing such issues directly with the faculty eased the transition. Items such as the need for "break" times in long blocks of class time and other logistical details can be smoothed out with direct discussion. Adjunct faculty training to which full-time faculty are also invited can be very helpful.

Administration Support and Expectations

An administration that has goals it wants to accomplish and is therefore supportive is a big plus. Often expectations are too high for the short term. But a few early successes and keeping administrators informed can help. Large systems may not accept the variability needed by continuing education: nonstandard semester starts and endings, contract courses whose students are not billed in the usual way, or nonstandard registration procedures. If the registration program is linked to the billing program in a mainframe computer without a code that can be applied for contract courses or off-campus differentiated tuitions, high-level meetings with unit administrators may be needed to solve some of the resultant problems. A chief information officer can head off such problems when new technology is in the planning stages by looking carefully at the "business process" of the institution before re-engineering it with technology.

Budget

Having a good sense of what the budget is at the start is important. As one new administrator said, "Know where the extra pots of money are." For example, if personnel pays for recruitment advertising, access this fund. If graphics and printing are fee-for-service departments, know this before large sums are suddenly deducted from the continuing education budget. It is important to know what the unit will be charged for and what it won't. Some institutions have cost-center budgeting; others have very separate income and expense budgets. Learning the history of the institution's budgetary decision making helps one to understand and deal with the limitations of different approaches.

SUMMARY

As institutions of higher education rethink who they are and what they will do into the next century, there is a tremendous educational opportunity for them in the movement of society into the Information Age. A number of chief information officers both in the public and private sector believe that education is the key to ensuring that government agencies and corporations successfully make the transition into this new era (Rand, 1995). Many lament that particular courses or degrees are not available nationwide by distance learning modes for their field offices. The need for more courses and degrees to be available to the adult work force, is a continuing trend and challenge to higher education. The use of information technology in support of institutional missions presents ongoing issues in many areas.

Clearness of definitions and a mission statement will help new programs get started well, as will faculty and staff development about adult learners. Many kinds of adult and continuing education found in nonprofit organizations other than colleges and universities also can benefit from clarity, making mission statements, and staff development.

Risk taking and adaptation to change have never been standard behaviors for institutions of higher education, whether in this transitional century or in ages long past. However, developing a better world and investing in people have always been foremost in educators' ideals, and meeting the challenges of continuing education in higher education will help institutions work toward these goals.

BIBLIOGRAPHY

Abecassis, Alan (1996). Personal Meeting/Interview with the Chief Information Officer of the French Education Ministry, March 28, Washington, DC.

Ackoff, R. L. (1970). *A Concept of Corporate Planning*. New York: Wiley.

Birnbaum, Robert (1988). *How Colleges Work*. San Francisco: Jossey-Bass.

Cosmos, Spencer (1984). Personal interview with Dean of Continuing Education, January 20. Washington, DC: Catholic University.

CIO/IAC (1997). Chief Information Officers Council and the Industry Advisory Council (1997), *Best Information Technology (IT) Practices*, Washington, DC: Author.

Jacks, L. (1930). *Journal of Adult Education, 2,* 123.

Jones, C. C. (1986). "Mission Statement for Off-Campus Programs," Draft. Washington DC: George Washington University.

Kantor, Rosabeth Moss (1983). *The Change Masters: Innovations for Productivity in the American Corporation.* New York: Simon & Schuster.

Kayser, E. L. (1970). *Bricks without Straw.* New York: Appleton-Century-Crofts.

Knowles, Malcolm (1978). *The Adult Learner: A Neglected Species* (2d ed). Houston, TX: Gulf.

Likert, Rensis (1961). *The Human Organization.* New York: McGraw Hill.

Lynch, William (1994). "Distance Learning." Speech given at the U.S. Government Training Officers Conference, Washington, DC: October 11.

Meredith, J. R., and S. J. Mantel (1995). *Project Management: A Managerial Approach.* New York: Wiley.

Naisbitt, John and P. Aburdene (1990). *Megatrends 2,000.* New York: Random House.

National Information Infrastructure Awards Contest Conference (1996). "Beyond the Barriers" panel presentation, March 19. Washington, DC.

Peters, Ed (1996). "The Virtual Data Warehouse and Middleware." Paper presented at Data Management Association Conference, April 3, Rosslyn, VA.

Rand, Cynthia (1995). Speech given at Association for Federal Information Resource Management Seminar, October, Washington, DC.

Senge, Peter (1990). *The Fifth Discipline: The Art and Practice of the Learning Organization*. New York: Doubleday.

Whitaker, Roger (1995). "Position Paper on Distance Learning." Paper presented at the Division of University Programs meeting, March 24, Washington, DC.

White, W. (1994). "Challenges for the Future." Speech given at Information Management Solutions Conference, Third Annual Conference of SIGCAT/Special Interest Group on CD-ROM and Applications Technology, April 26, Fairfax, VA.

Zuckerman, M. B. (1996). "Crumbs for the Majority." *U.S. News and World Report*, February 26.

▶ Section II

Leadership for the 21st Century in Continuing Education

The leadership and management of continuing education in higher education now and into the twenty-first century will need to rise to meet the challenges of the times to provide traditional, non-traditional, and distance educational opportunities. Understanding leadership, and the sources and use of power, and institutional lag, or why a large institution or a large market might need 6 years before it can be judged, will be of key importance. Planning and implementation of programs must be done well, and this will mean tapping the creativity of all involved in the continuing education organization in one way or another. Creativity is an underutilized resource in most organizations, including higher education. Creativity, however, is the attribute that mixes and expands past experiences so that new, "nonobvious" concepts, variations or extensions are generated (Meredith and Mantel, 1995). Often the small administrative units of continuing education have a tremendous amount of outreach to large numbers of prospective students. Two-way communication to the increasingly large adult market is essential to keep offerings synchronized with new directions and emerging needs.

Organizations that survive and thrive in the future will be those that foster creativity today. But even if this statement is obvious, creativity is often stifled and innovation frustrated. "Don't make waves" is a common admonition in large bureaucracies, and change stirs up organizational waters rather than smoothing them. Indeed, creativity can be like pepper in food—too much can be unsettling. Change is a likely result of creativity, however, as continuing education adapts to the fast-changing needs of adult learners in a fast-changing society. Many modern managers are taught to be risk avoiders, which generally includes avoiding creativity. This can slowly undermine the revenue stream, which can take 5 years or more to restore.

Carefully assessing risk, making group decisions whenever possible, and using teamwork to empower staff, faculty, and even students are all part of the participative style of management needed in a growing, expanding continuing education division in higher education. Much in the chapters in this section will help institutions of higher education find ways to enhance rather than discourage creativity, even in a fairly political organizational culture or climate. Leaders should foster the creativity of employees and then reward the creativity that results. Because creativity requires a mutually supportive leader–employee relationship, not a competitive or autocratic one, participative management seems to be most productive. Some educational institutions may be bureaucratic, some autocratic, or some political rather than collegial, due to size and other factors, in their management styles (Birnbaum, 1988; Bergquist, 1992), but fostering creativity with productive, two-way problem solving, is still possible within a particular continuing education division. Creative extensions of existing ideas and creative applications of new technology resulting from enabling leadership can be relatively low-risk beginning steps.

Techniques that allow people to think creatively are discussed in Chapter 8. The less understood a problem is, the greater the need for creativity there is. Questions such as "Who is the market for this?" "What courses and degrees will serve these needs?" and "What is the best way to market these programs to that population?" are representative of the ambiguous, unstructured problems that arise in continuing education, both for credit and noncredit. The group process for planning and creativity brings together knowledge and skills that are not possessed by a single individual. This process eliminates errors and mistakes more effectively than does unilateral decision making and allows individuals to stimulate each other's thinking and build on suggested ideas. Furthermore, it produces solutions that are more likely to be accepted as the group members participate in developing them. Much in education is ambiguous at all levels—there's even disagreement as to what the goal is, and the fundamental reason for seeking creativity through a group process is that the problem structure is ambiguous and unclear (Meredith and Mantel, 1995). Skill in creative problem solving can be acquired and developed.

Chapters 6 and 7 offer ideas on team building and motivation, which along with staff development are important elements in effective leadership for change.

Distance learning also requires leadership in continuing higher education and is a somewhat less than clear task or problem (see Chapter 6 for suggestions about unclear tasks). Planning for technology in support of the entire institution's mission and components is usually a needed first step. Surprisingly, this planning is often not connected to actual distance education classes, although implications for administration and distance classes impact upon each other. Models for classes, library support, administrative procedures and other higher education support services using technological enhancement are becoming more abundant. Legal issues and evaluative research lag behind, but as "best practices" become available, especially via the Internet and through Associations for Distance Learning (see Appendix G), some of the mystery about how to implement and manage distance education will subside. Chapter 9 discusses these issues in more detail.

Noncredit programs are discussed in this section also, in Chapter 10. Noncredit courses lead students into new areas of learning and provide a different educational service from an institution. They are also a promising part of creative leadership and management of continuing education into the next century.

BIBLIOGRAPHY

Bergquist, W. H. (1992). *The Four Cultures of the Academy.* San Francisco: Jossey-Bass.

Birnbaum, R. (1988). *How Colleges Work.* San Francisco: Jossey- Bass.

Meredith, J. R. and S. S. Mantel (1995). *Project Management: A Managerial Approach.* New York: Wiley.

▶ 3

Leadership in Continuing Education

Leadership principles drawn from management theorists can offer new insights to those responsible for providing well-run, quality programs in continuing education in institutions of higher education. The divisions or departments that run continuing education programs are often nontraditional in structure and mission, but they need to mesh with the traditional structure and organization of a college or university. There is, therefore, often a natural tension between the traditional organizational structure of most colleges and universities and the participative organizational structure of the continuing education/marketing/outreach division of the same institution. Leadership includes creating a vision and developing strategies to accomplish the vision in addition to the management tasks of planning, implementing, operating, and evaluating. Two-way communication is essential in continuing education, as the marketplace needs and economic trends change, affecting the program needs to be communicated to the institution and the program availability to be communicated to the adult student market. Leadership principles can help with the meshing of the two structures, as the traditional institution of higher education is primarily affected by the ebb and flow of the 18- to 22-year-old age group in the current demographic trend, rather than trends in mature adult demographic and marketplace needs.

It's important to help institutions of higher education see their leadership roles in continuing education and distance education in the society at large. With new goals and new processes, leaders in charge of continuing and/or distance education have some new solutions to some historically difficult internal political problems, especially space and facilities power struggles. In the high-context organizational culture of an institution of higher education, as described in the literature (Birnbaum, 1988), new numbers of learners in the over-22 age group will hopefully force the investigation of new solutions, not increase old power struggles and intrigues. The history of higher education shows that some of the same issues of power and internal political influence and struggles that exist on the main campus or the residential campus are extended to continuing and distance education issues.

Faculty tenure, for instance, is a nationwide issue, and the problems of tenure can be addressed when one looks at the main incentive of tenured faculty. Is it educating students? Doing research? Not seeking more than the allotted number of full-time enrollments(FTEs)? Or is the main incentive keeping enough free time to do outside consulting? If the latter is true, institutions of higher education have lost control of internal incentives for faculty, except that of spending less time at the institution. When institutions maintained a monopoly view of higher education, faculty wishes were largely ignored, and perhaps this is a contributing factor to faculty attitudes today. It certainly works in opposition to the goals of new (read "energy-consuming") programs, courses, locations, and technology. As one large department chairman said, "Universities are the last bastion of individual entrepreneurs" (referring to individual consulting work). This person has been re-elected chairman for 18 of the last 20 years.

Budget and resource allocation issues are also not new to higher education with the advent of continuing and distance education, but again, a new revenue stream from adult students can help bring new solutions to old problems (more on budget and finance in Chapter 12). Diversity of students and faculty is a newer but on-going issue as the demographics of the nation change and the changes are reflected in public and private institutions.

LEADERSHIP

Leadership in continuing education administration is built upon planning for change. Effective leadership behaviors are designed to accomplish change for the improvement of the organization and/or the programs—not just for change's sake. Leaders may also be required to carry out administrative behaviors and responsibilities, but these just keep things going: systems, policies, regulations—these are the areas that fall under administration. Administration alone is not leadership, however; it is just using old processes to obtain old goals. Leadership, on the other hand, uses new processes to achieve ongoing goals, or even new processes to reach new goals (Figure 3.1).

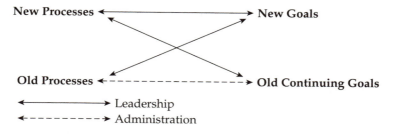

FIGURE 3.1   Leadership versus Administration

In continuing education an example of an old goal might be the providing of numerous well-run courses. A new process to gain this might be to offer additional new formats, such as five Saturdays all day or five weekdays all day for 1 week for courses with appropriate content. A new goal gained through old processes might be to add a lecture series for one credit or continuing education units (CEUs) to a group of credit courses or a degree program. A new goal accomplished through old processes might also be to open another branch of a graduate education center in a new location, using the same administrative foundations and sequence of steps used to open the first center. An example of a new goal accomplished through a new process might be to set up programs at a new off-site location and then increase to having several off-site locations and satellite downlinks identified by location codes or section codes.

Leadership in organizations and in society has been documented throughout history. Knowledge of the components of leadership is an invaluable asset to an individual charged with new kinds of tasks in higher education. Natural ability to lead has always been an asset, but knowledge of the various behaviors that increase the effectiveness of a group and aid in planning new goals and/or new processes focuses any leadership effort for greater success.

Perhaps a review of the basics would be valuable. The original human relations management perspective sprang from experiments at Western Electric's Hawthorne plant near Cicero, Illinois in the 1920s. The results of this experiment came to be known as the "Hawthorne effect," in which a seemingly nonintrusive experiment produced striking results in human behavior. The purpose of the study was to determine the relationship between working conditions and the level of employee productivity. It was found that no matter whether the lights were made brighter or dimmer the workers produced more (Gay, 1992). It was the attention the employees received and not the illumination of the workplace that made employees feel important and subsequently increased their productivity. The conclusion is that leaders and managers *can* affect the behavior of their subordinates. In many cases improved morale and working conditions influenced workers' productivity and attitudes more than financial incentives. It has always been assumed that faculty receive stimulation and encouragement from each other and from their professional associations. This may or may not be true, but as staff and administrative employees fill many jobs in continuing education of all kinds, without necessarily having extensive backgrounds in higher education, peer attention and encouragement may not be sufficient to gain desired results. In considering leadership knowledge, skills, and behaviors it is interesting to note the source of the material on leadership behaviors.

The behavioral approach to predicting leadership ability draws its data from descriptive observations of: (1) how managers/leaders spend their time at work and (2) comparisons of the behavior of effective and ineffective leaders. Behaviors were documented through job descriptions, direct observations, reviews of managers' diaries, anecdotes, and questionnaires. Researchers identified specific behaviors that could serve as guides for effective leadership. A synthesis of these behaviors later became the basis of an instrument used to describe leadership entitled the *Leadership Behavior Descriptive Questionnaire*. This instrument was developed at Ohio State University and is still in use today (Likert, 1961).

Likert's early studies with managers identified other behaviors that made individuals successful. He identified five specific actions that effective managers and leaders took that made them more successful than their counterparts in the same company. These behaviors, with their specific associated tasks, created a climate of (1) understanding, (2) mutual trust, (3) respect, (4) success among their subordinates, and (5) high task orientation. The five behaviors and their accompanying interpretations are discussed later in this chapter in the section on effective and ineffective leaders. Likert (1961) determined that another important behavior involved informing. *Informing* is defined as a process by which a leader communicates task-relevant information needed by subordinates, peers, or superiors. Likert believed that informing serves as a linchpin connecting the work unit, the rest of the organization, and the outside environment.

The situational approach to leadership that was developed by Blake and Mouton (1982) looks at: (1) work performed by the leader's organizational group, (2) the organization's external work environment, and (3) the characteristics of the followers. Their *Managerial Grid* has been used in organizations to assess the way that work is performed and the relationship of these three variables to that work.

Yukl (1994) emphasizes that "the assumption underlying situational leadership is that different leader behavior patterns will be effective in different situations, and that the same behavior pattern is not optimal in all situations (p. 14)." In his book *Leadership in Organizations*, Yukl (1994) identifies specific leadership behaviors that facilitate the "management of the work" and the "management of relationships." The depiction of each of these functions was the result of studies of managers and leaders who had been successful since the early 1950s. Yukl compiled and analyzed the research and pinpointed the following behaviors as important. Effective leadership behaviors to manage human relationships include:

- Supporting
- Developing
- Recognizing
- Rewarding
- Team building and conflict management
- Networking

Specific behaviors for managing the work include:

- Planning
- Clarifying
- Monitoring
- Problem Solving
- Informing

In summation, Yukl (1994) states that research on these specific categories of managerial behavior is limited. Nevertheless, the findings suggest that each of these categories of leadership and managerial behavior has the potential to improve leadership and managerial effectiveness if they are skillfully used in appropriate situations.

THE DIFFERENCE BETWEEN MANAGEMENT AND LEADERSHIP

Briefly stated, *management* provides consistency, control, and efficiency—with or without new ideas or processes. *Leadership* fosters purpose, creativity, imagination, and drive. The specific roles of manager and leader have been analyzed frequently in the field of business. The research points out that there are differences between these responsibilities and that individuals who manage have specific roles that are determined by their organizations. Organizational leadership, on the other hand, can come from a variety of people in a number of roles. In a time of change and challenge, managing well requires elements of leadership.

Other useful insights include Gardner's (1990) definition leadership as "the process of persuasion by example by which an individual induces a group to pursue objectives held by the leader or shared by the leader and his or her followers" (p. 1). Gardner describes managers as individuals who hold a "directive" post in an organization. They also preside over the resources by which an organization functions, allocate resources prudently, and make the best possible use of people. Gardner views leadership and management not as separate entities, but as a delicate balance between two roles. He calls individuals with the ability to play both these roles "leader/managers." Gardner does, however, differentiate between leadership and management with respect to the role the manager accepts in the workplace. He suggests that the word *manager* indicates that the individual so labeled presides over processes and resources, including personnel.

Yukl (1994) suggests that most definitions reflect the assumption that leadership involves a process of social influence, wherein intentional influence is exerted by one person over other people in order to structure the activities and relationships in a group or organization. Yukl and others view effective leadership as a "group or organizational process that contributes to the overall effectiveness of a group or organization" (Yukl, 1994, p. 8). Administration and management are similar in the description, as shown in Figure 3.1. However leadership differs, as leaders must deal with the issue of implementing long-term change and must use new processes (e.g. technology might be one) to achieve on-going goals, old processes to reach new goals, or new processes to reach new goals.

How does a dean or director make significant changes to achieve better-quality results? Usually this requires long-term changes that may take 1 or 2 years to plan and 2 to 3 years to implement. This requires leadership, which does not operate in a vacuum. In terms of social exchange, leadership is:

an interaction between persons in which:
1. One presents information, of a sort, and in such a way that
2. the other is convinced that the benefits to him/herself will be greater than to you (cost-benefits improved), and,
3. the interaction avoids direct confrontation
4. and moves the persons or groups towards goals without making status or power differentials obvious. (Jacobs, 1971, p. 237)

A good example of social exchange as a leadership function can be found in the story of a dean of a large continuing education center of a midwestern state college. Her center was in a small town in the middle of flat, hot, dusty farmland. She always managed to hire crackerjack assistant deans—competent, productive people. How did she do this? She told them that if they would do their best work for her for 4 years, she would write a glowing letter of recommendation to the dean of any of the biggest continuing education programs in the country that they chose. (They could see their cost–benefits as being improved.) The dean made it clear that she didn't expect them to stay with her forever, just for the 4 years. Without this leadership gesture, which gave young professionals a chance to see their own direct benefits in giving their boss their best efforts, this dean might have had assistants quitting in 1 year. Or she might have had a hard time enticing able people to her locality at all.

Obviously this type of leadership requires interpersonal interaction skills of persuasions. Some prefer an authoritarian type leader and some prefer a humanitarian type of leader. Which is better depends on the situation, the leader, or the followers.

SOURCES OF POWER

There are five different sources of power described in management theory, and leadership can be enhanced by combining two or three of these to widen one's power base. Remember, power is the *ability* to influence others and is always granted from below in this definition. These five sources of power, therefore, are ways one can seek to influence others' behavior.

1. *Reward Power:* This kind of power derives from the capacity of one person to reward another person in some way in exchange for their compliance with desired behavior. This compliance is expected to happen without supervision and works best when the results of the person's accepting direction and providing effort *can be seen.* If the compliance has been reinforced at the time, then it can easily be referred to later when the dean is giving the person a raise or selecting a "Staff Member of the Month" to be featured in some way.

2. *Coercive Power:* Coercive power is not just withholding rewards; it is the capacity to actually inflict something negative on a person. The outcome of the use of this kind of power is not good, and it tends to cause workers to "cover up," to lie, to turn in false reports and in general to sabotage the goals of the organization.

3. *Legitimate Power:* Legitimate power is just that: The dean *is* the dean, so people *expect* him or her to lead and ask them to do things. However, the leader's efforts to implement change must appear to be reasonable and correct to the group. If this is not readily the case, the leader will need to inform them of his or her point of view or help them understand more about the leader's responsibility. Elected officials also have legitimate power.

4. *Referent Power:* The source of referent power is that people find the leader so attractive, competent, and understanding that they want to *identi-*

fy with him or her. They wish to please the dean or director by seeking to do as he or she asks. This is the kind of leader who "inspires" people who often have no idea of the power he or she has over them. This is one of the most powerful sources of power and a valuable one for all continuing education leaders, as it is important for staff and administrators to also model ways to inspire the faculty and students.

When a person models his or her behavior after a leader, it allows the leader great influence over the person. People do things then because they like the leader, they want to do something the leader might like, and they want to *be* like the leader. People will have different areas in their lives, or groups of reference, that might each have a different referent person, such as work life, social life, family life, and religious life.

5. *Expert Power:* The source of expert power is the employees' view that the leader has more knowledge and ability in a given area. This is an easy power source to add to, by updating knowledge with workshops and conferences and keeping up with professional reading—*and talking about it,* whether in staff training or informally. People will support a leader and follow directions without supervision in relationship to how expert they think the leader is.

SOCIAL EXCHANGE—HOW TO MAKE INTERACTIONS WORK FOR YOU

The concept of social exchange is particularly useful to new leaders in continuing education in higher education confronted with a myriad of issues and charged with the task of creating new growth in many areas. The concept can be very useful, especially in deciding how fast to move on new initiatives.

The basic concept behind social exchange, which can be applied to leadership, is much like a checking account. Leaders can have a plus or minus balance of "credit" and they can add to this or subtract from it. In exchange theory the central question is *why* a group member subordinates himself or herself to someone of higher status. When leaders start out, they usually have a neutral balance. Then:

1. Everything leaders say builds plus or minus credit.
2. The follow-up on what they say builds plus or minus credit—getting resources as promised, et cetera.
3. The reward or punishment of those doing well or poorly toward organizational goals builds plus or minus credit.

Many times, leaders start off with a slight plus credit, because they are "the leader," unless the leader or director before them has done an unusually poor job. In the latter case, leaders would start off with a slightly minus credit and need to allow a longer time to build trust, remembering the three steps listed here. Implementing two major new initiatives every 6 months builds this trust, as people notice steps 1,2, and 3. Saving smaller, superficial changes until later can help prevent using up leaders' "plus credit" in advance, say into the following year or so.

When leaders begin their job, there is limited carry-over effect from past leaders, as credit is mostly based on the new individuals and what they do. New leaders also have a small plus credit as people just assume they have access to resources. Their organization can put a publicity item in a newsletter or college paper to add to their plus credit start.

Good change often comes slowly and deliberately. New deans or directors need to have their group at least not in opposition to them. If the group doubts the leader, they may try to split the cohesiveness of the group. Some individuals will work slowly and cautiously to split the staff. This, of course, ruins the organization. In order to prevent this, leaders have to make proposed rewards great enough to keep people quiet and working, and they shouldn't promise anything they can't deliver.

Leaders always need to get more credit. They have a plus to begin with and it grows, but, as they implement change they also get more criticism. Deans and directors should decide if they want this and have the competency to handle it. Perhaps they have other competencies.

Social exchange is popularity-based. Mostly it is based on people *liking* to be with leaders. The leaders make people feel good about themselves. The followers feel that they are helpful to this kind of leader and like being helpful to them (referent power).

Popular leaders can tolerate, accept, and appreciate a wide range of values—they are not dogmatic. Of course, leaders never know exactly how employees will interpret their behavior or what they'll do. Leaders can hope, though. Most groups develop fairly strong informal organizations. The goal is to have the goals of this informal network be the same as the formal goals of the division (e.g., being the best continuing education unit in town).

GETTING MAXIMUM EFFORT

Usually when employees start a job there is an employment contract, either written or unwritten, that affirms that the employees will accept direction and provide effort without question. This is called a "minimum effort"— basically, what must be provided without serious risk of being fired. In continuing and/or distance education this concept might be applied also to departments and professors, as their cooperation is essential to most new program initiatives. It is important to look at the incentives for cooperation with the continuing and/or distance education unit, and address them directly if necessary. Is there a revenue incentive? Does the department get a percentage of the net income from new programs? Do they get research opportunities? More teaching assistants?

One goal of leadership is to obtain, at least part of the time, group or individual effort that *surpasses* the minimum. To obtain this greater effort, there must be some sort of process that leads the group or individual to be concerned about the achievement of organizational objectives for reasons other than just pay and fringe benefits or immediate short-term returns such as research, consulting, and publication opportunities. Long-range marketing and showcasing of a faculty member's or department's content area might be one incentive that could inspire cooperation. Employees or departments must be genuinely concerned about the goals of the continuing education division itself (identify with them, usually in terms of finances) or must feel that the goals themselves are right and proper (e.g., appreciate the worth of the work—helping students develop to their full potential). Either will lead to superior effort. People who identify with or appreciate the worth of a unit's goals take pride in saying, "I work for a top university (or college) with a continuing education program that reaches far and wide."

Commitment in the marketplace and with faculty and students is very slow to build but very easy to destroy. Perhaps the most important aspect of the interaction between adults and the higher education institution in building commitment is that the interaction must reflect to the adults that the institution considers them important and of personal worth in themselves, whether student or employees. Everyone has a strong need to feel accepted and esteemed by others. To the extent that the institution communicates a feeling of personal worth and support to individuals or departments, staff or faculty, they will feel rewarded and *in exchange* will feel motivated to repay the institution through greater cooperation and encouragement of other adults, whether students or employees. (However, this happens best when they know that they or the department will get even more esteem or income—or both—if this behavior is continued and improved upon.)

When dealing with another person's ideas, work, or property, one should always maximize the person's self-esteem and give credit at the end of a project when it is successful. The person will also be grateful to be saved from the embarrassment of criticism.

An interesting system of rewarding professors who perform extra services, in this case, offering engineering courses on satellite television, can be seen at a large state university. The professors are given a teaching load of just one course on campus that is also on distance technology, and they are also given the services of a half-time research assistant. In addition, 10-month professors are paid also for the month of August when they come for some training and practice in front of the TV camera. Interestingly enough, the school finds that good instructors can practice very little and still do well, and poor instructors are not helped much by the training. The goal is acclimatization to on-line presentation, however.

Likert (1961, 1967) found that organizations generally have three sets of variables. If you want to effect long-term change, you must have input into the first set, which then affects the second set, and then the third set. These variables are:

1. *Causal Variables:* The organization has some control over these variables which include policies, interpersonal relations, salary, fringe benefits, rules and regulations, and hours.
2. *Intervening Variables:* These include perceptions, attitudes and loyalty that build based on the causal variables.
3. *End Variables:* These result from the attitudes and loyalty in a continuing education department or division and include as an end goal competent students and profitable programs (one definition of productivity); cooperative staff or faculty; or, on the negative side, waste, pilfering, turnover of employees, noncooperation of departments, and absenteeism.

The Likert continuum of organizational variables is summarized in Table 3.1. Don't forget to consider the time factor in the process depicted in the table. The organizational lag is usually 6 months to 2 years between sets of variables for each column to effect a change in the next column. A total of 6 years may be needed for a change affecting a large market or a large university.

If undesirable behaviors in the end variables are found when the Likert model is applied to a specific division or center, or even to an entire institution, plans can be made for changes in causal variables. Perhaps it is time to have the leadership group review and update staff and faculty policy. Salary is often controlled directly by the continuing education unit, but almost all of the other causal variables can be changed to better benefit or accommodate the faculty and staff, creating better feelings and more loyalty.

TABLE 3.1   Likert Model of Organizational Variables

Causal	Intervening	End
Policy	Perceptions	Happy, Competent Students
Rules	Attitudes	Productivity
Salary	Loyalty	Waste, Pilfering
Interpersonal Relations		Lateness
Fringe Benefits		Turnover, Absenteeism
Hours		Cooperative Staff/Faculty
Time lag:	6 months—2 years	6 months—2 years

An example illustrating the effects of a simple change in a causal variable can be seen in the story of Mary, a secretary. Mary needed to take a summer job waiting tables to help pay the taxes on her graduate tuition benefits at a private university. Her boss adjusted her schedule two afternoons a week so she could leave at 3:30 p.m., in time to get to her other job. Mary was very grateful (intervening variable) for her director's understanding attitude and remained loyal to the division and was polite and enthusiastic with the students and faculty for the rest of the time she was employed there (several years). There was no perceptible time lag in this change in Mary's feeling that hers was just a job with inconvenient hours and low pay to a feeling of gratitude—but exceptions to organizational lag do occur, especially at the individual level.

Unfortunately, the variable continuum moves in reverse, too, and where there is waste, absenteeism, staff turnover, unhappy students, and uncooperative departments, a director or an observer might find disloyal staff or faculty who perceive the policies and regulations as harsh and unfair or have other complaints (whether justified or not). This would be a larger problem and might take 2 years or more to overcome, after some of the causal variables have been changed.

It is important never to judge a program or initiative, and perhaps drop it, after only 1 year. When a new dean or director comes in, he or she sees many possibilities for change. The director should write these change areas in a notebook and start changing the two most important ones. This is a trust building time, so the changes should be implemented gradually. Two more changes can be activated in 6 months. If, after a year, the director looks at the four areas he or she has chosen to work on, noticeable improvement may be hard to find. The Likert model and the idiosyncrasy credit concept, discussed later in this chapter, suggest the benefits of waiting another year before dropping these efforts, as changes in attitudes and perceptions develop slowly, but are well worth waiting for.

CHARACTERISTICS OF SUCCESSFUL LEADERS

Likert (1967) compared the thirty most successful leader/managers of large companies with many branches, with the thirty least successful leader/managers of the same companies. He found that the major differences between the two fell into the five categories described earlier. The successful leaders and managers were able to:

1. *Provide social support for people and groups.* This was found to be the most important characteristic and is a causal variable that a leader can control to build good attitudes.

2. *Provide high task orientation.* These leaders were always clarifying the overall goals of the organization, translating the vision, and reminding people of their importance.
3. *Provide a high degree of technical expertise.* These leaders knew their fields. They took courses and workshops and read books to keep up professionally, and thus they were able to be problem solvers and help train their people.
4. *Maintain a high degree of role differentiation.* While these leaders were friendly with their staffs, they didn't go out and drink with the staff or share details of their recent divorce. By doing the things that only leaders can do and not being tempted to "pitch in with everyone" they served their organizations better. This is not to say that they did not pitch in sometimes, but they reserved time for planning and keeping up with professional reading.
5. *Provide general supervision.* The successful leaders/managers did not provide close and specific supervision, but met with groups of people in a *general* way. The concept here is that people are hired because they are competent, and they are trusted to do a good job. General training and direction are offered at staff meetings. It was found that specific, close supervision makes people feel mistrusted. Even "nosy praise" can hem people in. People who feel mistrusted or constantly watched develop attitudes of disloyalty and nonsupport for organizational goals.

By providing these five elements—social support, task orientation, technical expertise, role differentiation, and general supervision—the successful leaders/managers created a climate that led to happy, competent employees and other positive results.

People want a leader who can be a focal point. They are more likely to follow a leader who gets supplies (increases resources), provides goal orientation and facilitates group attainments, and resolves conflicts between people.

Likert divides organizations into four types, or systems: (1) "exploitative authoritative," (2) "benevolent authoritative," (3) "consultative," and (4) "participative group." Some of the characteristics of these systems are shown in Figure 3.2. Looking at the figure, which type are you?

In over 300 studies, Likert found that when organizations changed from System 1 to System 4 management, their income/revenue changed from 15% to 20% *less* than their projected budget to 15% to 20% *more* than their projected budget. In System 1 management, without two-way communication, bad news is often kept from the leader, and the "surprise" of it comes when it's too late to untangle, or correct well. These mistakes can be costly, especially in marketing, and can be averted with early information about them, from free-flowing two-way communication. This benefit of a System 4

FIGURE 3.2   Likert's Four Systems of Management

System 1	System 2	System 3	System 4
People afraid to talk to management or are told not to. Unpleasant "surprises" with little or no notice.	People less afraid to talk to management. Mistakes still kept from the leader.	People fairly free to talk. Some problems surface earlier.	Extensive friendly interaction. People really working with you. Productive problem solving, not win-lose. Two-way communication. Management knows what people's problems are.

management style, which is characterized by extensive, friendly interaction and problem solving with people, reflects the fact that the most valuable asset of any organization is its personnel. When directors become overly "task oriented," or have "control" as a top priority, they sell short their most valuable resource—people. In fact, when the "let's run a tight ship," "clean up the budget," or "follow the organizational chart" attitudes come in, the most productive employees leave first, as they get offers elsewhere.

Comptrollers and budget officers often do not have the vision to build toward a System 4 management and suggest short-term, budget-oriented solutions to problems. The specifics of how leaders apply System 4 management goals varies with their individual organizations. People have to be treated well in order to want to put any extra effort into changes and organizational improvement. The essential fact is that leaders need to respect each individual's human dignity, within his or her own framework.

If directors would like to find out what system their programs are, they can ask any employee, "How much confidence and trust do you feel your superior has in you?" The formula for a successful organization is supportive relationships (including opportunities to advance), plus high performance goals and technical competence. Most of Likert's research is based on *perceptions*, which may not reflect what's really going on, but the perceptions are what counts (they affect the end variables).

When one first starts to build attitudes, loyalty, and perceptions, "productivity" may decline in the first 6 months. This productivity decline, related to human factors, has been called the "implementation dip" in the change management literature. Because *all* resources were previously put into productivity, some people may have been "just waiting" to let their problems be known. To survive in this phase of building attitudes leaders can "use up inventory," "borrow," or "cut back" in other ways.

In the long run, people who feel respected will be much more willing to give the institution their maximum effort. This leads to it really becoming the best continuing education program in the area and to everyone associated with it taking pride in providing excellent programs for adult students.

THE USE OF POWER

Sometimes power is erroneously defined as negative and coercive because the positive aspects of power have been listed under leadership. However, the following definitions of power, as distinct from authority, will be used here.

Definitions of Power

Power is—*the ability to influence others' behaviors* (always granted from below, that is, by the people over whom it is exercised).

Authority is—*the vested right to try to influence others* (always granted from above).

Power has to be earned.

Power actually increases when you give it away—when there are more ideas and more people involved (Figure 3.3). Some people think the more power they give away the less they have (a few powerful academic deans are good examples of this). For example, suppose Dean Joseph Jones approaches his staff and says, "We need more active showcasing and marketing of this program. I want you each to call ten companies." What happens? Two people find suddenly that they are much too busy with administrative duties, two others have car trouble, and another thinks it's a bad idea that will never work and says so (politely). However, if Dean Jones turns the power of deciding how to solve their marketing problems over to the professional outreach and counseling staff, he may find that he winds up with four or five components of an elaborate marketing campaign: an education fair, a direct mail piece, advertising, corporate calls, and listing the course description and schedule on their Web site. Because the contributors are each confident about the success of their own components (and know how to get help to make them work) and like their own ideas so well, they are ready to work on them, and the unit benefits. The total amount of "power" multiplies. To achieve new growth in changing times, this participative

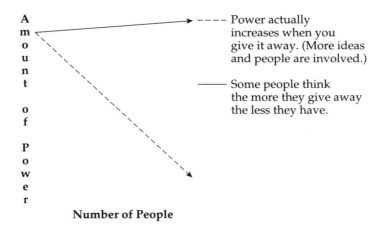

FIGURE 3.3   Amount of Power and Number of People

approach is almost an imperative. The collaborative learning that can result from the participative approach also produces increased learning, creative insight, higher productivity, higher achievement, and a higher quality of decision making (Johnson and Johnson, 1989).

There are times when a director needs to take the lead and be "in charge." Two factors determine whether or not power attempts will work: (1) The potential costs and the potential consequences of the change the leader is initiating, and (2) The view subordinates have of the director's responsibility. The Director needs to consider the subordinates' view and change it by giving them information about his or her responsibilities if necessary. This is a good time to develop joint goals to solve the problems creating the need for changes. Working as a group to develop joint goals also implies that positive potential consequences of the change being initiated include the leader's valuing the staff's input and ideas. Naturally, this would help to offset a potential cost of the change being initiated, large or small, such as the rearranging of schedules or classrooms or even coffee breaks.

If the staff is brought into coalition in the leader's favor, they will accept many more of the leader's ideas. Coalition building involves talking one to one with staff members. The coalition would ideally include the entire staff, but if the majority or even a few people understand the changes and have had time to make suggestions in informal chats, the coalition will help the leader reduce his or her costs. A coalition does risk costs to the leader (i.e., the costs involved with presenting an idea and having it turned down), but it more often will help the leader avoid costs.

IDIOSYNCRASY CREDIT

Idiosyncrasy credit, sometimes called "personality credit," develops slowly, over time. It is important for new leaders to remember this. The term *idiosyncrasy* refers to the number of idiosyncrasies, or peculiarities, the director, or new leader, is generally allowed to have.

New directors may come in and see many things they want to change in a program. In workshops for directors, experts advise new leaders to write all these good ideas in a notebook to use later when their fresh perspective may have worn off and they cannot identify the needs as clearly. Then they should choose only two ideas to begin implementing the first 6 months. They can choose two more for the second six months.

One director writes a "letter to the staff" that is the first page in her staff notebook. In this staff letter, following the paragraph on philosophical topics, she includes a paragraph on her two idiosyncrasies, plus thanks for each person's special efforts. For instance, one wrote "I appreciate your patience with the changes in office space. I think the work flow will be smoother this way. I also appreciate your extra patience with foreign students. I was one myself once, so I have a special concern for their problems." The idea here is that she can initially get away with having two quirks—just because she *is* the director. The acceptance of her idiosyncrasies builds with time and with her abilities in social exchange and interactions. Generally, leaders have a greater positive balance of idiosyncrasy credit.

Studies show over and over again that people at least want a fair exchange or even prefer getting more back in return for their efforts. If they feel they gain self-esteem and status from working in a good work climate where their extra efforts are especially valued, they will begin to feel they are getting a fair exchange. The amount of credit a leader has is based on the perceptions of the group members relative to the accomplishment of group goals. A leader, therefore, should let the group know when the division or unit is praised or group goals are being met in a way in which the staff may not be aware.

To gather credit, a leader must

1. Facilitate group attainments and group awareness of successes (remembering that people gain their perceptions through interactions)
2. Resolve conflicts
3. Increase resources

Exchange behaviors for leadership are partly learned in early childhood. Children build high self-esteem and a strong self-concept at an early age. They learn that they are desired, loved and popular. This in turn helps them to take risks and to make decisions. Because they are popular, they are asked to make decisions or to take risks first. This may be the source of charisma and what seems like "natural leadership."

But adults as well as children can learn to value the payoffs that result from risk taking (such as asking the staff to implement one change). Adults can learn to accept failures that can result from risk taking. By learning from their mistakes, adults and children can say, "I won't make the same mistake twice" or "I can usually do *something* to help correct a wrong decision."

Adults can learn leadership behaviors, to take risks, and to value the payoffs. It is difficult to change one's behavior and to maintain adaptations over a long period of time. In stress situations a person's behavior won't change too much, if it's fairly consistent with the person's most comfortable style, whether it is "human oriented" or "task oriented."

Some leaders understand how others perceive them and some do not. The ones who don't keep going out on a limb and getting no support. To pick up on perceptions, leaders have to "read" peoples' behavior—their slouches, for instance. If leaders do not feel they have support, it is better *not* to take a stand, but to discuss the issue more before group interactions, informally, in one-to-one conversations. Stress can block meaningful discussion or awareness of feedback, so a relaxed situation, over coffee or food of some kind, might be beneficial. (At one spring staff meeting a director provided fresh strawberries and powdered sugar to dip them into. He had gone out at noon to pick up the berries and sugar at the store. The originality of the idea gave everyone a lift.)

The more valuable a leader is perceived as being, the greater the credits and rewards—including salary—that he or she can receive. If directing one graduate education center helps students develop to their full potential, directing three continuing education centers will help even more students and thus provide more return to the institution of higher education. The Continuing Education Leadership Questionnaire in Figure 3.5 at the end of the chapter gives some more ideas about the knowledge, skills, and abilities that enhance a leader's value and resultant rewards, both tangible and intangible. These concepts were also discussed in Chapter 1. (Herzberg's "hygiene factors" are discussed more fully in Chapter 7.)

ORGANIZING STRUCTURES

A leader's powers, behaviors, and credits operate within the organizational structure of his or her particular environment. There is no typical organization of a continuing education division, department, or unit in higher education, but it is usually different from the traditional college or department organization. A college or department organization might look like the organizing structures A or B in Figure 3.4. Other useful structures look like C, D,

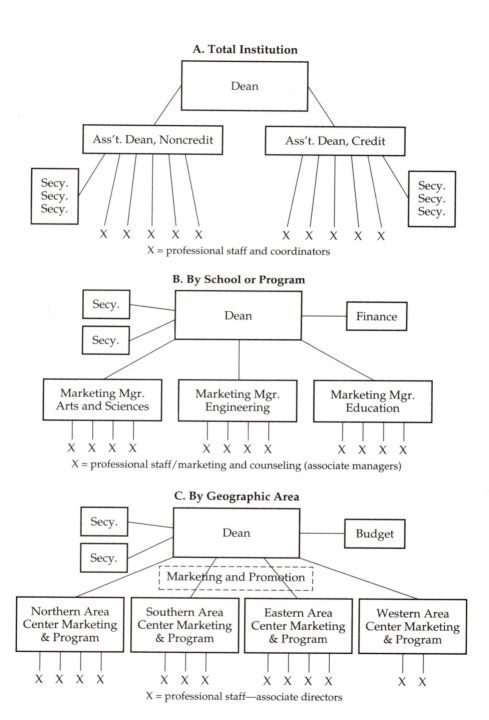

FIGURE 3.4 Organizing Structures

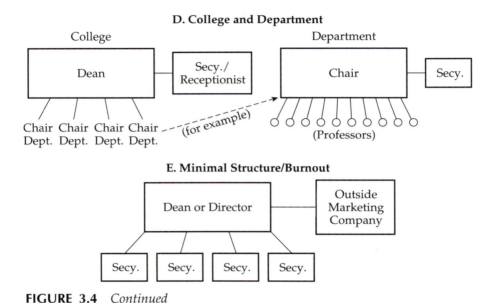

FIGURE 3.4   *Continued*

or E, arranged by geographic area; by school or program; or, lastly, a minimal or "burnout" structure, in a humorous representation.

Continuing education organizations might try to follow the "organizational chart" shown in E of the figure, with three or four able secretaries, a good computer system, and outsourced marketing functions. The disadvantages of this structure include that there is no provision for growth, as there is no professional-level staff to help with counseling, marketing calls, and information sessions; and it is possible to lose control of the marketing style and direction quickly when relying too much on outsourced business-world marketing and/or advertising companies.

These models, whether organized by area or school and program (or in a matrix combination of both to meet special requirements), allow for the programs to grow. Directors or managers can be added by program or area, and associate or assistant directors can be added for professional-level marketing outreach, counseling, handling information sessions, and off-site course administration. Management "by walking around" (Peters and Waterman, 1982) is necessary for the leader using either structure, as professional staff may be dispersed into several locations. Attending information sessions for prospective students when possible and in general being in touch with the staff and the market in each area will yield benefits.

As a program grows and changes, reassessment of areas, programs, and duties will be needed. The National Center for Education Statistics (1997) predicts that by the 21st century the proportion of adult students in higher education will approach 50 percent. A large contract program with six or eight courses may be added. Another program may "saturate" and need to be closed down. This ebb and flow can be accommodated and is quite normal in continuing education. The role of the associate director is most frequently overlooked in the "staffing up" of continuing education programs, and deans and directors wind up attending education fairs and giving information sessions themselves, as more and more companies outsource their training and education needs, which have now become a fast-growing new "market" for higher education.

SUMMARY

As risk taking is an inherent part of leadership but is not a traditional cultural norm in higher education (Birnbaum, 1988), many deans or directors of continuing education accept their positions only if they are tenured professors in their own disciplines. Knowledge and understanding of higher education are already part of the new dean's attributes, but the person has to rely on personal discretion and local tradition for leadership knowledge and skills, for management, and for marketing strategies and techniques. Often the individual is a likable, entrepreneurial type of person who may see the need for delving into the literature on marketing and on leadership or management. One successful assistant dean, a Ph.D. in management, overcame the gaps between the three fields of higher education, marketing, and management, but he was an exception. The framework for continuing adult education requires a leader who has knowledge and expertise in higher education, leadership, and marketing if a successful (and growing) continuing education unit is to develop within the institutional context. The unit usually works better with its leader chosen for these multiple backgrounds and experiences. Balanced risk taking with risk assessment can be done; understanding the institutional lag in a large institution and a large market is possible; and utilizing persuasion and idiosyncrasy credit helps the leader to be successful. Careful planning and decision making, with the group of staff members or the group in an academic department cooperating whenever possible, also help (and are addressed in the next two chapters). Leadership behaviors that follow as leadership skills and knowledge are acquired help the internal group, and even the institution, become more effective as the mission and vision for continuing education are defined and developed.

FIGURE 3.5   Continuing Education Leadership Questionnaire

	Knowledge	Skills and Abilities	Behaviors
I. Is Skilled in Setting the Direction for the Centers, Programs, and the Institution of Higher Education.	__Knows the vision he or she has and tells staff, informally.	__Articulated vision when started in the role. Set goals and implemented them.	__Tells them this vision at meetings but doesn't invite their participation in developing the vision. __Does invite their participation.
A. Conveys and translates this vision to staff.	__Tells them formally once or twice a year.	__Re-articulates the vision often and translates it. __Tells only senior staff this vision. __Makes sure the group moves toward the goals.	__Has a retreat once a year.
B. Understands and believes in high expectations for students.	__Yes __No	__Yes __No	__Has a strong vision of what the centers and programs should look like. __Translates the vision for the division or unit.
C. Takes the time to be highly visible in centers and with staff.	__Manages by walking around. __Stays on the main campus only/mostly.	__Chats with all levels of people while walking around—has frequent one sentence interactions. __They never see him or her—uses e-mail.	__They see him or her dropping in for planned and unplanned visits.
D. Understands and is committed to staff achievement.	__Knows that their good work will reflect well on him or her—therefore is encouraging to all.	__Guides planning for problem solving as needed. __Influences behaviors and attitudes of staff. __Provides and encourages opportunities to promote improved programs.	__Maximizes the effort made by staff through recognition.

FIGURE 3.5   /*Continued*

	Knowledge	Skills and Abilities	Behaviors
II. Staff Development			
A. Maintains and increases own knowledge through participation in courses, reading, conferences.	—Takes courses and workshops in marketing and direct mail, etc. —Sends e-mail notices giving date and time of new technology presentations.	—Attends conferences. —Takes managers to conferences. —Helps with problems and center evaluations.	—Sends and forwards e-mail on topics of usefulness. —Holds meetings for staff development. —Brings in useful literature and shares. —Keeps marketing and higher education textbooks on a "library shelf." —Has staff rotate conducting seminars on useful articles and books. —Provides positive feedback to staff. —Spots problems and takes action early.
B. Discusses course work and readings at staff meetings.	—Understands how to empower staff through their involvement in the decision-making process.	—Encourages staff attendance at workshops, conferences, and university courses to facilitate professional growth.	—Shares useful literature and articles.
III. Instructional Leadership			
A. Understands and is aware of student needs. B. Sets and clarifies performance expectations for the entire staff.	—Knows various educational and instructional approaches. —Is aware of student needs in various programs.	—Uses some of this knowledge in meetings with staff. —Gets library privileges and career center privileges for off-campus students. (Provides resources for activities and instruction.) —Provides maps and building diagrams on the Web site.	—Doesn't use a seminar approach for staff development meetings. —Maximizes the efforts made by staff. —Encourages professional growth. —Encourages staff to go to conferences and courses.

FIGURE 3.5   */Continued*

	Knowledge	Skills and Abilities	Behaviors
IV. Internal Environment			
A. Has know-how about the politics that take place in the organization. B. Uses his or her power with the organization to achieve goals for centers and programs.	—Knows that empowerment comes through participatory management and brings strength and creativity to the unit.	—Doesn't use an autocratic approach with a lot of structure and no two-way communication like much of higher education administration. —Maintains the structure he or she does have. —Builds friendly interactions at meetings to aid problem solving and risk taking.	—Gets along will with staff and provides Herzberg's hygiene factors. —Provides (or sees that Herzberg's motivator factors are provided): autonomy, recognition, esteem, worth of the work, sense of achievement and growth.
V. External Environment			
A. Uses his or her power outside the organization to achieve goals for the centers and programs.	—Knows to reach out to build liaisons, and to build up the budget and other resources from all parts of the university or college. —Builds connections with the community.	—Tells the staff about these efforts and how well they're working. —Develops external liaisons to achieve goals for the centers and programs.	—Takes various staff members to meetings on occasion. —Creates supportive coalitions and alliances within the community to make things happen for the centers and programs. —Encourages professional and marketing staff to create alliances also, to develop contract programs and build public relations. —Takes time to be highly visibile, visits each location once every week or two.

BIBLIOGRAPHY

Allen, R. W., D. L. Madison, L. W. Porter, P. A. Renwick, and B. T. Mayes (1979). "Organizational Politics: Tactics and Characteristics of Its Actors." *California Management Review, 22* (4), 77–83.

Baldridge, J. V., D. V. Curtis, G. Ecker, and G. L. Riley (1978). *Policy Making and Effective Leadership: A National Study of Academic Management.* San Francisco: Jossey-Bass.

Banfield, E. C. (1961). *Political Influence.* New York: The Free Press.

Bass, B. (1981). *Stodgill's Handbook of Leadership.* New York: The Free Press.

Beach, D. S. (1975). *Managing People at Work: Readings in Personnel.* New York: Wiley.

Birnbaum, R. (1988). *How Colleges Work: The Cybernetics of Academic Organization and Leadership.* San Francisco: Jossey-Bass.

Blake, R.R., et al., (1964). "Breakthrough in Organizational Development." *Harvard Business Review*, Nov.-Dec.

Blake, R. R., and J. S. Mouton (1982). "A Comparative Analysis of Situationalism and 9.9 Management by Principle." *Organizational Dynamics*, Spring, pp. 20–42.

Blake, R. R., and J. S. Mouton (1985). *Managerial Grid III.* Houston, TX: Gulf.

Blau, P. M. (1964). *Exchange and Power in Social Life.* New York: Wiley.

Bolman, L. G., and T. Deal (1994). "Looking for Leadership: Another Search Party's Report." *Education Administration Quarterly, 30* (1), 77–96.

Boyatzis, R. (1982). *The Competent Manager.* New York: Wiley.

Brearley, A. (1976). "The Changing Role of the Chief Executive." *Journal of General Management, 3* (4), 62–71.

Drucker, P. (1967). *The Effective Executive.* New York: Harper & Row.

Drucker, P. (1974). *Management.* New York: Harper & Row.

Fiedler, F. E. (1967). *A Theory of Leadership Effectiveness.* New York: McGraw-Hill.

Fiedler, F. E. (1971). *Leadership.* New York: General Learning Press.

French, J. R., Jr., and B. Raven (1996). "The Bases of Social Power." In M. T. Matteson and J. M. Ivanevich (Eds.), *Management and Organizational Behavior Classics.* Boston: Irwin.

Gardner, J. W. (1990). *On Leadership.* New York: The Free Press.

Gay, L. R. (1992). *Educational Research: Competencies for Analysis and Application.* New York: Macmillan.

Herzberg, F., B. Mausner, and B. Snyderman (1959). *The Motivation to Work.* New York: Wiley.

Hollander, E. P. (1958). "Conformity, Status, and Indiosyncrasy Credit." *Psychological Review, 65*, 117–127.

"The 100 Most Effective College Leaders, Named in a Survey of Their Peers." *Chronicle of Higher Education*, Nov. 5, 1986, p. 13.

Jacobs, T. O. (1971). *Leadership and Exchange in Formal Organizations.* Alexandria, VA: Human Resources Research Organizations.

Johnson, D. W., and R. T. Johnson (1989). *Cooperation and Competition.* Edina, MN: Interaction.

Jones, C. C. (1980). *Leadership and the Use of Power.* Rockville, MD: ECEA Institute.

Kotter, J. P. (1973). "The Psychological Contract: Managing the Joining Up Process." *California Management Review, 15*, (3), 91–99.

Kotter, J. P. (1977). "Power, Dependence, and Effective Management." *Harvard Business Review*, July/August, pp. 125–136.

Kotter, J. P. (1978). *Organizational Dynamics: Diagnosis and Intervention.* Reading, MA: Addison-Wesley.

Kotter, J. P. (1979a). "Managing External Dependence." *Academy of Management*, 4 (1), 87–92.

Kotter, J. P. (1979b). *Power in Management.* AMACOM.

Kotter, J. P. (1982). *The General Managers.* New York: The Free Press.

Kotter, J. P., V. A. Faux, and C. C. McArthur (1979). *Self-Assessment and Career Development.* Englewood Cliffs, NJ: Prentice-Hall.

Likert, R. (1961). *New Patterns of Management.* New York: McGraw-Hill.

Likert, R. (1967). *The Human Organization.* New York: McGraw-Hill.

Likert, R. (1996). "Human Organizational Measurements: Key to Financial Success." In M. T. Matteson and J. M. Ivanevich (Eds.), *Management and Organizational Behavior Classics.* Boston: Irwin.

Lorsch, J., and S. A. Allen (1973). *Managing Diversity and Interdependence.* Cambridge, MA: Harvard UniversityPress.

McClelland, D. C. (1970). "Two Faces of Power." *Journal of International Affairs, 24* (1), 29–47.

McClelland, D. C. (1975). *Power: The Inner Experience.* New York: Irvington.

Miles, R. H. (1980). *Macro Organizational Behavior.* Santa Monica, CA: Goodyear.

National Center for Education Statistics (1997). In PBS Video Conference downlink "Best Practices in Marketing to Adult Students," Nov. 12, Washington, DC.

Nichel, W. G. (1982). *Marketing Principles* (2d Ed.). Englewood Cliffs, NJ: Prentice-Hall.

Pascale, R. T., and A. G. Athos (1981). *The Art of Japanese Management.* Simon & Schuster.

Peters, T. (1978). "Symbols, Patterns, and Settings." *Organizational Dynamics*, Fall, pp. 3–23.

Peters, T. J., and R. H. Waterman (1982). *In Search of Excellence.* New York: Harper Row.

Pettigrew, A. (1973). *The Politics of Organizational Decision Making.* London: Tavistock.

Pfeffer, J. (1981). *Power in Organizations.* Marshfield, MA: Pitman.

Presthus, R. (1962). *The Organizational Society.* New York: Vintage Books.

Richman, B. M., and R. N. Farmer (1974). *Leadership, Goals, and Power in Higher Education: A Contingency and Open-Systems Approach to Effective Management.* San Francisco: Jossey-Bass.

Rickarts, T. (1975). *Problem Solving through Creative Analysis.* Epping, England: Gower Press.

Rumelt, R. P. (1974). *Strategy, Structure, and Economic Performance.* Cambridge, MA: Harvard University Press.

Salancik, G. R., and J. Pfeffer (1974). "The Bases and Use of Power in Organizational Decision Making: The Case of a University." *Administrative Science Quarterly, 19*, 453–473.

Salancik, G. and J. Pfeffer (1977). "Who Gets Power and How They Hold On to It: A Strategic Contingency Model of Power." *Organizational Dynamics*, Winter, pp. 3–21

Sayles, L. (1964). *Managerial Behavior.* New York: McGraw-Hill.

Sonnenfeld, J., and J. P. Kotter (1982). "The Maturation of Career Theory." *Human Relations, 35* (1), 19–46.

Tannenbaum, R., and W. H. Schmidt (1973). "How to Choose a Leadership Pattern." *Harvard Business Review*, May-June.

Weick, K. E. (1983). "Managerial Thought in the Context of Action." In S. Srivastva and Associates, *The Executive Mind: New Insights on Managerial Thought and Action.* San Francisco: Jossey-Bass.

Yukl, G. A. (1994). *Leadership in Organizations.* Englewood Cliffs, N J: Prentice-Hall.

▶ 4

Planning for Continuing Education in Higher Education

Leadership means planning for change, as discussed in Chapter 3, whether through new goals or through new processes, or both. Facilitating group goal attainment requires involving the whole institution of higher education as graduate and undergraduate continuing education and distance education become distribution channels for more and more academic programs. Good planning is the key to smoothly running programs for continuing education in higher education or in any setting. Planning anticipates decisions, it can help handle interdependent decisions, and it can provide a process by which staff and faculty can have input and "buy into" the goals and strategies of the organization. Due to problems of faculty power struggles and intrigues, faculty tenure, issues of diversity, and budget and space issues, instructional and educational leadership and marketing in the external arena can be pulled down by lack of leadership on internal political issues on two levels: within the institution and within the unit. Good planning, with participation and empowerment of all stakeholders, is important in both these arenas, if a program is to be successful in its outreach efforts. In this chapter various planning strategies and tools will be discussed as they affect developing and translating a vision for the continuing education division, department, or unit.

As the division deals with issues in the external and internal political environments and with topics that come up for staff development and in educational/instructional leadership areas, various planning philosophies and strategies will be useful. Leadership for change and planning for change affect these different arenas, but with or without change, these are areas that need attention and planning.

DEVELOPING A VISION

Developing and translating a vision for the continuing education division is an important first step in leadership. Whether developed individually or as a group, this vision and philosophy must be translated into action to be effective. The sections on scenarios in planning will help with these translations into action. But first, a discussion of one approach for planning a vision with the staff group, and later with academic departments, is in order.

Involvement of Staff and Faculty

In identifying problems and solutions for an education center it is helpful to be clear on the vision and style or values of the continuing education division. Discussion of this vision and philosophy with both the staff and the faculty of academic departments will help to define the programs to be presented more clearly. This can be done by first brainstorming statements for the philosophy and then the market needs and requests in a staff meeting. This can be followed by a vote on the five or ten most important elements in the philosophy. This list can then be taken (on a flip chart or large poster) to a meeting that includes faculty, and the faculty can brainstorm *their* ideas about the philosophy and the program. When the faculty reach some sort of final consensus about their list and then the two lists are put together, usually an impressive vision and goal statement results. This can be placed in publicity brochures, on bulletin boards and wherever else information on good higher education continuing education is needed. A sample program vision or philosophy statement can be seen in Figure 4.1.

The opportunity to vote on elements of the philosophy gives faculty a feeling of involvement and can be repeated every spring during the planning-for-fall period. Alternatively the philosophy can be communicated one to one by the dean or director of the continuing education division or unit calling on the heads of the academic departments or by presenting it at academic department meetings. Faculty who are directly involved in selecting elements of the vision hear the many expectations other faculty have for the education centers or unit, and in voting for the elements favored by the majority, they see that not all wishes can be met. If an adjunct professor feels strongly that his or her students should be allowed photocopier privileges (or other unusual privileges), for example, he or she may wish to look for another institution in which to teach. This will save the center director and faculty member a year

---

FIGURE 4.1   Philosophy of a Continuing Education Division or Center

The philosophy of the Higher Education Continuing Education Division is based on the belief that students are individuals, learning and growing. Within the framework of the current world situation, the focus of the Continuing Education Division (or Continuing Education Center) will be:

1. To provide programs that, in balance, enhance a student's development intellectually and build career abilities as appropriate.
2. To provide programs that are requested in the community and marketplace.
3. To provide an environment conducive to learning.
4. To provide an environment in which students can learn actively through research and hands-on experience.
5. To provide individualized attention within the context of a group setting.
6. To provide specialized student services including informal counseling, expediting administrative. matters, and making higher education "user friendly."
7. To work with faculty as active partners in their students' learning.

---

of complaints and unhappiness and thus can be a benefit. Or the faculty member may see that photocopying by students cannot be worked into the budget and suggest that students use outside photocopy shops.

Once the philosophy or vision and programming goals are decided upon, the dean or director can begin translating them into goals for the division and staff, and then into a schedule for attainment of these goals. A director's list of goals may look quite different from the philosophy, while still remaining relevant. These goals might include:

- Remaining financially afloat by increasing the division or a particular center's income
- Building quality into the program by focusing on specifics in the philosophy
- Improving safety and security throughout the center
- Building staff morale and student service

Three Philosophies or Processes of Planning

More ways to develop a vision or a philosophy statement, and the plans needed to carry them out, are demonstrated in the three following philosophies of planning. These include: satisficing, optimizing, and adaptivizing (Ackoff, 1970).

Satisficing is when one solution is arrived at that meets objectives and goals that are feasible and desirable. It implies "being satisfied." The satisficing planner sets a few simple goals and is happy to satisfy them. This approach has dangers in not being long-range enough or not considering the outside environment enough, but for some problems it is appropriate. An additional danger of satisficing is that sometimes at the end of a long meeting, when there is pressure of time, the single solution can look more and more attractive even though it is not the best or the most appropriate solution.

Optimizing is similar to the rational approach taught in business schools. The goal in optimizing is to do as well as possible, and many, many alternatives can be generated. Unfortunately, this takes more time than one often has. In the rational approach criteria are developed after the problem is defined, and three to five alternatives are considered against these criteria. The consideration of several alternatives can highlight some variables that may be combined in a new way. There are always variables that are uncontrollable, such as weather, economic conditions, the competition, technological developments, and preferences of students or employees. Unfortunately, the optimizer sometimes ignores these variables, and often ignores goals that cannot be quantified. (For example: the financial bottom line can be more important than the academic excellence, integrity, or applicability of the programs.) However, optimizing allows planning to get underway.

Adaptivizing is the name given to planning that "gets outside the box" or considers solutions from a very different perspective than satisficing or optimizing. Often this happens when a problem is redefined and looked at in new ways. The chapter on problem solving (8) suggests a number of ways to do this.

Adaptivizing provides for five different sets of plans based on the knowledge of the future which can be certainty, uncertainty, or complete ignorance. Planning for a future that is fairly certain is called *commitment planning* (plan set number 1); the administrative budget might be an example of this. Planning for an uncertain future that might be a little better or a little worse than the present situation is called *contingency planning* and requires two plans: one for the somewhat better (plan set number 2) and one for less good or somewhat worse conditions (plan set number 3). The aspect of the future that cannot be anticipated or that one is completely ignorant of, also requires two sets of plans: one for much better conditions (plan set number 4) and one for much worse conditions (plan set number 5). This is called *responsiveness planning*, and is frequently overlooked. It's labeled "responsiveness" because this planning builds responsiveness and flexibility into the organization. The Figure 7.4 in the chapter about adding Saturday and computer programs shows how responsiveness planning might be done for scheduling in a situation that was much more favorable than previously thought. A responsiveness plan for conditions being much worse (such as a major plant or military base closing near your town) might first require additional classes and then might need financial emergency measures or ideas, such as plans to rent out one or two classrooms for other uses or for an incubator for small businesses. Another emergency measure would be to eliminate the most expensive, least effective part of your program, such as programs that have saturated the market in their present location. New formats, new locations, and updated course descriptions and titles all help programs be responsive to new circumstances, whether much better or much worse.

The adaptive planner tries to change the system or the structure so that efficiency follows as a result. Organizations that plan this way tend to use their employees' best potential and therefore are very effective.

SCENARIOS AND OBJECTIVES FOR MANAGING CHANGE

Once the philosophy and programming goals are developed, the "style" of the educational programs and/or centers will be clear and possible scenarios for improvement and advertising of one aspect or another can be generated. A few are developed here as examples. A scenario is a description of what an organization might look like at some specified time in the future. It is a description rather than a financial plan. Use of scenarios is based on the idea that what continuing education becomes depends more on what it does than on what is done to it. It builds on the idea of making the future happen rather than letting events slide and then saying, "What happened?"

A continuing education division and its centers can design almost any kind of future they want for themselves with careful planning and involvement of staff and faculty. (See the section on revenue sharing with academic departments in Chapter 11.) A scenario allows room to plan for "wishful thinking" for the future and also may uncover unexpressed aspirations of the participants.

Commitment planning is sometimes is called "reference projection" and is essentially what can be predicted if nothing new is done. What one would like to have done can be referred to as a "wishful projection." The difference between the two defines the gap that needs to be filled by planning and setting objectives onto a time line—making a "planned projection." A scenario in the motion picture industry describes what people will do when acting out a story. Scenarios in continuing education management planning describe different models of what people will do or what must or might happen in striving toward different goals. They also allow for wishful thinking in various areas to be quantified so that decisions about possible goals can be made.

A good way to get at the wishful projections of a group and to determine if there are possible goal conflicts is to develop scenarios around different topics. Identifying and resolving possible goal conflicts early further enhances any project, by reducing conflicts and encouraging useful discussions.

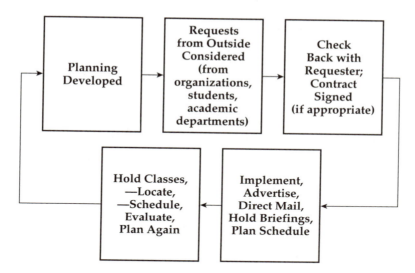

FIGURE 4.2   **A Model of the Continuing Education Planning Cycle**

It is possible to develop scenarios around policies, programs, procedures, practices, and courses of action. In each case, draw a picture (model) of the existing policy, course of action, or other item that needs to be examined. Put a box around each existing step. Then brainstorm alternatives for the steps described in each box of the model. A group or an individual can do this. As the four or five (or more) boxes are reviewed and brainstorming occurs, a scenario begins to emerge. Some ideas may clearly be inappropriate but may lead to more feasible suggestions.

An External Outreach Example of the Scenario Building Model

Dealing with the external environment in continuing education usually includes marketing open enrollment courses and increasing the number of group contract courses. Marketing will be dealt with more extensively in Chapter 11; here we will look at the scenario-building model through an example of external outreach for enrollment and income development.

The first step in developing a scenario is to draw a model of the activities done throughout the planning cycle in a continuing education division or center. See Figure 4.2.

The second step in developing a scenario for a particular goal is to brainstorm alone or perhaps with a group how that goal could be implemented in two or three ways around each box in the model. For instance, for the goal "Increasing the Center's Enrollment and Income" the scenario might look like

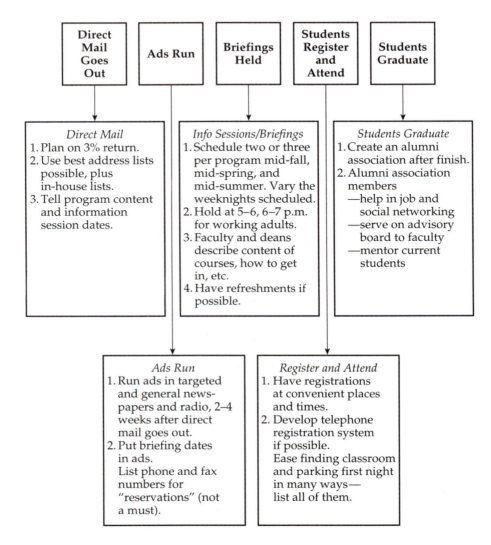

FIGURE 4.3   Increasing the Center's Enrollment and Income

the model in Figure 4.3. This scenario gives a Director many ideas from which to choose—three to five logical projects for development that might increase the center's income. Other ideas stay in the back of people's minds, and the director may hear more ideas or more possibilities about a given idea next year.

Scenarios are a tool for helping people take a long view in a world of great uncertainty. They are *not* predictions; they are vehicles for helping people learn. The end result is not an accurate picture of tomorrow but an aid to making better decisions about the future. Scenarios can be used to change others' view of reality. Another use of scenarios is to visually demonstrate future possibilities (or possible realities)—a "better," "the same," or "worse" scenario series such as the three possibilities shown in Figure 4.4 through Figure 4.6.

Figure 4.4 depicts a positive, "more growth" scenario. Such a scenario can be self-fulfilling, as it includes steps or boxes that would make the possibility more probable. Figures 4.5 and 4.6 are presented as a humorous way to show "less growth" and "no growth" scenarios. They map out some of the frustrations felt at some institutions of higher education. Although these models are negative, they show that when tenured faculty refuse to teach at inconvenient locations or will only sponsor programs with "underutilized" faculty, less growth or no growth will occur. Unfortunately, these figures represent "true stories" from large universities.

An Example of Scenario Development for the Internal Environment

Planning that impacts the internal environment may require some staff development. The leader may need to plan to do this to introduce the scenario activities and for some decision-making and problem-solving activities described later in this book. With new staff members who are not part of the traditional higher education milieu, staff development for new areas and tasks (and new thinking!) in continuing and distance education becomes important. Staff development has been acknowledged as important in other areas of educational leadership for many years, and now its usefulness for higher education staff and faculty is also becoming apparent. A scenario that might maintain and build quality into the program according to the philosophy in Figure 4.1 and that would also work toward building staff morale and development might look like Figure 4.7.

Space does not permit exploring all the ideas that can be generated from the philosophy when it is applied to the model of the planning cycle. More equipment, more imaginative use of what is there, or inviting outside speakers to a staff development meeting are a few that come to mind. The possibilities are limitless, and generating them is a good exercise for beginning-of-the-fiscal-year staff meetings. If the staff helps choose two or three goals for staff development for the year, the improvement of quality and morale is off to a good start.

A leader could use the decision-making-tree such as the one shown in Chapter 5 to help decide which projects might be best for group involvement. Some ideas generated would benefit from outside funding or would need cooperation from another group, which might entail networking and proposal writing. A section on writing proposals is included in Chapter 12.

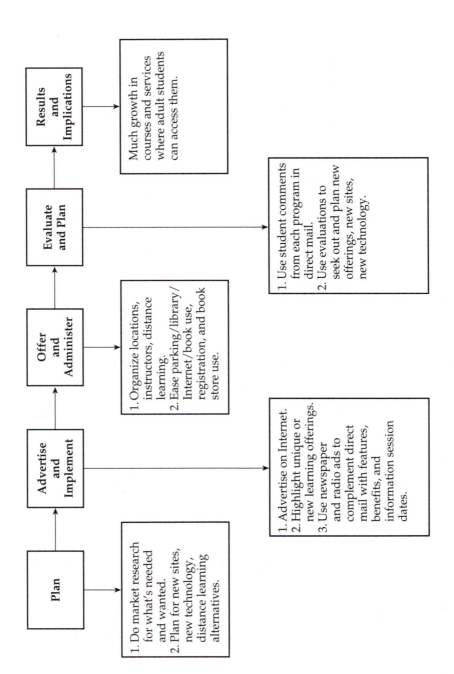

FIGURE 4.4   Scenario for More Growth

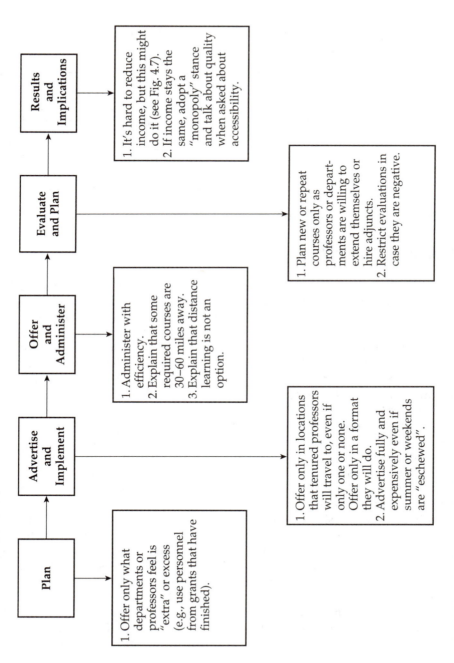

FIGURE 4.5 Scenario for Less Growth (Worse)

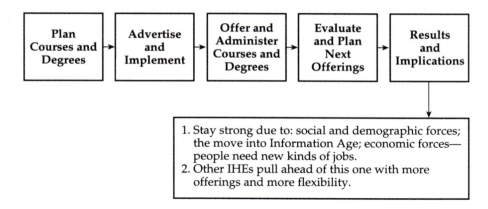

FIGURE 4.6   Scenario for No Growth (The Same)

STRATEGIC PLANNING

Strategic planning is the name that has been given to the process of looking first in an organized way at outside environmental opportunities and risks and then looking internally at the continuing education unit's strengths and weaknesses (i.e., available resources). It is better for an individual unit to develop plans and opportunities and not to just respond to the impact of outside events. At the very least, the planning process has the effect of adding some predictability to outside impacts, whether they come from the institution or from the society at large. A first step might be for a planning group to think of two or three significant events in society that will affect continuing education in higher education. It is not necessary to agree on these, but as the leader/facilitator goes around the group for each person's list, some consensus usually does emerge. This is called an "External Analysis" and is shown as Step I in Figure 4.8. Identified items might include such things as changing demographics, the society moving into the Information Age, and economic recession requiring new job or career skills.

At this point a "visioning" exercise of some type might be useful. Simply asking people what they envision being able to tell people about the continuing education unit or center in 5 years is a good start, or one can use the scenarios approach just described. With this information recorded, a review of the unit's mission or philosophy statement, possibly rewriting it and adding some policies, might be called for. This done, the group can review the external analysis done earlier and then review internal strengths and weaknesses to develop an "Internal Analysis," Step II in Figure 4.8. Strengths and weaknesses include a weak or strong financial picture that

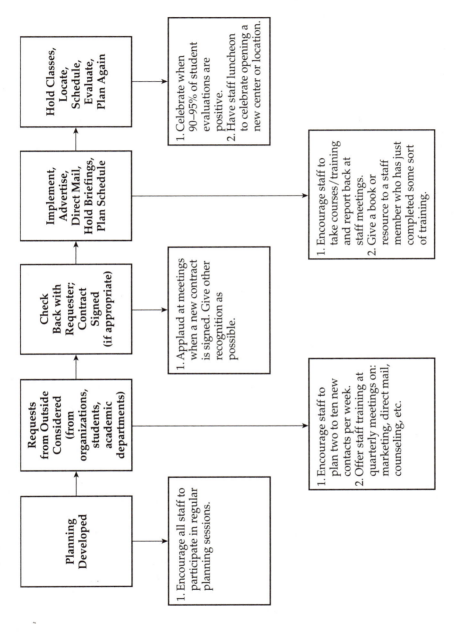

FIGURE 4.7   Scenario for Maintaining Quality and Staff Morale

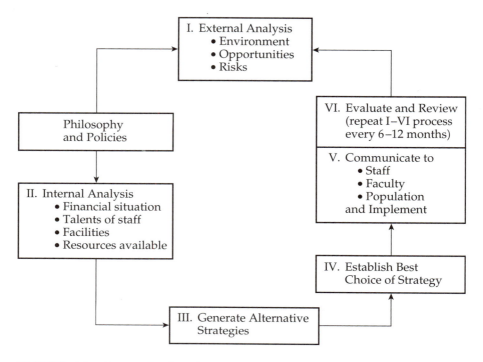

FIGURE 4.8   Strategic Planning Steps

would allow or would not allow for expansion. The depth of professional and managerial talent also must be considered. It is not necessary to reach a consensus on the internal analysis, either. Setting priorities and then writing objectives for the next 3 to 5 years comes next. Then the group is ready to write strategies for new programs and processes.

Generating alternative strategies can be done alone or in a group brainstorming session. Alternative strategies for long-range and short-range planning to solve a problem are discussed further in Chapter 8. "Shifting the burden" or making a "quick fix" can be done in the short range, but a more fundamental long-range plan is also needed. The choice of strategy and its implementation requires group involvement and outward communication to be most effective. This planning time can be the most valuable time that a dean or director spends. It is also a form of staff development, and it prevents management by default. Failure to plan can result in ineffective, undirected action (also called "planning to fail").

Once the alternative strategies for accomplishing priorities are generat-

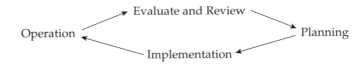

FIGURE 4.9   The Continuous Planning Circle

ed, the best choice of strategy can be agreed upon. (At this point it is important to keep a record of the other strategies generated, as they may become
useful as outside events change.) The best-choice strategy is then communicated widely—to staff, to faculty and to the public—as appropriate (Step V
in Figure 4.8). Optimally, all but the general public will have been involved
in one way or another before this juncture. A last step after these plans have
become operational, and one that may begin next year's planning session
(or next quarter's), is to evaluate and review this strategy and the choices
(Step VI in Figure 4.8), to build for the future. It is important at this review
point to find and fix any problems and plan to prevent the same problems
in the future. (This is the beginning of a quality system that will be discussed
more thoroughly in Chapter 11.) There is thus a continuous planning circle,
as shown in Figure 4.9

Unfortunately, the internal institutional political environment cannot
always be planned for, but having contingency plans and responsiveness
plans in place can help the unit react appropriately to new initiatives. These
plans can also help the unit be proactive with the institution in bringing in
new income and research opportunities.

EDUCATIONAL LEADERSHIP AND PLANNING FOR CHANGE

Educational and instructional leadership are often an assumed element in
higher education administration and management, but, again, modeling
attention to students' learning needs and planning with staff for new and
better ways of meeting them bring fresh thinking to the task of realizing an
institution's vision. One dean of continuing education, in thinking through
the individual student's experience, introduced distance delivery of library
resources and access to career center services to an institution that had not
previously provided these services to off-campus students.

Brainstorming a scenario for an individual student's experience is
another good staff development activity that generates new ideas. A model
of a student's experience and ideas for improving it is given in Figure 4.10.

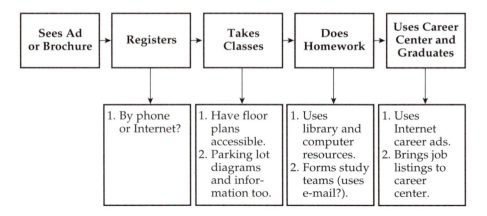

FIGURE 4.10   Scenario of a Student's Perspective

Because programs for adult students are affected by outside trends including demographics and economics, planning is essential. Figure 4.11, "Sources and Impacts of Change," shows the results of a brainstorming session on the effects of outside trends on programs in continuing education. It shows how even global and national concerns can be interpreted in the workplace, and for individual employees and students, and can require planning for managing their impacts. Such brainstorming is an interesting exercise for staff meetings, as the information or ideas in the boxes of the figure may change every few months. This also could be a first step in a strategic planning exercise in considering all levels of the environment, as demonstrated here.

A second meeting or a meeting using Figure 4.11 as a handout could include the next strategic planning step of considering opportunities and risks, perhaps beginning with impacts of change at the national and community level. The staff might choose one category to develop more fully for the workplace or for the individual level, such as social, physical or technological. After considering possible alternatives such as the ones listed for the workplace and the individual shown in Figure 4.11, and ones added by the group, the group can vote on the one or two best alternatives to pursue.

A leader working with the staff then skips to the level of communication in the strategic plan. In a simple example, the division could communicate to the public that it is having an initiative in technology (or another theme for the semester or the year) that will include credit and noncredit courses, with the lead feature being a noncredit series in multimedia technology and authoring of CD-ROMs. Announcements would list the degrees and courses (and their various locations) that fit into this theme. Different teams might

Figure 4.11 Sources and Impacts of Change in Continuing Education

Sources:	Political	Economic	Social	Physical	Technological
Global Impacts	New configurations on the globe are causing many changes.	Global economic cooperation is more and more a reality creating many learning needs.	Families and individuals will be moving to follow jobs and the education needed for jobs. Plan ways to offer continuing education courses internationally.	Easier to fly to distant places, or transcend physical distances with distance learning and e-mail.	Use of computers and the move into the Information Age are world-wide trends. Develop an Internet home page; include continuing education schedule.
National Impacts	Federal cutbacks are causing IHEs* to look to Continuing Education units and alumni for additional income.	International business initiatives and partners are becoming the norm.	U.S. demographics becoming more international. Have a partner IHE in another country.	More IHEs are opening satellite locations in other cities and states.	Learning "Information Age content" is a national need at all levels: management information systems and telecommunications, etc.
Community Impacts	Political support for state-funded IHEs will be needed. Fewer funds-dependent projects will be needed.	More and better continuing education will be needed for all economic levels.	Some communities have a high need for ESL (English as a Second Language) courses.	Place education centers near the students, e.g., in suburbs or on subway routes, etc.	Some communities are networking services and will help advertise continuing education programs available.
Impacts for Continuing Education Programs	Invite local legislators as guest speakers. Remind them that education is the "bridge" into the Information Age and to economic development.	Offer different tuition for different locations, populations, or contract groups. Consider offering some deluxe services to offset costs (e.g., such as résumé writing and counseling).	Provide social interaction times at Information Sessions and other events. Offer multicultural management courses as appropriate.	Share, regularly, news about different segments of your geographic marketing areas.	Network all locations in one geographic area on a Wide Area Network (WAN). Offer Information Age–relevant courses at all (or most) locations.
Individual Impacts	Encourage students to study legislative affairs. Do regular environmental scan on political issues.	Always tie economic benefits of programs into new student information sessions.	Have staff bulletin board—post news of places people have moved from and visited, so all can learn.	Encourage staff to use Internet and to come up with new ideas for types of distance learning for a 5-year plan.	Encourage staff to stay current with new computers, software, e-mail, and other technologies.

*IHE: Institutions of Higher Education

work on each alternative. More ambitious plans requiring more resources, such as opening a graduate education center across town, could be tested via the scenario process, which helps a group (or individual) simulate possibilities and probabilities for the new idea.

SUMMARY

The excitement and friendly interaction of brainstorming sessions help staff (and faculty members) learn and also make them feel stronger, more helpful, and more "empowered" as a team. Designing situations such as those described in this chapter in which people can succeed, in considering hypothetical scenarios and strategies unlocks creativity and puts joy and energy back into the sometimes taxing work of being in continuing education in the higher education setting. As people come up with ideas, they will be more likely to offer help. Innovation is attractive, and new ideas, even those generated by just one person, will be interesting and draw support. However, as noted in Chapter 3, if things have been discouraging for a while, a leader may need to hold two or three idea sessions to get useful planning underway.

A continuing education unit with high-quality innovations supported by staff and faculty will be "ahead of the game" when competition becomes stiffer. The programs will also have great "word-of-mouth" publicity and possibly more students in the center(s). It might be necessary to have special programs to help pay for some innovations, but being more in control of the continuing education unit's future will be worth it.

One point of view stresses that the main value of planning does not lie in the actual plans produced, but in the process of producing them. The interaction of people and ideas as people think about mid-range and long-range goals for a program or educational center is the main benefit. Therefore, planning cannot be done *to* or *for* a group but must be done *by* the group. Many "best ideas" of staff and faculty may surface and can be suitably adapted onto a time line joined with other best ideas. The implementation of every step of the plan is less important than the habit developed of sharing good ideas and planning for the future within a framework structured enough to allow good ideas to be captured and thought through. As with students, the process of learning can be more important than the product, and the planning process is a form of staff and faculty development.

As both the program being planned for and its environment change during the planning process, it is nearly impossible to consider all the variables. Therefore, it is necessary to continuously update and maintain any plan, individually and in a group. To prevent being "sandbagged" by change, it is important to try to understand the environmental impacts systematically on at least five levels: global, national, community, workplace, and individual. When changes in each of these levels are considered in relation to the impact(s) they might have on the programs for adult students, new insights emerge and actions and contingency plans can be developed. One can also: (1) try to alter the course of the change, (2) decide how to capitalize on the advantages of the change, or (3) plan to resist the change.

Anticipating change and planning for it help an organization and its people feel more "on top of things" and therefore to have good morale. Scenario building and strategic planning are just two of the many useful tools in the leadership process. Long-range planning that is hard to reverse and that affects many functions of the organization should also be considered in the light of techniques for decision making, discussed in Chapter 5.

BIBLIOGRAPHY

Ackoff, R. L. (1970). *A Concept of Corporate Planning*. New York: Wiley.

Ackoff, R. L. (1974). *Redesigning the Future: A Systems Approach to Societal Problems*. New York: Wiley.

Argyris, C., and D. Schon (1974). *Theory in Practice: Increasing Professional Effectiveness*. San Francisco: Jossey-Bass.

Bennis, W., and B. Nanus (1974). "Leadership and Organizational Excitement" *California Management Review*, Winter.

Bennis, W., and B. Nanus (1985). *Leaders: The Strategies for Taking Charge*. New York: Harper & Row.

Bradford, D. L., and A. R. Cohen (1984). *Managing for Excellence: The Guide to Developing High Performance in Contemporary Organizations*. New York: Wiley.

Foster, R. (1986). Innovation: *The Attackers' Advantage*. New York: Summit Books.

Kanter, R. (1983). *The Change Masters: The Innovation for Productivity in the American Corporation*. New York: Simon & Schuster.

Kelly, C. M. (1987). "The Interrelation of Ethics and Power in Today's Organizations." *Organizational Dynamics, 16* (1), 4–18.

Koontz, H., and C. O'Donnell (1972). *Principles of Management*. (3d ed.). New York: McGraw-Hill.

Lindbloom, C. E. (1980). "The Science of Muddling Through." In H. J. Leavitt and L. Pondy (Eds.), *Readings in Managerial Psychology*. Chicago: University of Chicago Press.

McGregor, D. (1960). *The Human Side of Enterprise*. New York: McGraw-Hill.

Naisbitt, J., and P. Auburdene (1990). *Megatrends 2000*. New York: Morrow.

Peters, T. J. (1987). *Thriving on Chaos: Handbook for Managing Revolution*. New York: Knopf.

Peters, T. J., and N. Austin (1985). *A Passion for Excellence: The Leadership Difference*. New York: Random House.

Rogers, C. (1977). *On Personal Power*. New York: Dell.

Shoemaker, C. J. (1995). *Administration and Management of Programs*. Englewood Cliffs, NJ: Prentice Hall.

Wack, P. (1985). "Scenarios: Uncharted Waters Ahead." *Harvard Business Review*, September/October, p. 72.

Weisbord, M. R. (1978). *Organizational Diagnosis: A Workbook of Theory and Practice.* Reading, MA: Addison Wesley.

Weisbord, M. R. (1987). *Productive Workplaces: Organizing and Managing for Dignity, Meaning and Community.* San Francisco: Jossey-Bass.

▶ 5

Making Decisions in Continuing Education

Leadership involves decision making. To lead effectively, one needs to plan for change that improves the organization. As discussed in Chapter 2, this change may involve achieving new goals using old processes, continuing to work toward old, ongoing goals using new processes, or aiming for new goals using new processes. Research has shown that whenever leaders involve staff, faculty, or students in the planning and decision making, they build commitment. But how is one to do this? And when? Furthermore, planning should be a continuous process as new resources, goals, policies, or needs arise. This is especially true in continuing and distance education in higher education, with changes in the economy, changes in the demography of the student body, and new calls on public institutions for scrutiny and accountability from legislative and governmental bodies. A plan can be considered an interim report, so it is essential that the planners get together at regular meetings to adapt and improve plans that have been made and to generate new plans to address these many issues.

The Greek word for administration is *kuberneseis*, which refers to the work of ships' pilots who steer the ships through rocks and shoals to the harbor. All administrators have days when they say, "Where is the harbor?" "The fog is too thick!" "Why are there so many rocks?" Administrators and leaders of all kinds need to have wisdom, for if an organization is not well administered, it cannot meet its goals. The fog rarely lifts when one is "paddling in permanent white water." Administrators and leaders also need to generate encouragement, confidence, and commitment on the part of staff, faculty, and students in order to have an excellent and growing continuing education division or unit. It is rewarding to be part of an organization about which staff and faculty can be proud and enthusiastic.

Having an outstanding continuing education division and/or education center(s) requires leadership and decision making. Other in-depth discussion of continuing education leadership and management material appears in the chapters on leadership and motivation and throughout this book. However, a basic premise behind leadership is that the more power a leader gives away by involving others in decision making, coordination, or supervision, the more total power a leader has. Not all decisions are appropriate for group involvement, however, so further analysis of the decisions to be made and of the decision-making processes is needed.

KINDS OF DECISIONS

Simple Decisions

In a decision with only two possible outcomes and in which the leader has no preference, the leader can flip a coin. Listing the pros and cons of a decision in separate columns on a paper is a useful strategy for slightly more complicated decisions. The benefit of decision making strategies is that they help the decision maker look at a problem more systematically and consider relevant questions that may not at first have been apparent. The context in which higher education decisions are made is also a factor. An effective leader delegates most "simple" decisions to an appropriate staff member, after setting parameters. For example, "The annual picnic can be held at any of these three parks. Let's have a vote." (Or have a committee investigate, or have Mrs. Smith choose this year, et cetera.) Much has been written about the benefits of delegating decisions to the lowest feasible level, to build commitment all through a staff's organizational system. For example, "This year the secretaries will vote on where to have the picnic."

More Complex Decisions

A decision tree is useful for decisions that are a little more complex. A decision tree can be generated with staff and faculty participating in a meeting setting and can be useful in encouraging discussion and informing people before a vote is taken. Or a simple tree can be used at home, alone, to solve personal problems such as whether to buy a new car, repair the old one, or buy a used car.

A simple decision tree for the annual picnic might center on whether the meal was lunch or dinner and whether it would be barbecued or brought cold. The tree might start out like this:

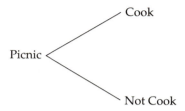

Then discussion (or information getting) focuses on whether Parks A and B allow cooking, at what hours, and with how much advance notice. The tree begins to look like this:

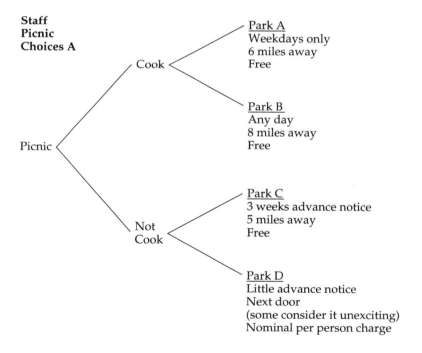

This tree could have additional branches placed to the right as one considers more details—possible swimming, amusements, or carpool arrangements. In dealing with this tree, the group or decision maker first decides on the items farthest to the right. To start deciding, one might first rank all the considerations on a preference scale of + 1 to + 10 or -1 to -10. The tree then looks like this:

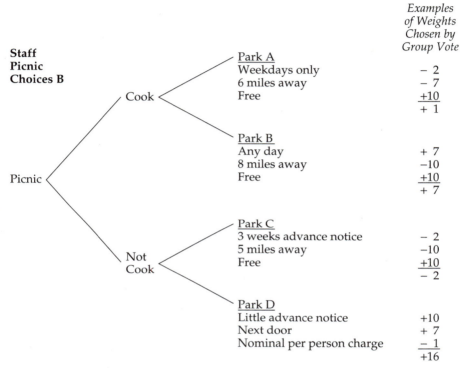

Examples of Weights Chosen by Group Vote

Staff Picnic Choices B

Cook

Park A
Weekdays only — 2
6 miles away — 7
Free +10
+ 1

Park B
Any day + 7
8 miles away −10
Free +10
+ 7

Picnic

Not Cook

Park C
3 weeks advance notice − 2
5 miles away −10
Free +10
− 2

Park D
Little advance notice +10
Next door + 7
Nominal per person charge − 1
+16

Park D becomes the favorite if people don't mind not being able to cook. If they still want to cook, Park B seems better. This question could now be presented to the large staff meeting with a choice between Park B and cooking or Park D and no cooking. The factor of whether the same people consider Park D exciting or not, or whether that is even important to the attendees, would surface. The next decisions to be made are whether to have lunch or dinner and who should be invited from the institution at large outside the unit, if anybody. This example may seem very simplified, but in today's workplace, with the diverse group of people in various ages and stages in life, with different backgrounds and cultures, who make up an excellent continuing education unit staff, it is a "safe" practice exercise in group decision making.

Using a simple tree of this sort is helpful in making other group decisions either with staff or faculty. For instance, the staff picnic example gets people interested, and they will go out and research other parks and bring in new information for next year. This is building commitment and interest.

This formula worked quite well, in one true story, for several years. Then an autocratic decision maker became leader and just selected the park and set the hours. Results included leaders, who were not involved in the choice coming, but coming quite late and not eating. Others came late or left early, and there was no generalized "buy-in" into the activity. The following year the picnic was canceled. However, good effects in worker relations did result, as further described in Chapter 7 on motivation under "hygiene factors." The remaining question for a leader is how many people should be involved in a given decision? And *how* does the leader involve them?

THE DECISION-MAKING PROCESS

The Fishbone Decision-Making Tree

A "Fishbone Decision-Making Tree" can be used to suggest a series of questions to be asked about a decision in order to decide how many people to involve in the decision-making process. These questions appearing in the sections of the "fishbone" in Figure 5.1 merit clarification. The issues around topics that can usually impact a decision are people, resources, the surrounding environment, and technology. These are the section headings in Figure 5.1. More sections can be added to the fishbone for more factors in a particular decision.

The first question about the decision is: Is one solution likely to be better than another in that a large amount of resources would be used, and/or it is not an easily reversible decision, so other options cannot be "tried out"? Examples of answers to this question might include opening a new education center across town (this would use a lot of money and time), changing a major part of the programming, or changing in a major way the information processes the university or the center uses to track its students. Because "people time" is a scarce resource in continuing education programs, the amount of time a dean or director would have to put in is always a consideration. Other hallmarks of an important decision, in addition to the percent of money, people power, or materials used, are answers to: Does the decision use scarce resources? And is it easily reversible? These questions should be asked *first* in all sections to uncover additional elements that might be present.

The next question in three of the sections, People, Resources, and Technology, involves information about the challenge or problem and the decision one needs to make. Do I have enough information to make this decision? Do I know where to get more information? Who does? Where can they or I get it? Who needs to be involved? Can technology be used to gain this information or share it? How much people time would a leader have to put

Environment
1. Does it use a large amount of resources? Is it easily reversible?
2. Is conflict likely among staff members and colleagues in chosen solutions?
3. Do they have enough information to help decide?

People
1. How many people are needed to decide? Is it easily reversible?
2. Do I have enough information to make this decision? Who needs to be involved?
3. Do staff members or colleagues have to accept my decision for this to happen? Is this likely?
4. Do they share the goals of the organization?

Goal

Resources (time, materials, money)
1. Will scarce resources be used?
2. Is it easily reversible?
3. Do I know where to get the information I need? Who does, or where is it?
4. Do I know where to get the money or materials or people-time I need? Who does?

Technology
1. Does it use a large amount of resources? Is it easily reversible?
2. Can technology be used to help staff or colleagues gain more information? To stay in touch with each other?

FIGURE 5.1   A Fishbone Decision-Making Tree

into making a decision? Often the leader does not have sufficient information to decide alone, but knowing that much, at least, is a start. For example, if a leader is sure of wanting to start another education center across town but also knows that he or she does not know all of the necessary steps (or can't decide between one location closer in or one 3 to 4 hours drive away, with good reasons for both), the leader can then start reading professional materials about others' experiences and asking people for more information. If the leader has gone through the fishbone decision-making tree and has decided to involve the staff at this point, the dean or director might invite guest speakers to staff meetings who have successfully started second centers. The dean might also ask the staff to start researching this problem by saying, "The division is looking into it," without necessarily stating that the division plans to open a satellite branch. Alternatively, the decision maker might talk informally at a professional conference with a few administrators from other institutions of higher education who have started new education centers in satellite locations.

The questions under "Resources" asking, "Do I know where to get the information and the money, materials, and people?" means "Does the leader know exactly what information is needed, who possesses it, and *how* to collect it?" In terms of starting a new center, the answer would probably be no. Then one needs to ask who might know *how* to get this information. If the question were "What is the VCR with the lowest price?" the answer would probably be yes, the leader does know *how* to get that information. This is a very important question as one may need the resources of the group or information the group may have about resources in order to move forward. If the answer to these two questions is no, then it is likely that the group will need to be involved. However, "knowing what you don't know" is a great strength because at least one can start to find out the answers (or the questions that need to be asked). By opening the problem to the group, more resources and more ideas will be brought into the whole initiative. The process of looking together for information and then for solutions builds commitment and interest in any project.

"Is acceptance of the decision by subordinates critical to effective implementation?" This question is very important to ask about many decisions, as are the questions "Is conflict likely if I decide?" and "Do they (subordinates) support the goals of the organization?" If staff members and colleagues will be the ones carrying out a decision (such as implementing a new academic program or a new student relations program), then giving them enough information and a large enough range of choices to gain their acceptance will be the key to success or failure. In the question of opening an education center across town this question of needing staff support might have a yes or no answer, depending on whether a totally new staff would be sought or whether two top staff members would be asked to transfer for 1 or 2 years or longer.

"If I were to make the decision myself, is it certain that it would be accepted by my staff and colleagues?" This question relates to the previous question, obviously, but it serves as a reminder to a leader who might be tempted to go out on a limb. It is always better to allow more time for understanding and discussion if it is apparent that the limb could be sawed off. It also helps the leader to assess the climate of feeling around a given issue.

"Does the institution or the staff share the continuing education division's goals to be attained in solving this problem?" One would hope that in a continuing education organization the answer would be yes—the staff members and colleagues are working toward a goal of satisfied students gaining knowledge and competencies in their programs. However, in reality, some staff members may take a job just to earn money, and if that is the majority of the staff's attitude, staff training, motivation build-up, and perhaps some selective hiring and firing are needed. If the majority of the staff does identify with the goal of an education center being the best education center in that location (or any goal that benefits students, faculty, and the institution of higher education, and agreed to by all or most), then involving staff in decision making will enhance staff commitment and the organization. When staff members and colleagues share the goals, the group can search together for solutions that are in the best interests of the organization. In any organization, people tend to share the goals that they helped to select.

Is conflict likely among colleagues or staff in preferred solutions? This question will be skipped on the fishbone decision tree if colleagues and staff share the continuing education division's goals. But if colleagues and staff do not share organizational goals, it is important to pre-plan how to handle possible conflict, or to decide if one even wants conflict to arise. The leader should think of how to deal with various objections.

Do colleagues and staff have sufficient information to make a high quality decision? Often they do not, and this leads to a natural opportunity for new learning and staff training on a given topic. Faculty members can be invited to attend, or even to speak about their programs at the staff training, too, if that is appropriate. In discussion, or ahead of time, the leader can identify the problem more clearly and, by using the fishbone tree, decide which solution and degree of staff involvement are appropriate.

After looking over the fishbone tree, the leader turns to possible decision methods for group or individual problems. Sometimes involving the group is the *fastest* method for solving the particular problem just "broken out" on the fishbone tree. For instance, in a move to a new location, if it is just announced as a flat statement (the autonomous, autocratic method), staff members may complain for several years after the move. If 3 to 6 months of discussion occurs, complemented by gathering more information about the new location, the fastest solution of 3 to 6, or even 12 months may be the fastest, best, and smoothest, even though it *appears* slow.

How Much to Involve the Group

The group becomes involved in more and more ways as solutions progress from autonomous to group decisions. In autonomous decisions the leader makes the decisions himself or herself using the information available at the time. In the case of opening another education center across town, often the decision is made in just this way.

If the leader needs more information, the decision maker can obtain necessary information from employees, then decide alone. The leader could ask staff and faculty, "Do you think this city could use another graduate education center? Where would be a good location? What special programs might be an asset?" and so forth. The leader can tell them his or her plans or not, as the leader thinks best, but the staff and faculty are not part of the decision, only information providers.

In a cooperative solution the leader talks one to one with staff and faculty, without meeting with them as a group. This can be done informally, at a social gathering, over time, or in a number of ways. Finally the leader makes the decision, which may or may not take their views into account. In another version of a cooperative solution the leader may finally decide alone, perhaps not even using the employees' advice, but this time they come together in a group to give their suggestions. This allows everyone to be familiar with the question and also provides a situation in which they can build on each other's ideas. If the leader decides later that their help is needed, at least they would know what the leader was talking about. Of course, if the decision maker does follow their advice, or straw vote, he or she lets them know and praises them for their help. If the leader doesn't use their advice, he or she can explain that circumstances were such that another solution seemed better at this time, if an explanation is appropriate or needed.

A group decision maker shares the problem with the group and then acts as a discussion leader while everyone generates as many solutions as possible. The majority vote on the best solution is one the leader is willing to adopt and implement, and, of course, it has the support of the entire group. This might be helpful if the leader knows he or she wants to start a new education center across town but is not sure where to locate it. The leader would probably want to have it fairly convenient for new enrollees. It may be that some staff members will *volunteer* to work there when they hear that they will have a say in the new location and the new equipment. This group solution is especially useful when the decision maker knows that he or she wants to do something big but doesn't know how to go about doing it or even where to learn how. Opening the problem to the group allows more resources and more ideas to flow in the whole group. They may decide they want to know more. Guest speakers can be invited and literature provided as everyone learns more and has time to solicit information from friends and acquaintances. Interesting problems attract able people, and the leader will find all sorts of resources becoming available. Also, allowing some time gives "the grapevine" time to work; a staff member might ask a competitor's brother, or some other informal network person, key "how-to-do-it" questions that would be inappropriate at higher levels.

Solutions for individual problems follow the same pattern but are appropriate for one-to-one problems. As usual, politeness in seeking information or asking advice is essential.

POWER, ROLES, AND GOALS OF ADMINISTRATORS AND FACULTY

Decision making is complicated in the context of higher education due to differences in the perceptions of administrators and faculty members about the power, goals, roles, objectives, status, and work load of the other group. Many administrators, of course, have been faculty members and so have some understanding of both sides of the equation. At the present time however, when many administrators come directly from another institution or organization and have not served as faculty in their present institution, wrong assumptions can creep in as to how business is done in *this* institution (or in this organizational culture). Many of these differences in perception could be called "structural conflicts" (Kotter, 1985), as the structure of the higher education organization has conflicting components built right into it.

There have been a few institutions of higher education with faculty representation on the board of trustees in the early days when faculty lived in the dormitory, but that is not (and was not) the general practice. Since that time a gap has grown between administration and faculty as the faculty usually has no formal representative on the board of trustees, which traditionally hires the president and sets policy. In the labor relations field this situation is akin to the classic category of labor not being represented to management, which generates a number of predictable problems and sometimes even unions. It is helpful to look at the understandable differences in focus between the two groups as an aid to understanding decision-making dynamics.

In a generalized way each group thinks the other has more power. The *goals* of faculty are usually lifelong, career goals, whereas the leaders in continuing education and the rest of the administration often have 1-year (or 5-year) goals and budgets to worry about. The *role* of the faculty is a professional one, and while the role of administrators is also professional, there is more need for personal discretion and for local tradition to be used as a guideline. This can be seen in the refusal of a senior professor to travel to a satellite center to teach a required course in the degree program offered there. He did not see this as part of his role, and certainly not as one of his goals. Yet he had been in agreement when his department approved offering this degree at that location, as this would reflect well on the department and bring administrative credits for income earned. The Dean of Continuing Education used a great deal of tact and pointed out that the tradition of this institution was to offer a whole degree at satellite centers when it had been advertised. Later this degree may have been closed down at that site due to this problem.

The *objectives* of faculty are again related to 20- and 30- year or lifelong goals: publish more, research certain specific areas, et cetera. The administrators' objectives tend to be tied to yearly goals for marketing, enrollment, and income versus expense concerns. The *pay* is perceived to be different by the two groups, but there is variability in who thinks the other gets more. The *status* differentials also vary, with faculty having a professional status (and using a "status veto" when individual members feel their power is low) (Birnbaum, 1988) and administrators, except for at the highest levels, having a lower status. This can be of particular importance in continuing education, as leaders and administrators may be dealing with several "layers of prima donnas," as one observer put it. Lastly, the *workload* of each group is frequently misperceived, as the faculty work long hours and feel high pressure at paper grading and exam time, and administrators feel a more generalized, year-round pressure and may envy what appear to be long faculty vacations. These areas are necessarily simplified here for reasons of space, but the discussion continues in most institutions.

These dynamics merit reflection, as often the key to understanding an interaction lies somewhere in this realm and can be developed with more detail for a specific situation. Furthermore, the answers to the differences lie in getting to know each other as people, with real human needs and aspirations. Using this knowledge, framing a decision that is likely to be successful becomes more likely. Hypothesizing faculty responses in a scenario before actually discussing possibilities with faculty will become more realistic when these dynamics are remembered. These discussions could be from any of the blocks in a scenario as described in Chapter 4 on planning.

SUMMARY

Decision making is indeed key in leadership processes; however, the ability to structure decisions and then break them down into manageable parts is necessary in decision making, and these skills can be learned. Sometimes making a decision alone can be the *slowest* way to a resolution when group support is needed and group involvement would be better (and faster). Taking 3 to 6 months to involve the faculty, the staff, and even the students is often the fastest decision approach possible when a large decision is involved and when an individual decision on the same issue might result in years of backsliding or controversy. This chapter discussed some of the parameters to consider when approaching a decision; the following chapters on team building, motivation, and problem solving provide additional tools that may be useful to leaders.

BIBLIOGRAPHY

Alber, H. H. (1961). *Organized Executive Action: Decision Making, Communication, and Leadership.* New York: Wiley.

Anderson, J. G. (1968). *Bureaucracy in Education.* Baltimore, MD: Johns Hopkins Press.

Argyris, C. (1985). *Strategy, Change and Defensive Routines.* Boston: Pittman.

Birnbaum, Robert (1988). *How Colleges Work: The Cybernetics of Academic Organization and Leadership.* San Francisco: Jossey-Bass

Blake, R. R., and J. S. Mouton (1964). *The Managerial Grid.* Houston, TX: Gulf Publishing.

Dale, E. (1960) *The Great Organizers.* New York: McGraw-Hill.

Fiedler, F. E. (1958). *Leader Attitude and Group Effectiveness.* Urbana, IL: University of Illinois Press.

Fishburn, P. C. (1973). *The Theory of Social Choice.* Princeton, NJ: Princeton University Press.

Goldman, T. A. (1967). *Cost Effectiveness and Analysis: New Approaches in Decision Making.* New York: Praeger.

Hellreigel, D., J. W. Slocum, and R. W. Woodman (1998). *Organizational Behavior.* Cincinnati, OH: Southwestern College Publishing.

Horowitz, I. (1970). *Decision-Making and the Theory of the Firm.* New York: Holt, Rinehart & Winston.

Kotter, J. P. (1985). *Power and Influence.* New York: Macmillan.

Millett, J. D. (1968). *Decision Making and Administration in Higher Education.* Kent, OH: Kent State University Press.

Paine, F. T. (1975). *Organizational Strategy and Policy.* Philadelphia: Saunders.

Shirley, R. C. (1976). *Strategy and Policy Formation: A Multi-functional Orientation.* New York: Wiley.

Staw, B. M.(1996). "The Escalation of Commitment to a Course of Action." In M. I. Matteson and J. M. Ivanevich (Eds.), *Management and Organizational Classics.* Boston: Irwin.

Strata, R. (1989). "Organizational Learning—The Key to Management Innovation." *Sloan Management Review*, Spring, pp. 63–64.

Stodgill, R. M. (1974). *Handbook of Leadership.* New York: The Free Press.

Tosi, H., J. R. Rizzo, and S. J. Carroll (1994). *Managing Organizational Behavior.* MA: Blackwell.

Vroom, V. H. (1967). *Methods of Organizational Research.* Pittsburgh, PA: University of Pittsburgh Press.

Vroom, V. H. (1973). *Leadership and Decision-Making.* Pittsburgh, PA: University of Pittsburgh Press.

Vroom, V. H. (1995). "A New Look at Managerial Decision Making." In J. L. Pierce and J. W. Newstrom (Eds.), *Leaders and the Leadership Process*, Boston: Irwin/Austen.

Vroom, V. H., and A. G. Jago (1996) "Decision Making as a Social Process: Normative and Disruptive Models of Leader Behavior." In M. I. Matteson and J. M. Ivanevich (Eds.), *Management and Organizational Classics*, Sixth Edition. Boston: Iriwn.

Walker, C. D. (1979). *The Effective Administrator: A Practical Approach to Problem Solving, Decision Making, and Campus Leadership.* San Francisco: Jossey-Bass.

▶ 6

Team Work, Team Building, and Small Groups

Small groups, whether in the workplace or in voluntary organizations, provide a source of satisfaction to the group or team members that is of great importance. What goes on in small groups is vital to any leader. It is necessary to understand some of the processes that go on in small groups (or teams) in order to develop group stability, group health, and group effectiveness. Internal dynamics and factors within a group can make it more less productive. A small group is usually considered to be less than twenty and is often less than twelve. Many small continuing education units' staffs comprise just one "small group," so it is important that it be productive.

DYNAMICS OF SMALL WORK GROUPS

The basic reason for group membership is that groups provide their members with social support and a feeling of personal worth. The foundations for mature social exchange are established early in life through child–child, and child–adult interactions that are favorable, thus indicating acceptance and approval. Acceptance and approval continue to be important in adult life and in the workplace.

It has long been found that small groups or teams in the workplace will be more effective if they contain "friendship groups," that is, if they take into account the smaller groups that exist in the "informal organization." Individuals like to be surrounded by people who like them, even if it is a small number. Sometimes the attitudes and opinions of others are the only basis on which a person can evaluate his or her own opinions and attitudes. People like to have a feeling of certainty about their beliefs, opinions, and attitudes and gain affirmation through shared values in a small group.

A negative aspect affecting small groups is that people with low self-esteem tend to find frustrating conditions more frustrating than do those with higher self-esteem. Those with very low self-esteem may give up in a situation in which a person with higher self-esteem might stay.

Stages of Small Work Groups

In any new small group there are three observable stages: "forming," "storming," and "norming" (Tuckman, 1955, Jacobs 1974). These stages can be observed during the planning of an evening information session or briefing for inquiring students or on a 3-month work group assignment.

The *forming stage* occurs as the group gets going and a status hierarchy develops in the group. Status can be based on a person's performance skills, interpersonal skills, or the job he or she holds. Emergence of different roles can be seen in the group during this stage: the tough leader, the friendly helper, and the clear thinker. Clear expectations help speed this process; for example, by having an appointed discussion leader, a group will get into a discussion more quickly. Sometimes the leader is just the person who has the pencil and paper or some other needed resource.

The *storming stage* can cause tensions. Storming occurs when one or more group members think the leader of the group is going in a direction with which they disagree. An example of this occurred during a staff training small group activity for which the assigned task was to write out a philosophy for an education center. (Several groups were working on the same task as a first step toward developing a unified written statement.) One person started the group off with a strong statement about her views favoring a fairly harsh philosophy of no eating, no drinking, no moving of chairs or rearranging furniture, and so forth. Another person said, "Now, *wait* a minute." A "clear thinker" type in the group suggested checking other written philosophies and thus broke the possible deadlock—and also, incidentally, became the leader. It should be noted that this is an "unclear task" according to the definitions given later in the chapter, which contributed to the group's rough start.

The third stage, or *norming* is defined as creating a social norm for the group. In the workplace a "norm" can be a performance standard or a standard of behavior expected of informal group members. (An informal group is two or more people associated with one another in ways that may be different from the formal organizational structure.) The "norming" stage follows quickly for an information session planning meeting or can last several weeks or years for a work group assigned to a large task. Norming is based on shared beliefs and opinions in at least some areas of reference (social, work, church, political). Group members need to feel that their objectives are worthy of attainment. They develop expectations about how people should feel about certain issues. There is usually some agreement about what is relevant and what is not. Interestingly enough, if group members perceive a difference in one of these areas, they will talk *more* about it rather than less, perhaps trying to persuade the others to their point of view.

Group norming leads to pressures for conformity that include defining "a fair day's work" in the workplace. Group norming can increase group effectiveness when the goals of the group are in line with the goals of the organization. On the other hand a negative group norm can be detrimental to the organization. If the informal group, for example, defines a fair day's work as very limited, it can pressure other workers to not go beyond that "norm."

Rules or norms can help group or team effectiveness and make the group fairer for all. They reduce the need for decisions on routine matters and also reduce the need for the use of personal power. A more elaborate model of the stages of small groups comes from Drexler and Sibbet (1995), who present a seven-step model. This model addresses additional elements of the early establishment of trust and acceptance; agreement about goals, procedures, and timing; and the exchange of information. The interdependent elements, which are not necessarily chronological, are orientation, trust building, goal/role clarification, commitment, implementation, high performance, and renewal and return to orientation.

An interesting exercise for a class, a staff meeting, or just a review of an interaction with persons is to check off behaviors listed on Table 6.1 as they occur. These are behaviors that can be seen in the progressive steps of the two models of group formation. This is also good practice in observation. The behaviors are listed in order of increasing benefit, with 9 and 10, clarifying group goals and facilitating group attainment, being the most beneficial. Comments such as "What date shall we set for our next meeting?" demonstrate facilitation of group attainment. Achieving number 6, "awareness of the high cost of coercion," helps group members avoid an approach that sets back the whole interaction. These ten behaviors might be seen as a sequence in a few directors' first 6 to 12 months on the job, also.

Specialized Roles in Work Groups

As a group emerges, two or even three types of leaders can be seen. While one person focuses on the task and competes for, or takes over, the position of power and influence in the group, another person can be seen reducing tensions in the group and having a high interaction rate within the group.

TABLE 6.1   Observing Social Exchange

Tally behaviors used	Interaction Behaviors
	1. Agreeing, complimenting, conforming (generally spontaneous) to obtain approval of others.
	2. Rewarding others: asking advice, complimenting, giving positive responses—generally calculated.
	3. Reciprocating: interacting or responding on the same level.
	4. Obtaining small returns: supplying rewards that benefit, yet obligate the other person.
	5. Maximizing cost–benefit ratio: consulting indirectly, i.e., talking about a problem to get advice rather than asking directly for it. Seeking advice from a group member perceived to be more like self.
	6. Being aware of the high cost of coercive attempts. Shrewd manipulation of the group toward the leader's point of view. Perhaps using debts from past exchanges.
	7. Indicate superior bargaining position such as having the only copy of a book, or having a skill, technique, or knowledge needed by the group.
	8. Making a unique and valuable contribution in return for status. Presenting of knowledge that is superior to that given by other members of the group. Taking more responsibility than other members.
	9. Developing or clarifying group goals. Taking action to ascertain that group members are certain of group goals.
	10. Facilitate attainment of group goals: structuring the group. Keeping the group goal-directed.

The first person could be said to fill the role of "tough leader" and the second to take the role of "friendly helper." A third role can often be seen in the "clear thinker," which occasionally is combined with the "tough leader." Some writers call these behaviors "goal behaviors" and (group) "maintenance behaviors" and the roles "task specialists" and "social specialists."

These roles are so important for group or team success that a certain individual might find herself or himself filling different roles with different groups, just because it's so obvious that the group won't be effective without someone stepping into that role. Also, a particular person might fill different roles at different stages in life. A person in a beginning career might be the "friendly helper" more of the time, for example. A person new in the education community might offer to be on a telephone task force. These different role structures in a group permit the rapid achievement of assigned tasks.

Informal group leaders can be powerful and may be chosen by consensus or to fill a leadership vacuum, but they are usually trusted. This is a good person to have on a leader's side at work and to explain things to in the community. They are sometimes called "opinion leaders" in sociology.

PREDICTION OF WORK GROUP OR TEAM PERFORMANCE

Frederick E. Fiedler (1967, 1995) integrated other work he had done and developed a model to predict group or team effectiveness based on leadership style, group variables, and task variables (1967). He found that three main factors within a situation affected group performance:

- Leader–member relations, or how well they got along
- Task structure, or clearness of task (e.g., can it be written down?)
- Leader position power, or the actual power to hire and fire

The task structure variable was further defined showing four ways a task might be clear or unclear:

- If a decision can be shown to be correct in an impartial manner (such as with enrollment statistics or other quantitative or measurable behaviors)—this is called *decision verifiability*
- If the group members understand the requirements of the task
- If more than one procedure can be used to accomplish the task (such as different marketing strategies)
- If the problem has more than one correct solution

The goal or task of higher education continuing education is not a clear task—there are several right ways to do it and several correct solutions to most problems. Anything that adds clearness will be a help.

Fiedler (1967) found that any group that had two out of three of the major factors (leader–member relations, task structure, leader position power) would probably be effective. If one looks at education and sees the task as unclear, one can see that leader–member relations (also called collegial relations), and leader position power become essential. Conversely, anything that can be done to make the task clear (written goal and vision statements, course descriptions, checklists, faculty or staff handbooks, or anything that is written) will help a group in the field of higher education continuing education be more effective.

The Connectedness Factor

In continuing higher education the basic administrative model of the larger institution structures some of the small group interactions. Continuing education can be located on a continuum of connectedness (Figure 6.1), with one end of the continuum being the model of a unit very connected to the institution of higher education. This means the regular campus academic departments hire all the adjuncts, supervise all coursework for credit, and say yes or no to new program and location initiatives depending on the faculty support available and other commitments of faculty. This model has the lasting benefit of keeping the coursework current and up to date to the same degree that the main campus coursework is refreshed and relevant. Faculty do not administer the continuing education courses beyond this, however. The disadvantage of this model is that occasionally tenured professors turn down opportunities for fairly frivolous reasons including time and trouble involved, or their car is too old to go that far, or the like.

The model at the other end of the continuum of connectedness is the totally separate model, with courses, faculty, degrees, *and* administration completely separate, which leads in some cases to splitting the unit off from the institution of higher education completely to become a separate institution of higher education with a separate president. The benefit of this model is that the short-term revenue expenditure and planning are much more efficient and are in the control of the continuing education unit. Courses can easily be kept relevant. The disadvantage of this model is that course quality can erode, and highly technical degree programs are hard to offer and sustain over time.

The middle of this connectedness continuum (50-50) is filled with varying degrees of connectedness, including credit programs supervised by academic departments, plus noncredit or conference programs not at all connected or supervised, or other variations all within the same unit.

Different factors can be seen in small groups or teams, in the varying categories of Fiedler's small group theory, that are affected by the amount of connectedness also. Connectedness and other factors are significant in Fiedler's leader position variable, as discussed next.

Least connected	50-50	Most connected

FIGURE 6.1   Continuum of Connectedness

"Loose Coupling" in Higher Education

Higher education institutions can be characterized as "loosely coupled" (Lutz 1982; Weick 1976), which means that units do not have a direct effect on each other, neither for good nor for ill. The characterization of loose coupling implies that coupled events and units are responsive to each other but that each maintains its own identity and separateness. This can be seen with academic departments and the continuing education unit, the library, the career counseling center, and other administrative institution units. The attachment between units in an institution of higher education may be infrequent, weak, unimportant, or slow to respond, partly due to the fact that they have little in common. Glassman (1973) rates the activities of the variables into two categories. One category has few variables in common and the other category is when they are weak or unimportant variables. An academic department that presents courses off campus infrequently might be an example of this "little in common." If these infrequent classes are always small, this class activity would become unimportant as well as infrequent. The coupling concept relates further to the idea that activities in one or another unit can be expanded, minimized, or severed within the organization (Birnbaum, 1988). An example of this would be the closing of the classics department in a large university having little adverse effect on other departments or other schools in the same university except in the realm of morale.

There may be also loose coupling between the intentions and the actions of two units such as a department planning to do a new degree program at a satellite location, participating in proposal writing, and withdrawing after winning the award due to individual caveats of faculty. Benefits of loose coupling (Birnbaum, 1988) include that it allows some elements of the organization to be able to persist, thus freeing the rest of the organization from the need to constantly adapt to new changes in the environment. Continuing education is frequently the place where new, relevant, market request–driven courses are offered. Having many independent elements, only externally constrained, and *not* standardized, allows the continuing education unit to be more sensitive to the outside environment's requests for programs. Loose coupling allows for local adaptations, allowing one graduate education center to offer an array of programs particularly suited to its geographic location and different from those at another site. The system can retain a greater number of mutations and innovative solutions to problems than a standardized approach would allow. It also allows a greater sense of efficacy and effectiveness for its participants and their (somewhat) autonomous units than a tightly coupled system would. And, lastly, units in a loosely coupled system can be sealed off from other units if there is a breakdown (or embarrassment) in one part of the system, such as wrong advertising copy or an incorrect description of a degree or program. In the early days, when institutions of higher education held "marketing" in low esteem, having a continuing education unit keeping the name of the university or college before the public took advantage of this "sealed off" attribute of a loosely coupled system. (If they had a misstep, they could always be blamed as "separate.")

Furthermore, a loosely coupled system can be relatively inexpensive to run, as there is a reduction in the (expensive) necessity for coordination. However coordination *is* important for smooth-running continuing education in higher education, so clarifying the task (courses, programs, degrees, formats, etc.) as much as possible and having good leader–member (collegial) relations are very important, especially in situations where there is no hiring-firing power, as discussed next.

Predicting Success in Small Groups: Examples of Different Factors

Lack of Leader Position Power

At many meetings and situations involving continuing education there will be no one present who has any (or very much) "hiring and firing" power over the others present. Therefore, having a clear task and good leader–member relations is essential for effectiveness of the outcome. An example would be two leaders of units discussing, planning, or meeting for a variety of continuing education reasons. Anything the continuing education leader and unit can do to clarify the task at hand, such as drafting or writing the proposal in question, submitting multiple copies of printing deadlines and information session dates well in advance of due dates, and establishing a yearly ebb and flow of activities that are recognizable and fit faculty schedules, will help. Because some faculty members will be tempted to use their veto power just to establish (or maintain) their status, it is important to have a number of clear task projects going so that "overloading the system" reduces frivolous vetoes (Birnbaum, 1988). Having two out of three of these success factors present will help in the predictability of any initiative.

Institutions of higher education, one hopes are collegial, so that good leader–member relations, the other essential in effectiveness, are possible.

Leader–Member Relations	Task Structure	Hiring–Firing Power
+	+	0

FIGURE 6.2   Lack of Leader Position Power

The situation of lack of leader position power, which occurs fairly frequently in continuing education units, is diagrammed in Figure 6.2. In a tightly coupled situation, such as when the continuing education unit hires some or all of its faculty, the instances of this situation would be fewer.

Unclear Task

A different combination of factors can be seen in many continuing education marketing situations. This is frequently an unclear task although many efforts can be made to clarify it with direct mail, advertising, and more (see Chapter 8). The need to choose which programs to place in a new location can demonstrate the need for strong leader–member relations with academic departments and for hiring-firing power, in order for the unit to make effective long-range choices. (See Chapter 7 for an analysis of possible market and content choices). An example of this can be seen in an unconnected continuing education model, in a state university continuing education entity, that did hire its own faculty but was unable to offer or sustain a highly technical degree in telecommunications electrical engineering. This was badly needed by 50 companies in one satellite location. It was hard to hire adjuncts with enough expertise for this degree program. The need was never met, as the hiring goals had not originally clearly included providing professors with a high enough level of expertise for this degree to be offered. The continuing education future tasks had not been clear; otherwise some balance in expertise and full-time faculty might have been established. Five years later this opportunity was wide open for a competing private institution's continuing education unit. The private institution was more tightly connected than the state university, with a competent staff of full professors in the field (but still with loose coupling—the department could refuse to travel and provide this M.S. degree, if they chose). Figure 6.3 diagrams the unclear task; the diagram could also be an example of marketing—which is always an unclear task. If one of the two plusses become a minus, this task is unsuccessful, with two out of three minuses.

Leader–Member Relations	Task Structure	Hiring–Firing Power
+	0	+

FIGURE 6.3   Unclear Task

Leader–Member Relations

A third illustration shows poor leader–member relations between an academic vice-president and an academic department. The vice-president told the department to hire contract professors to fill two formerly tenured slots.

Attempts to correct this approach failed (poor leader–member relations), and two contract professors were hired at somewhat higher pay then the beginning tenured slots would have carried. After 2 years these two left (for even better jobs) and the department was left unable to fill the two slots at the lower pay rate, now tenured positions again. The lack of leader–member relations plus a task (hiring) that looked clear but became unclear (Figure 6.4) caused this department to have to turn away not one, but two large contract programs that had been carefully developed from the proposal stage by the continuing education unit. These would have brought in $800,000 or more for the initial 2 cohorts of students to the university, but the income was lost to this university, as was that from ongoing cohorts of students. Two out of three minuses could predict this unsuccessful and costly result.

Leader–Member Relations	Task Structure	Hiring–Firing Power
0	0	+

FIGURE 6.4   Poor Interpersonal Relations

TEAM LEARNING AND SHARED VISION

Now that some of the group dynamics of small groups have been analyzed and understood, a better understanding of "team learning" is possible. As a team becomes more aligned, a commonality of direction emerges and individual energies harmonize (Senge, 1990). A commonality of purpose, a shared vision or philosophy leads to an understanding of how to complement one another's efforts, and there is less wasted energy. A jazz ensemble or an orchestra is an example of the whole becoming greater than the sum of its parts—the definition of this synergy. However, they may have leader position power (a director) and a clear task (sheet music) so thus can manage without much in the way of leader–member relations. Learning organizations that build team learning can work together to build energy and enthusiasm. But they require good leader–member environments in which people continually expand their capabilities to understand the complexity, to clarify vision, and to improved shared mental models (Senge, 1990), whether they are mental models for a balance of academic programs or scenarios for the Division or for one education center (see Chapter 3 on planning). Being responsible for learning—adults', students', and one's own—is a first step for team builders. Peter Senge (1990) sees leaders as designers, stewards, and teachers and says that while learning disabilities are tragic in children, they are fatal in organizations.

THOUGHTS ON TEAMWORK AND
KNOWLEDGE BUILDING

> *"Coming together is a beginning; helping together is
> progress; working together is success."*
>
> —Henry Ford (1863–1947)
> American industrialist

> *"There is nothing good or bad per se about a group. A group can be a
> roadblock to progress, enforcing 'group think' and conformity upon its
> members, paralyzing decision-making processes, and smothering individual
> initiative. Under other conditions, a group can be a powerful synergism of
> talents, strengthening its members, speeding up the decision-making
> process, and embracing individual and personal growth."*
>
> —Rensis Likert (1930–1981)
> Director of the Institute of Social
> Research, University of Michigan

> *"The modern knowledge economy turns on the better use of
> knowledge. . . . The key is the ability to learn."*
>
> —John Seely Brown
> Xerox Corporation

> *"Many agree that developing, using, and leveraging
> knowledge is essential."*
>
> -Tom Peters
> "Excellence" consultant and author

> *"Together the units know more than they could as separate
> entities. . . . Power stems from constant cooperation among units."*
>
> —Percy Barnewick
> BB Asea Brown Boveri Corporation

> *"Success becomes possible the minute you realize you can't do it alone."*
>
> —Robert Shuler
> "Possibility Thinking" speaker and author

> *"Let each of you look out not only for your own interests,
> but also for the interests of others."*
>
> —Philippians 2:4

In assessing the continuing education unit's team and "teamness," one
can construct two rating scales (Eitington, 1984). A list to assess "Team
Empowerment" such as that shown in Figure 6.5, with each item rated on a
1 to 5 scale, gives a measure to work from for improvement. A rating instrument to assess team communication and empowerment can be constructed
with eight or ten statements about communication when it is at its best (Figure 6.6). A rating review to assess team problem solving and creativity
might consist of statements about group problem solving and request for 1

FIGURE 6.5   Team Empowerment Survey

(Please rate each from 1 to 5)	
Sense of ability	Empowerment
Cohesion	Cooperation
Pride, sense of competence	Communication
Decision making	Goal setting
Openness	Creativity
Trust	Conflict
Team self-assessment	Support
Team membership identification	Mutual respect
Leadership	Commitment
Feedback to leader	Atmosphere

to 5 ratings. Such scales, once developed and adapted for the division, can be added to and distributed to staff for self-assessment. They can be used as springboards for discussion at staff meetings, and they can be especially useful as an occasion for praise and recognition of a staff that is really working well together.

SUMMARY

A group exists when two or more people have a unifying relationship, such as common goals or physical proximity. When physical proximity is missing, team building is even more important, and frequent visits, telephone, fax, and e-mail communications become a must. Utilizing the characteristics of groups is an important skill of leadership, and understanding their dynamics as described by Fiedler or other theorists can be useful.

Teamwork is as necessary in higher education as in other organizations, no matter how loosely coupled the teams are. While the teams will evolve and have an ebb and flow with academic departments in the higher education context, the continuing education unit needs to stay strong as a working team. All three factors in the Fiedler model need to be present as often as possible: leader position power, clear (or structured) tasks, and good leader–member relations. Since the task often will not be clear (for instance in marketing choices), it is good to be aware of these dynamics and put in the extra effort that is needed. Any activities that clarify the task will help. These might include having marketing textbooks or article copies on a unit resource shelf, seeking out advice from experts, or hiring particular expertise such as a local area network or other technological consultants.

FIGURE 6.6   Team Communication and Empowerment Review

Criteria	Strongly Agree	Agree	Undecided	Disagree	Strongly Disagree
1. Team members listen to each other.					
2. The team leader listens to all group members.					
3. Everyone feels free to be candid with everyone else.					
4. All team members "check things out" with all concerned before action is taken.					
5. Constructive feedback is given freely to group members to improve their functioning.					
6. Broad participation is strongly encouraged at all group meetings.					
7. No one uses disproportionate amount of the available "air time" at group meetings.					
8. Resources and people are available to secure information needed.					
9. Information is shared willingly and no one hoards information.					
10. Information of interest to team members, such as information on new policies, new projects, and pay, is not categorized as "secret."					
11. Information about one's performance is communicated regularly and candidly by the team leader so that there are no surprises at performance measurement time.					
12. Team members are not afraid to give the boss the "bad news."					
13. Team members give feedback to faculty.					
14. We communicate well with other groups in the organization.					
15. We feel "empowered" as a group.					

Characteristics of groups include norms, a standard of behavior expected by group members; and roles, which can consist of the total pattern of expected behavior or the behavior during a certain situation. The synergism and energy that teams and small groups can provide are a beneficial force for accomplishing an organization's objectives.

BIBLIOGRAPHY

Argyris, C. (1962). *Interpersonal Competence and Organizational Effectiveness.* Homewood, IL: Dorsey Press.

ASTD Information Center (1994). "The Key to Self-Directed Teams." In *Resource Guide, Team Building.* Washington, DC.

Birnbaum, Robert (1988). *How Colleges Work: The Cybernetics of Academic Organization and Leadership.* San Francisco: Jossey-Bass.

Bonner, H. (1968). *Group Dynamics: Principles and Applications.* New York: Harper & Row.

"Building a Self-Directed Work Team" (1992). *Training and Development.* December, p. 24.

Cartwright, D. (Ed.) (1968). *Group Dynamics, Research and Theory.* New York: Harper & Row.

Covey, Stephen R. (1992). *Principle Centered Leadership.* New York: Simon & Schuster.

Drexler, A. and D. Sibbet (1995). *Team Performance Model.* Rockbridge Baths, VA: Grove Consultants International.

Eitington, J. E. (1984). *The Winning Trainer.* Houston, TX: Gulf.

Fiedler, F. E. (1967). *A Theory of Leadership Effectiveness.* New York: McGraw-Hill.

Fiedler, F. E. (1995). "How Do You Make Leaders More Effective? New Answers to an Old Puzzle." In J. J. Pierce and J. W. Newstrom (Eds.), *Leaders and the Leadership Process.* Boston: Irwin/Austen Press.

Glassman, R. B. (1973). "Persistence and Loose Coupling in Living Systems." *Behavioral Science,* 18, 83–98.

Hackman, J. R. (1976) "Group Influences on Individuals." In M. Dunnette (Ed.), *Handbook of Industrial and Organizational Psychology.* Chicago: Rand McNally.

Hertzberg, F. (1996). "New Approaches in Management Organization and Job Design." In M. T. Matteson and J. M. Ivanevich (Eds.), *Management and Organizational Classics.* Boston: Irwin.

Hitchcock, D., and M. Willard.(1995). *Why Teams Can Fail and What to Do about It.* Chicago: Irwin.

Jacobs, T. O. (1974). *Leadership and Exchange in Formal Organizations.* Alexandria: Human Resources Research Organization.

Jaffee, C. L., and R. L. Lucas (1969). "Effect of Rates of Talking and Correctness of Decisions on Leader Choice in Small Groups." *Journal of Social Psychology,* 79, 247–254.

Kiefer, C. and P. Stroh (1984). "A New Paradigm for Developing Organizations." In J. Adams (Ed.), *Transforming Work*. Alexandria, VA: Miles Riler Press.

Lutz, F. W. (1982). "Tightening Up Loose Coupling in Organizations of Higher Education." *Administrative Science Quarterly*, 27 (6), 653–669.

Osburn, J. D., L. Moran, E. Musselwhite, and J. H. Zenger, (1990). *Self-Directed Work Teams*. Homewood, IL: Irwin, Business One.

Schon, D. (1983). *The Reflective Practitioner: How Professionals Think in Action*. New York: Basic Books.

Senge, P. M. (1990). *The Fifth Discipline: The Art and Practice of the Learning Organization*. New York: Doubleday.

Tuckman, B. (1955). "Development Sequence in Small Groups." *Psychological Bulletin*, 23, May.

"25 Stepping Stones for a Self-Directed Work Team." *Training*, December 1991, p. 44.

"Ways to Sink Self-Managed Teams." *Training*, September 1993, p. 38.

Weick, K. E. (1976). "Educational Organizations as Loosely Coupled Systems." *Administrative Science Quarterly*, 21, 1–19.

Weisbord, M. R. (1987). "Transforming Teamwork: Work Relationships in a Fast-Changing World." in *Productive Workplaces*. San Francisco: Jossey-Bass.

Wellins, R. S., W. C. Byham, and J. M. Wilson (1991). *Empowered Teams*. San Francisco: Jossey-Bass.

Motivating and Empowering Staff, Faculty, and Students

The best deans, directors, and leaders of all kinds agree on one thing: People support what they help to create (Senge, 1990). When people are involved in thinking through the vision, goals, and strategies, a task structure is more likely to evolve that will capitalize on the natural motivation inherent in all people. Everyone is motivated all the time by something, so the dean's or director's task is to create a supportive climate with high performance goals to try to access this natural motivation (Senge, 1990). This climate will promote a self-fulfilling prophecy that this is an excellent continuing education division where excellent people work. By encouraging people to take responsibility and by constantly checking one's own assumptions about people, being wary of multicultural or gender filters, a director is well on the way to having a continuing education unit in which people motivate themselves. Two theories of motivation give new insights into what actions on behalf of employees in a service or education field might have desired effects. The first is two-factor or group motivation theory, developed by Herzberg. The second theory discussed here is Maslow's, which can be called one-factor or individual motivation theory. Of the many theories of motivation, these two are particularly useful in administering and leading continuing education programs in institutions of higher education.

ORGANIZATIONAL GROUP MOTIVATION THEORY

"What would motivate my staff to really work toward our division goal of able, satisfied, competent students and graduates?" wonders a director. "I

wish I could pay them more money. Maybe I can give Sue a small raise—
that's only a few dollars a week more. Then I think I'll ask Mary if she'd like
to attend that all-day conference next month. It has a moderate cost but it's
only a one-time cost." What will be the results of these two "trial balloons"?
A staff member who got the raise asked for another raise 6 months later, but
the staff member who received the training used new skills for several years.

In two-factor motivation theory as outlined by Herzberg (Herzberg,
Mausner, and Snyderman, 1959) and diagrammed in Figure 7.1, two types
of factors are needed to motivate employees. The first type of factors are the
dissatisfaction or *hygiene factors* shown at the left in Figure 7.1. The second
type, at the right, are called *motivator factors*. Many motivator factors are an
inherent part of higher education work, such as achievement and the worth
of the work. The previous story about Mary and Sue illustrates this theory,
in part.

Dissatisfaction or Hygiene Factors

Hygiene or dissatisfaction factors mean the extrinsic or outside factors—the
things in a continuing education division that a director can do something
about. They are group-oriented factors that are all around a person at work,
and they set the working atmosphere. Included are salary, working conditions, interpersonal relations, policy, hours, status, and security, as shown in
Figure 7.1. Quality of supervision can be measured by observing whether
the director follows staff around and is nosy or whether the director trusts
the staff. Trust is also a major component of empowerment for employees
(Peters, 1994). These factors are those usually chosen for improvement when
a leader or manager wants to strengthen motivation in an organization.
However, Herzberg found that even if all of these factors are excellent, this

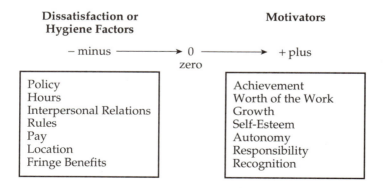

FIGURE 7.1   Hygiene Factors and Motivators

excellence will merely prevent an employee from being dissatisfied. On the diagram this is shown by the arrows bringing the employee from a minus position up to a zero position. He or she may not complain as much now but the individual is still not motivated to do his or her best work.

Many people think that when they want to motivate people, they should increase the pay, improve the hours, have more staff parties (improve interpersonal relations), or improve on some of the hygiene factors in the lefthand box in Figure 7.1. In numerous studies it has been found, however, that all that improving the hygiene factors does is to keep people from being dissatisfied. It is important not to ignore the hygiene factors, however, because if a person is too dissatisfied, he or she will not even be interested in the motivator factors. However, in any organization one or two of the hygiene factors may be beyond the administrator's control. In continuing education the hours and the salaries are somewhat controlled by outside factors but the two factor group theory of motivation is particularly applicable in continuing education organizations because all of the motivator factors can be developed within a given continuing education division or program at little or no cost.

Motivator Factors

The second type of factors needed, according to Herzberg, are motivator factors, like those listed in the righthand box in Figure 7.1. It has been found that, in order to motivate people, leaders need to build motivators that are really internal. Feelings of job satisfaction and motivation are more likely to come from the work itself. These include a sense of achievement, a sense of responsibility, and a sense of the worth of the work. In continuing education there is a tremendous benefit from this latter factor because the work that people are doing with higher education continuing education is inherently worthwhile. Persons active in higher education continuing education will have a part in shaping the future. It is important to remind staff and faculty of this and to say, "Thank you: This is *important* work. You are enhancing people's lives. You are empowering people to take more control of their own futures."

Being an educator can be a psychologically draining job. Faculty and staff are on duty long hours and may have repeated crises. On the other hand, it is an important life's work because one is helping people improve their lives and develop their potential in ways that may have far-reaching consequences.

In any continuing education program or center this factor of the importance of working with people and helping them develop is a built-in motivator, inherent in the job itself. In contrast, persons who work in most factories, turning three bolts all day long or inserting three computer chips every day, will have to be turned to other motivators, as the work itself will never be as inherently important and as far-reaching as working with people (students) who are improving their lives. Factory owners know that they have this problem so they pay assembly line workers increasing wages and just assume that they will always have morale problems.

The motivators are some of the things that can be developed by any leader or manager, so that employees feel a real sense of satisfaction in their work, not just an absence of dissatisfaction. Other motivators include building self-esteem, encouraging people to grow and learn, giving them opportunities for professional growth and advancement, and giving people some autonomy. Giving people autonomy means allowing them to work on their own, whether they are an exempt or nonexempt employee or are faculty.

Studies have found that people will stay in work longer if the work really satisfies (or motivates) them, even though it doesn't pay well. Some people say, "If I only earned more, I wouldn't care what I did," but studies have found that this is not true. Earning more in an unrewarding job may please a person for a year or two, but really satisfying life's work is one of the finest rewards one can seek in life.

Recognition is another important motivator for all ages, adults or children. All people like to be recognized for something—for a bright smile, for a job well done, for having the most registrations, for bringing in a new contract program, or for their own unique qualities whether job-related or not. These motivating factors are the important variables that really cause people to be motivated and happy.

Hygiene factors are important and lead to and build job commitment. But if the motivating factors are also present, it leads to job and *organizational* commitment. Organizational commitment is commitment to the goal of the particular program, which may be having the best-quality continuing education program in town or developing happy, competent, satisfied graduates. The continuing education division has some overriding goals beyond just keeping the division going. The center goal might be for the students to have a sense of pride in being enrolled in such a fine program. However, all of the staff needs to be committed to the division's primary goal of being the best continuing education division in town, or whatever goal is selected. Developing motivator factors within the working environment really helps to secure this needed commitment of staff and students.

It is interesting to take this list of motivators and brainstorm ways that more motivators can be written into the job description of a staff member, a faculty member, a dean, or a director or into the plans for an education center. The lists of motivators to involve faculty more in a center, were developed by a "staff meeting" role play group in a motivation segment of a college credit workshop. Like most brainstorming results, the items may be overlapping or repetitious, but they have great potential for polishing and extending.

Brainstorming Motivating Strategies

Achievement and Recognition

1. Give a certificate of commendation (with a gold seal on it?) at a meeting to a faculty member for her or his first contribution to a center.

2. Mention names of those who have helped in unusual ways in a newsletter.

3. Give thank-you notes at the end of the semester to those who have helped in extra ways.

4. Feature a "Professor of the Month" on a bulletin board or in the newsletter. Tell hobbies, interests, scholarly achievements, and family news, if appropriate. List compliments given that person or solicit them from adult students. (Adjunct professors especially, get little recognition, other than an annual dinner or reception at some schools. They often serve a vital role in continuing education, and low-cost motivators like this validate their efforts. Since adjunct salaries tend to be low, many individuals serve in this role because they love teaching or love their subject or because it balances their other work, but efforts to smooth their path and to help them to get to know the staff, the students, and each other are appreciated.)

5. Acknowledge and implement faculty members' ideas whenever possible. Validate their input at meetings for solutions that are useful.

6. Praise faculty members in front of their adult students. Reinforce and compliment faculty members' positive interactions with adult students.

7. Do paragraphs on one or two adjunct faculty and full-time faculty each month in the continuing education division newsletter (whether hard copy or e-mail). This also helps staff members answer prospective students' inquiries and questions from a more solid information base.

8. Involve adult students in writing paragraphs for the newsletter for recognition or for thank-you notes.

9. Share information about other higher education institutions' practices of inviting adjunct faculty members to attend department or discipline meetings and/or orientations. This is a form of academic recognition.

10. Encourage the academic vice-president and schools or departments to grant faculty status at the quarter- or half-time level to key adjunct professors.

The Worth of Work

1. Send "happygrams" to the staff and faculty for their efforts. Include current statistics, when possible; also include the benefits of getting a college degree (at any level), and how their work is helping enhance people's lives.

2. Ask a faculty member to be a guest speaker at a staff meeting, telling about his or her degree program, course content, and view of the trends for the future in that particular discipline. This helps staff members pick up new leads for new programs, helps them counsel students, and helps generate advertising copy that is timely and accurate.

3. Share good ideas on academic teaching; distribute the best ideas in the newsletter and with group e-mail.

4. Praise faculty members in the newsletter or in person when they build a support network for each other. Include the department chairs or lead program professors in this praise, as they put in hours organizing and often are unsung heroes and heroines.

Responsibility

1. Invite and train professional staff members to hold briefings and information sessions for potential students on their own, with faculty members who cover degree and course information.

2. Train staff members who are creative to make suggestions for brochures and direct mail pieces and to help in proofreading them. Try to have each item proofread at least two to four times.

Advancement and Growth

1. Invite staff members to attend workshops and conferences.

2. Train staff members to advance to responsible positions and then allow them to attend selected conferences or, when appropriate, faculty meetings.

3. Share information about adult stages of human development and adult supports needed at different life stages at a staff meeting, perhaps as one of several "themes" covered at different meetings. Distribute a photocopied article on this topic ahead of the meeting.

4. Share information about resources in the community.

5. Encourage staff to read library books on different topics such as marketing, management, or higher education for adult students or adults in general, and then at a meeting vote on which books to give their "seal of approval." Have a staff library shelf. (This is especially good for books on marketing, as they inspire new ideas and insights.)

6. Invite faculty members to attend continuing education conferences.

7. Share adult student development and marketing demographics information frequently.

Further Motivation Ideas

In looking for a job, one job seeker uses the two-factor motivation theory as a criterion for selecting a job. When she goes for an interview, she says to the other people working there, "What is it you like about working here?" If they reply, "The pay is regular," "The hours are good" (hygiene factors), she doesn't take the job. If the employees reply, "They let you try out your own ideas," "They'll support you when you get going in an initiative," those are motivators and she listens, even if the job in question pays a little less than the first job described.

It is important to spend time thinking how to get more motivators into the higher education faculty and staff work settings, because, by and large, these motivators are free, or at least easily affordable. It is important to remember that the goal is job enrichment, not job enlargement, however. The payoff in commitment and motivation is to get a good job done for the continuing education division or center and to get the "maximum effort" at least some of the time. (The minimum effort is the minimum an employee does to avoid being fired. Of course, tenured faculty have a different set of dynamics.) The goal is to help people realize their full potential.

If there is a secretary or staff member in the center or division who is very creative, give him or her more opportunity to do bulletin boards, newsletter drawings, ad or brochure sketches, or to develop a marketing plan, or to use that creative talent in another way that helps him or her to grow. The organization has an obligation to recognize the potential in people; in turn, recognition leads to payoffs for the organization. If the division or center believes in people, they will reward the unit by being motivated and by expending more effort on the unit or center than on something else. Many organizations lose a lot in talent because they do not motivate people with these motivators. This results in an economic loss as well as a loss in human happiness. The hygiene factors can recharge people, but with motivator factors they become their own generators.

This theory of motivation parallels what adult educators believe in: the importance of building employees' self-esteem and of helping employees reach their potential. Good theory about people can apply to any age or stage of adulthood. Adults respond to those who believe in them and who recognize their potential, as any age students do. Adults like to be helped to create and achieve, to be responsible and to grow, also. There is often an *expectations* gap between what a person does and what he or she is capable of (Figure 7.2). The more the organization can help close that gap, the more of a sense of commitment it will build in its employees toward the organization's goals.

People need to be trained to handle more *responsibility*, however, and they have to find satisfaction in it. People need to build competence and confidence and have a sense of being able to grow. It is not wise to simply require a lot of extra responsibility and say, "Aren't you fulfilled?" Ways to train people might include giving or delegating a small section of a market plan to another person, or allowing a new marketing representative to accompany a more senior representative on a week or two of calls. A support staff member can be trained in the same partnership way on a regular

What one does ⟶ What one is capable of, or
what one is expected to do

FIGURE 7.2   Gap in Expectations

basis, with something specific to do. This builds a *sense of achievement* into an adult's job and also some responsibility.

Emphasizing the *value of the work* itself is one of the easiest motivators to reinforce, but it is often not done. Remind people of the continuing education division's philosophy regularly, in a newsletter and on bulletin boards. Say, "We believe in having an excellent program for adult students— respecting adult students and the learning that is occurring—helping them develop to their full potential" or whatever simply stated goals you may have. (The goals can vary every year, to keep interest in them high.)

Recognition is also easy to give. For staff, have a "Highlighted Person of the Month" (or Week) bulletin board near an entrance or in a faculty area. Show a picture of him or her and list his or her birthday, hobbies, names of any children, favorite jokes, or pets. Faculty members see it as they come in and can better greet the staff member. Anything that gives the staff a lift just naturally helps them to be nicer to the students and to prospective or inquiring students.

Deans and directors need a lift too, and it is important for them to attend workshops, conferences, or courses to gain new ideas and to receive some recognition for what can be a lonely and isolated job. There are many problems a dean or director cannot complain about to the staff, so it is important to go to a program where people have similar problems.

Growth can be provided by paying a staff or faculty member's way to a local or regional conference or by offering regular staff and faculty training at the center. Often training for staff ends up educating a faculty member about more options and opportunities in the marketing arena. Even if only two or three people seem to be getting something out of training provided at a center, training on a regular basis is an opportunity for growth. College courses are in this category also. Tell the staff, "We want you to grow professionally, so you can apply for an even better job in the future." People need to feel that they're getting something back from working with the organization. The most usual benefit in higher education is the tuition benefit package, but often staff members may need to be encouraged to take advantage of this. It should not just be assumed that no staff development is needed because most of the staff are enrolled in courses. Feeling they are growing is one of the best things people can gain from employment. In a field where people are asked to give all day, units and centers have to give staff something in return—refill them—so that they can be informative and responsive to the adult students. Studies on stress show that people can only give out so much. As a general rule, the more that an administrator can support staff, help them feel self-esteem and a sense of personal worth, and help them feel that what they are doing is really worthwhile, then the more they will feel good about themselves. The director can encourage staff to realize their importance to the continuing education unit, to the adult students, and to the faculty. People like to feel good about themselves. It is an innate human need. Helping people feel good about themselves is something that is not very hard to do. Administrators who are discouraged may think "How come *they* get to feel good about themselves when I've got this budget problem?" However, this is dead-end reasoning. If the unit can give staff something (recognition, self-esteem), it is likely that the fruits of this will eventually cheer up the director, and perhaps even improve the budget, too. To build any kind of marketing program, morale build-up is an ongoing need, because representatives of the institution are being asked to risk rejection for their efforts in the outside world every day.

The questionnaire in Figure 7.3 can help leaders find out just how their staff feels and in what areas motivating factors might be increased. Now that higher education continuing education is becoming less of a monopoly (with new schools, satellite centers, and distance learning options entering the field), *maximizing* the way the institution of higher education's programs are presented by all concerned will help the bottom line of the institution. Respondents should check off or circle the number for one response to each question and then total the numbers.

The questionnaire probes feelings about thirteen factors—seven hygiene factors and six motivator factors—as listed in Figure 7.4. As mentioned before, hygiene factors are easy to complain about and when rated at 100% still only keep people from being dissatisfied. The motivator areas in the other questions are much more important for lasting success and an optimistic outlook for the future of the division of continuing education. A total score of 44 to 66 is good. Below 44, look into the motivator factors for an additional area to boost. Below 22, a director may begin to see absenteeism and high turnover.

Leaders can ask themselves this question as a "self-management" exercise to see if they need to praise themselves more or reward themselves for the efforts they make: Does my "self-talk" (conversation with yourself) only include the "shoulds," as in "I *should* do this more" or "I *should* do that more"? Being kindly in speech to yourself will help you to be kinder to those you lead.

Figure 7.3 Staff Motivation Questionnaire

Question Fantastic	Pretty Good	Just Okay	Not So Hot

1. How do you like the work you do?

Great, highly exciting, the work I always wanted to do	Better than average	Average, so-so, worthwhile	Routine, dull, meaningless
SCORE_3_	SCORE_2_	SCORE_1_	SCORE_0_

2. Does your work call for you to do jobs on your own?

Always	Often	Sometimes	Never
SCORE_3_	SCORE_2_	SCORE_1_	SCORE_0_

3. How much control do you have over the way you do your work?

Do it my way	I think how to do it and get approval	Director and I decide together	I do as I'm told
SCORE_3_	SCORE_2_	SCORE_1_	SCORE_0_

4. How much time and freedom does your work allow you?

My time is my own, freedom to come and go to do the job as I see fit	Better than average, many late nights	Some free time, work Saturdays	Constant surveillance
SCORE_3_	SCORE_2_	SCORE_1_	SCORE_0_

5. Have you received any acknowledgment for a job well done in the past year?

Every time	Occasional pat on the back	Almost never	Don't know what you're talking about
SCORE_3_	SCORE_2_	SCORE_1_	SCORE_0_

6. Are you given opportunities to attend classes, conferences, or other events in the areas of interest and specialization?

Regularly	Once in a while	Rarely	Never
SCORE_3_	SCORE_2_	SCORE_1_	SCORE_0_

7. Does your job encourage you to be competent in the areas of your choice and to achieve?

Yes, it's great	Often	Too much, I'm overworked and need help	Never
SCORE_3_	SCORE_2_	SCORE_1_	SCORE_0_

Continued

Figure 7.3   *Continued*

Question Fantastic	Pretty Good	Just Okay	Not So Hot
8. *What kind of guidance do you receive from your leader?*			
Well planned and helpful, individual attention	Periods of no guidance	Occasional vague guidance	Poor, little, or no guidance
SCORE_3_	SCORE_2_	SCORE_1_	SCORE_0_
9. *Does your leader and/or co-workers recognize your efforts when you pitch in and help?*			
Usually	Occasionally	Almost never	What are you talking about?
SCORE_3_	SCORE_2_	SCORE_1_	SCORE_0_
10. *How do you feel about the progress you've made this year?*			
Am learning new and more challenging things	Have some new tasks	Routine learnings and tasks	Not going anywhere, same old thing
SCORE_3_	SCORE_2_	SCORE_1_	SCORE_0_
11. *Have you been given a raise in salary, promotion, or better work location this year?*			
Every 6 months	Once a year	Every 1 1/2 to 2 years	Never
SCORE_3_	SCORE_2_	SCORE_1_	SCORE_0_
12. *What kind of relationship do you have with your leader?*			
Great, effective, really understands me	More often effective than not	Average	Ineffective, so-so
SCORE_3_	SCORE_2_	SCORE_1_	SCORE_0_
13. *To what extent do you participate in decision making?*			
My ideas are asked for and often used constructively	My ideas are asked for	Not involved in decision making but informed of what I need to know	Not informed of job-related matters
SCORE_3_	SCORE_2_	SCORE_1_	SCORE_0_
14. *Do you have responsibility or authority over any others?*			
A lot	Somewhat	Very little	Not at all
SCORE_3_	SCORE_2_	SCORE_1_	SCORE_0_
15. *How well do you get along with your co-workers?*			
Great group, I like them	Some likeable	Pleasant but dull	Boring or much conflict
SCORE_3_	SCORE_2_	SCORE_1_	SCORE_0_

Figure 7.3 *Continued*

Question Fantastic	Pretty Good	Just Okay	Not So Hot
16. All in all, how do you feel about your pay?			
Top dollar	Generous	Average, ordinary	Plenty of room for improvement
SCORE_3_	SCORE_2_	SCORE_1_	SCORE_0_
17. Do you like where your job is located?			
Ideal	Sub-ideal	Too far, could be closer	Too far from everything
SCORE_3_	SCORE_2_	SCORE_1_	SCORE_0_
18. What kind of fringe benefits do you receive?			
Vacation, tuition, medical coverage, pension	Most of these	Some of these	Few of these
SCORE_3_	SCORE_2_	SCORE_1_	SCORE_0_
19. How is your work setting?			
Luxurious, lots of resources and equipment	Comfortable, nice place, sufficient resources and equipment	Run-down hot, stuffy	Dismal, sick building
SCORE_3_	SCORE_2_	SCORE_1_	SCORE_0_
20. Who evaluates your progress?			
I evaluate my own	Cooperate in evaluation with Director	Given a chance to review and discuss evaluation given me	Given an evaluation
SCORE_3_	SCORE_2_	SCORE_1_	SCORE_0_
21. How secure do you feel?			
Secure	More secure than insecure	More insecure than secure	Don't know one day to the next
SCORE_3_	SCORE_2_	SCORE_1_	SCORE_0_
22. Do you have input into marketing plans, direct mail list selection, program development?			
It's my main job	Once in a while	Occasionally (or as an afterthought)	Not at all
SCORE_3_	SCORE_2_	SCORE_1_	SCORE_0_

Hygiene Factors	Motivators
Salary (#16)	Autonomy (#2, 3, 4)
Leader/Director (#12, 20)	Worth of Work (#1)
Co-Workers (#15)	Recognition and Achievement (#5, 9)
Location (#17)	Growth Needs (#6, 7, 8)
Fringe Benefits (#18)	Advancement (#10, 11)
Working Conditions (#19)	Responsibility (#13, 14, 22)
Security (#2, 21)	

Figure 7.4   Key To Motivation Questionnaire

INDIVIDUAL MOTIVATION

Abraham Maslow (1970) is quite well known in the field of psychology, and his work on the hierarchy of human needs (Figure 7.5) is also used in management. The theory states that the bottom level of needs in the triangle or hierarchy must be met before individuals can or want to move on to the next level. Individuals therefore are motivated by one factor: whether their needs on their level are met or not. The theory, in terms of motivation, assumes that meeting individuals' needs on their level will *motivate* them to go on to the next level. When the need is filled, they are satisfied and ready to move. Maslow's theory of motivation looks at individuals, whereas Herzberg's theory looks at motivation within organizations and organizational groups. Maslow's theory is based on the assumption that those things absent will satisfy when they are present.

The Needs in the Hierarchy

Maslow says that to motivate people, one needs to meet them on the level where they are and help move them forward to the next level. Of course, it is difficult to be certain of estimating the level of need correctly.

Physiological Needs

Human beings tend to concentrate on meeting physiological needs before being concerned with higher-level needs. When the needs at this level are partially satisfied, other needs emerge. The classic example of this is of the early missionaries attempting to preach to people who were starving. Starving people have to eat before they can hear any message being brought to them. Severe dieting and sleep deprivation can cause a lack of focus, also, with employees.

Figure 7.5   Maslow's Hierarchy of Needs

Safety and Security Needs, Anxiety

One can see the effect of security needs on a personality by observing elderly people who live in big cities, who worry about being mugged, and have twelve locks on their doors. This fear and worry need is so great (and with good cause) that the higher-level needs do not concern them. If a continuing education center requires a public transportation ride into the inner city to take courses (due to expensive or inadequate parking), it might be time to consider some suburban satellite centers for safety reasons. An individual at a higher level may also experience needs at this level after a traumatic experience such as an auto accident. The person might be quite fearful and worried about safety while driving or riding in a car for several months following the accident. It is important according to Maslow's theory to "meet people where they are."

Love and Belongingness Needs

Maslow believes that most of America is at this level. Love and belongingness needs can be seen in adult students who seek companionship.

Self-Esteem Needs

If a person has a feeling of being cared about, is not really feeling unsafe, and is not really hungry or in need of rest, then that person would not mind being chair of a work group or something similar, being open to gaining self-esteem in some way. Individuals with pressing needs in another area do not need or want status responsibilities on top of their other worries, however.

Self-Actualization Needs

The highest-level needs for development and self-actualization are satisfied only after needs at the four lower levels have been met. At this fifth level, individuals are concerned with the development of their potential. These people have peak experiences of insight or understanding. Individuals at this stage, which many people never reach, have a better perception of reality, accept themselves and others, are more creative, and are better able to become completely human in the realization and development of their full potential. Truth, goodness, beauty, and meaningfulness are recognized and enjoyed by these people.

Some writers say that only older people can be at this level, people like Winston Churchill or Eleanor Roosevelt. This writer has found many positive people in continuing adult education who periodically have tremendous moments of feeling really good about their work with adult students of all ages. One example is a director who planned a good staff training program and can see that it has really helped the staff. It is important to take time to value this kind of feeling, as it is a sort of payoff for the effort expended. A dean or director might take a moment to think, "I worked hard on that, and it really seems to be clicking." Similarly, people must value the insights that come to them about what they might do next. They can write down these insights and review them until they are ready to put them onto a goals list, either for long-range or short-range goals.

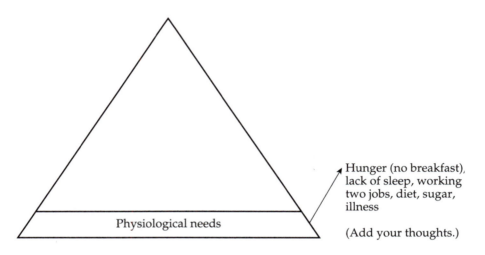

Figure 7.6   Lethargy Problem Considered from First-Level Perspective

Practical Application of One-Factor Motivation

Maslow's needs hierarchy can be applied to adult students' needs and motivations, as well as to staff and faculty members. The first step is to think of the different reasons a person could present a problem based on each level of Maslow's hierarchy of needs. For instance, an adult who seems unmotivated and lethargic could be reacting to any of the five levels of needs on the hierarchy. What could cause an adult to be a lethargic and unmotivated problem on the physiological level (Figure 7.6)? What safety concerns, fear, or anxiety could cause a staff member to be lethargic and unmotivated (Figure 7.7)?

What love and belongingness needs could cause an employee to be lethargic and unmotivated (Figure 7.8)? *Idea*: The "Staff Member of the Month" activity is particularly good for the staff employee with needs at this level. One education center obtained a photograph of Tom (or a picture could be drawn), mounted it in the center of a poster, and had all Tom's co-workers write compliments about him all over the poster. The poster was given to Tom, after a week of public spotlighting. Tom was proud enough to post it on his refrigerator at home. The activity is good for all adults, because, besides receiving their poster, they like to see nice things said about themselves. This has become rare in today's mass media culture in which the put down for a laugh has become so popular. Therefore, this type of activity becomes doubly valuable and needed. Adults respond to esteem-building activities—especially if they add a light touch to the office. Fourth-level self-worth and self esteem needs are also at play here (Figure 7.9).

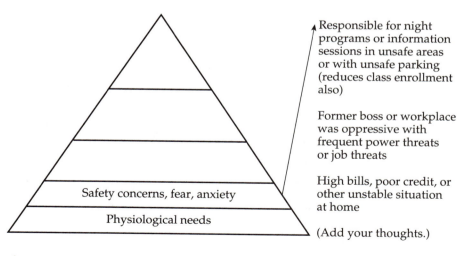

Figure 7.7   Lethargy Problem Considered from Second-Level Perspective

Self-actualization needs, at the fifth level, can also be observable, but people at this level are almost never lethargic. If they are lethargic it is usually due to a serious problem. This level is therefore not usually diagrammed, but a diagram might look like Figure 7.10 for a lethargy problem. Otherwise, one can first inquire about the well-being of the person in a compassionate manner and secondly think of creative or intellectual challenges for a person at this level

From this exercise of considering a problem (lethargy) from different need-level perspectives one can see that adults or (children) might act the same way for many different reasons. For example, one staff member came to work and was sarcastic with almost everyone every morning. This person was feeling ignored and was acting out of a belonging need.

The analysis of what level an employee is on needs to be on target, which is a challenge that may be eased by training. One looks at the employee who is lethargic and unmotivated and realizes there could be a number of causes. If that person is really exhausted or hungry, more attention or expanded duties will not help much. If someone really needs something, solutions based on another level of need will not be effective motivators. For example, a staff member who had grown up in a large family and never had a room of her own was having problems over sharing an office with other staff members. By giving her assigned office space of her own, the director met her need to have her "stuff" protected, to have her own space. This solution met this employee's need better than sending her to a workshop on interpersonal office relationships might have.

A leader or manager can think about each employee, decide if there is a

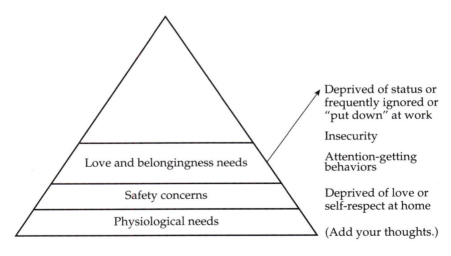

Figure 7.8 Lethargy Problem Considered from Third-Level Perspective

pressing need, identify it, and then try to work with that level. Adults can be operating on the level of physiological need: coming to work without breakfast, too little sleep, or having a problem with alcohol or other substances. Other problems or needs that faculty members, staff, or adult students might have, in addition to those on a physiological level, might be:

Anxiety level:	worried about a health problem,
	worried about financial problems,
	spouse lost job,
	sudden divorce, spouse abuse
Love and Affection level:	single parent,
	conflict with spouse
Esteem level:	loss of job or spouse
Self-Actualization level:	not enough opportunities to use talents, skills, and abilities

Obviously a dean or other leader's job is not to deal directly with many of these problems, but understanding their existence and helping find referrals to appropriate community resources might be a first step. Encouraging adults involved in the unit to be supportive and kind also builds a positive climate in the workplace.

Occasionally a leader or manager may have an employee who has a need so strong that it precludes working in continuing education. One example is that of a support staff member who had been wonderful answering prospective

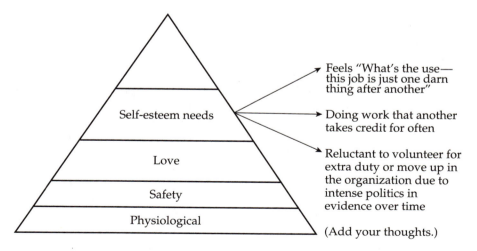

Figure 7.9   Lethargy Problem Considered from Fourth-Level Perspective

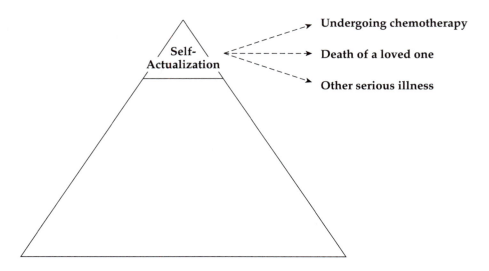

Figure 7.10   Lethargy Problem Considered from Fifth-Level Perspective

students' questions on the telephone but who was having tremendous problems at home with an alcoholic husband and a divorce. The director did not know all this, but the rest of the staff noticed that the individual had started being rude and abrupt with telephone inquiries. The director realized that there was no way that she could meet the staff members' needs, which were great. The unit found another job for this employee with less student interface for a year or two. Not all jobs require patience with people all day long. There are other jobs available for someone who cannot reasonably be expected to change his or her behavior at a given point.

Maslow's one-factor theory encourages leaders to look carefully at individuals, try to identify their levels (or the leaders' own) correctly, and work toward solutions based on the levels. It is helpful to draw out the hierarchy triangle chart and brainstorm (even alone) some of the possible causes for a person's behavior at each level. This will help prevent identifying the wrong level and then going down a blind alley.

Two other process theories about motivation, not often seen in continuing education but still observable, are an "expectancy" theory and an "equity" process theory. The expectancy theory states that persons fill positions because they *expect* better positions to evolve from them (e.g. Dean? Academic Vice-president? Alumni Development Director? Business School Professional Development Director?). The equity theory states that persons are in jobs because they see them as "fair" and "equitable" (Hillriegel, 1997). One hears about this often in political campaigns. However, the agonized comment of a government worker of "That's not fair!" upon hearing a downlinked speech by Peter Drucker about workers having 8 jobs and 5 careers demonstrates a trend away from "cradle to grave" or "career until pension" job likelihood.

Encouraging staff, faculty, and students to do their best, to reach for their full potential and to feel good about themselves is a valuable life's work. This encouragement will reap tremendous returns to the organization and persons who engage in it.

SUPPORTIVE AND DEFENSIVE WORKPLACES

Certain generic themes run throughout this chapter (and this book) which are known to facilitate any organization and are particularly appropriate in adult continuing education programs. These include the provision for a "supportive workplace" rather than a "defensive workplace" which allows for the openness, caring, and good morale so needed for all adults who work with students. In a supportive workplace there is empathy and a realistic concern for the self-esteem of all persons involved (students, staff, and faculty). Equality of all concerned to take part in problem solving regardless of rank or status is another hallmark of the workplace climate needed in an open, caring continuing education division. The climate needs to be focused on problems to solved rather than interpersonal fault finding, and on use of technical expertise and training to solve issues. The focus is on how to do it better, with concern for mutual learning and strategies-to-do-better. In short, a supportive climate would be:

- descriptive (of behavior)
- solution oriented
- vision driven
- empathetic
- collegial (friendship among equals)
- experimental

Therefore many of the chapters in addition to this one, mention involving many persons in the planning and implementation of programs for adult students. This is also the most professional approach as developed in the next chapters.

SUMMARY

Both organizational and individual motivation are applicable in the continuing education workplace. This chapter has examined two major models of motivation. Herzberg, in two-factor motivation theory, claims that motivators, such as job challenge and worth, lead to job satisfaction, not to job dissatisfaction. However, the hygiene factors, such as working conditions, only prevent job dissatisfaction and don't/can't lead to job satisfaction.

One-factor motivation, as demonstrated here with Maslow's theory, assumes that needs motivate people and when a need is satisfied, it no longer motivates a person. This can be very helpful in understanding the behavior of individuals, but if the analysis targets the wrong level, it can be misleading. Knowing one's employees, and friendly one-to-one interaction build the trust to make this understanding clearer and more on target.

Assuming that motivation is "built in" to the continuing education workplace can be a mistake. Professional interaction and inspiration may be available, but creativity and risk-taking need to be recognized and supported, with recognition and credit freely given. Since this often is not the norm in higher education, extra effort needs to be made in these directions, coupled with adequate staff development. The rewards of these extra efforts will be seen in almost all the areas discussed in this book: planning, decision-making, and especially in problem solving and marketing, which are discussed in the next chapters.

BIBLIOGRAPHY

Adler, N. J. (1991). *International Dimensions of Organizational Behavior*. Boston: PWS-Kent.

Barley, J. E. (1986). "Personnel Scheduling with Flex-shift: A Win-Win Scenario." *Personnel*, September, p. 63.

Bass, B. M. (1985). *Leadership and Performance beyond Expectations*. New York: The Free Press.

Bass, B. M., and R. M. Stodgill (1989). *The Handbook of Leadership* (3d ed.). New York: The Free Press.

Bennis, W. (1989). *Why Leaders Can't Lead: The Unconscious Conspiracy*. San Francisco: Jossey-Bass.

Birch, D., and J. Veroff (1968). *Motivation: A Study of Action*. Monterey, CA: Brooks/Cole.

Blake, R., and J. S. Mouton (1964). *The Managerial Grid*. Houston, TX: Gulf.

Cone, W. F. (1974). *Supervising Employees Effectively*. Ontario: Addison-Wesley.

Conger, J. A. (1989). *The Charismatic Leader: Behind the Mystique of Exceptional Leadership*. San Francisco: Jossey-Bass.

Cook, C. W. (1980). "Guidelines for Managing Motivation." *Business Horizons*, April, p. 23.

Driver, M. J. (1979). "Individual Decision Making and Creativity." In S. Kerr (Ed.), *Organizational Behavior*. Columbus, OH: Grid.

Drucker, P. F. (1977). *People and Performance: The Best of Peter Drucker on Management.* New York: Harper's College Press.

Eysenck, H. J. (1964). *Experiments in Motivation.* New York: Macmillan Co.

Fuller, J. L. (1962). *Motivation, a Biological Perspective.* New York: Random House.

Gellerman, S. W. (1963). *Motivation and Productivity.* New York: American Management Association.

Hamachek, D. E. (1968). *Motivation in Teaching and Learning.* Washington, DC: National Education Association.

Hammer, W. C. (1979). "Motivation Theories and Work Applications." In S. Kerr (Ed.), *Organizational Behavior.* Columbus, OH: Grid.

Hannaford, E. (1967). *Supervisor's Guide to Human Relations.* Chicago: National Safety Council.

Hersey, P., and K. H. Blanchard (1988). *Management of Organizational Behavior: Utilizing Human Resources.* Englewood Cliffs, NJ: Prentice-Hall.

Herzberg, F.P., B. Mausner, and B. Snyderman (1959). *The Motivation To Work.* New York: Wiley.

Hillriegel, D., J. W. Slocum, Jr., and R. W. Woodman (1997). *Organizational Behavior* (8th ed.). Cincinnati, OH: South Western College Publishing.

Jones, C. C. (1981). Motivation. Rockville, MD: ECEA Institute.

Jongeward, D. (1973). *Everybody Wins: Transactional Analysis Applied to Organizations.* Reading, MA: Addison-Wesley.

Klein, S.M., and R. R. Ritti (1984). *Understanding Organizational Behavior.* Boston: Kent.

Klimoski, R. J., and N. J. Hayes (1980). "Leader Behavior and Subordinate Motivation." *Personnel Psychology,* Autumn, p. 33.

Kotter, J. (1988). *The Leadership Factor.* New York: The Free Press.

Lawler, E. E. (1973). *Motivation in Work Organizations.* Monterey, CA: Brooks/Cole.

Locke, E., K. Shaw, L. Saari, and G. Latham (1981). "Goal Setting and Task Performance 1969–1980," *Psychological Bulletin,* 90, 125–152.

Luthans, F., and T. Davis (1979). "Behavioral Self-Management (BSM): The Missing Link in Managerial Effectiveness." *Organizational Dynamics,* 8, 42–60.

Luthans, F., and R. Kreitner (1986). *Organizational Behavior Modification and Beyond.* Glenview, IL: Scott, Foresman.

Manz, C. C. (1983). *The Art of Self-Leadership: Strategies for Personal Effectiveness in Your Life and Work.* Englewood Cliffs, NJ: Prentice-Hall.

Manz, C. C. (1986). "Self-Leadership: Toward an Expanded Theory of Self-Influence Processes in Organizations." *Academy of Management Review,* 11, 585–600.

Manz, C. C., and H. P. Sims, Jr. (1980). "Self-Managment as a Substitute for Leadership: A Social Learning Theory Perspective." *Academy of Management Review,* 5, 361–367.

Mason, R. H., and R. S. Spick. (1987). *Management: An International Perspective.* Homewood, IL:Irwin.

Maslow, A. H. (1970). *Motivation and Personality* (2d ed.). New York: Harper & Row.

McClelland, D. C., and D. H. Burnham (1976). "Power Is the Great Motivator." *Harvard Business Review,* March, p. 54.

Murray, E. J. (1964). *Motivation and Emotion.* Englewood Cliffs, NJ: Prentice-Hall.

Peters, Tom (1994). *The Seminar.* New York: Bantam Books.

Quick, J. C. (1979). "Dyadic Goal Setting within Organizations: Role-Making and Motivational Considerations." *Academy of Management Review,* July, p. 4.

Rosenthal, R. (1973). "The Pygmalion Effect Lives." *Psychology Today,* September.

Senge, P. M. (1990). *The Fifth Discipline: The Art and Practice of the Learning Organization.* New York: Doubleday.

Stahl, M. J. (1983). "Achievement Power and Managerial Motivation: Selecting Managerial Talent with the Job Choice Exercise." *Personnel Psychology,* Winter.

Terry, G. R. (1974). *Supervisory Management.* Homewood, IL: Irwin.

Wagel, W. H. (1986). "Opening the Door to Employee Participation." *Personnel,* April, p. 63.

Weisbord, M. R. (1987). "The Learning Organization: Lewin's Legacy to Management." In M. R. Weisbord, *Productive Workplaces.* San Francisco: Jossey-Bass.

▶ 8

Creative and Analytical Problem Solving in Continuing Education

If decision making is a part of leadership, problem solving is too. Creative and innovative problem solving boosts leadership and attracts support from staff and students (and faculty). Analytical problem solving is always needed too, with a new look at the facts, the history, or at surveys done with fresh inspiration from, and complemented by, some creative approaches. Set in the context of higher education, with power struggles and intrigues due to issues of faculty tenure and diversity, budgets and resources, and space and facilities matters, continuing education leaders usually don't go looking for problems—they come to them. Because individual problem solving has been a natural tendency in higher education for many years, group problem solving will be discussed first in this chapter.

A leader's problems in continuing education in higher education are often a group of subproblems or activities. Breaking down these problems into parts can be helpful, but a dean or director also needs a feel for the total situation. It is helpful to state the problem open-endedly. Then a selection can be made from any or all problem-solving techniques that are appropriate. First though, one should ask some questions about the problem.

STEPS IN PROBLEM SOLVING

Ask: Is the Problem Within the Problem Solver's Sphere of Influence?

An initial question to ask is whether the problem is within the director's sphere of influence. If it is, then individual techniques may well be enough to solve the problem (Figure 8.1). These will be discussed later in the chapter. If it is not within the director's or leader's sphere of influence, then group techniques are a must. It is helpful to identify key persons and involve them in the group techniques. Aids to decision making such as the decision tree in discussed in Chapter 5 and brainstorming and synectics are group techniques that will be discussed in this section.

Ask: Are Time and Change Important?

Problems can further be divided into those for which time and change are important and those for which time and change are less important. Planning a new schedule for next year would fall into the second category as more static (not changing rapidly, less time pressure) and meeting a proposal deadline this month would fall into the first as more dynamic (with high time pressure and possible change). Obviously, there will be situations that fit both categories, with time and change both being important.

Individual—Creative	Either Individual or Group—Analytic	Group—Creative
1. Morphological analysis and attribute lists	1. Checklists and attributes lists	1. Brainstorming
2. Redefining the problem	2. Decision trees and other aids	2. Synectics
3. Reversals	3. Six-question approach	
4. How is it done in nature?	4. Computer-aided projections and scenarios	
5. Boundary examinations		
6. Drawing a model		
7. Wishful thinking, big dream, inspired approach		
8. Analogy and metaphor		
9. Questioning		
10. Ten ways this can be done		

Figure 8.1   Creative and Analytical Individual and Group Problem-Solving Techniques

GROUP TECHNIQUES

Analytical decision aids such as creating a checklist or listing pros and cons can be done effectively either individually or in a group. More analytical group techniques can be found in Chapter 5 on decision making. Just addressing the questions:

- What is the problem?
- Who needs to be involved?
- What more do we need to know?
- What would an ideal solution be?
- What would be the first step?

begins to generate answers (written on a board or flip chart) from group discussion that "break open" the problem.

Creative group techniques that will be discussed here include brainstorming and synectics. Brainstorming produces a large number of ideas but not necessarily a deep level of new insights. Synectics requires that someone play the role of the client with the problem; the process produces fewer, but more in-depth, solutions.

Brainstorming

Brainstorming works best when there has been some sort of warm-up, perhaps at a staff or faculty meeting on a certain topic. The warm-up can be just a detailed description of the issue to be considered. The questions ("What is the problem?" etc.) listed previously provide a group warm-up for many problems. The group can then begin brainstorming possible first steps. Another, individual warm-up is to ask each person to write down three or more ideas on the topic or possible solutions before the group time begins.

Brainstorming is divided into two parts. The idea-generation part is first, and there are some set rules for it. These are: (1) All ideas are given equal respect, (2) there is no criticism of any suggestion no matter how wild (faculty need to suspend their critical-thinking skills at this point), and (3) all ideas are written down on a board or flip chart that can be seen by the group. This allows people to see the ideas and build on other group members' suggestions. Reverse brainstorming can be used also, as in: "What are all the possibilities of what could go wrong?"(or whatever the reverse side of the question might be).

Writing the ideas down on a board or flip chart also sets the stage for the second part of brainstorming, in which the ideas are ranked or given priority. One approach to ranking is to give every group member three to seven votes (depending on the total number of ideas that will be ranked). Allowing three to seven votes rather than just one illustrates greater nuances within in a solution. As voting occurs, a natural ranking appears. If the person with the problem is present, it always needs to be stated that this person or "client" may choose among all the solutions generated by the group and need not follow the group's ranking. The client, after all, knows the problem most intimately and may have received new insights from the idea-generating that he or she prefers to use.

For example, the question "How can we be sure the education programs we present at this new center will meet the local community needs?" might receive a much wider spread of answers when run through a brainstorming session with the staff. Some answers are more obvious, like: "do a market research survey", or "do an environmental scan of local newspapers and other educational offerings." However, more ideas, like "ask my cousin who lives there" or "advertise more widely than planned in local newspapers" also emerge. This kind of question might be only one of a set of questions considered with the group using synectics as the problem-solving approach.

Synectics

Synectics is a group problem-solving technique that requires that there be a leader who serves as a facilitator and a client (who can be assigned) who has the ultimate say as to whether a solution will work or not and who "owns" the problem. The client also can say what could correct the factor that blocks a solution's usability. The group acts as a "think tank" for the client. *Synectics* is a Greek word that means joining together different and apparently irrelevant elements. While the client is the evaluator in this technique, others can see the ideas generated and written on a flip chart or board and use them in their own way.

After a suitable warm-up of the group that describes the situation, the facilitator writes out the problem, defined in an open-ended way, for all to see. Then solutions are generated by the group and written below the problem in columns (Figure 8.2). Then the client is asked to respond to the solutions and give them a plus or minus sign. A paraphrase of the comment about why a solution would not work is written on the visual aid if the solution is given a minus sign. The minus responses are then addressed with "How to Avoid" questions, and new solutions are generated, as shown in Figure 8.2 and in Figure 8.3, which addresses the broad current problem of "How to Have a University Policy on Continuing Education," which was discussed by a graduate higher education administration group. This topic is also a good springboard for discussion for a professional association meeting or other similar groups.

The plusses generated in this discussion included that:

1. Continuing education centers would be self-sufficient cost centers within 5 years. Healthy (growing) centers return 30% to 50% of revenue to the university.

2. Splitting costs and income between the university and the department budgets allows revenue sharing for new program initiatives for departments (and they receive a higher percent).

3. Full-time faculty who are "under load" (not fully busy) or those who want to teach one or two "overload" courses can keep busy for payment.

4. In the daytime the space can be filled with contract courses and non-credit courses to promote full use of the space.

5. Centers must be accredited at the accreditation visits to the university.

The minuses included the following, but these might vary according to the institution:

1. The educational reputation of the institution can be hurt by bad satellite programs, both credit and noncredit.

2. Only adults able to afford tuition costs might have access to programs.

3. The expense to the university might be too great.

4. The education programs might not meet the market requests or the local community needs.

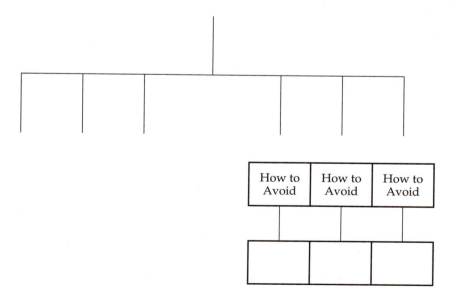

Figure 8.2 Framework for Synectic Problem Solving

Problem Stated: How to Have a University Policy on Continuing Education

Pluses

Have contract courses and noncredit courses to promote full use of space in the daytime

Centers must be accredited at accreditation visits to university

Self-sufficient cost centers within 5 years; healthy centers return 30–50% of revenue to the university

Split costs and income between university and department budgets; allow revenue sharing for new program initiatives for departments (higher percentage)

Full-time faculty who are "under load" or who want one or two overload can keep busy for payment

Minuses	How to Avoid
Education programs might not meet the market requests or community local needs	Careful market research and environmental scan help to ensure a "fit." Wider advertising for Centers helps.
Expense to the university might be too great	Self-sufficient cost centers within 5 years; healthy centers return 30–50% revenue.
Only adults able to afford tuition costs, have access	Give out financial aid and tuition assistance information at all briefing/info sessions. Solicit contract group of courses from local corporations and agencies (Employer sponsored).
Education reputation is hurt by bad satellite programs (credit and noncredit)	Meet accreditation and state certification standards. Have Advisory Boards by content area (Utilizing program alumni if possible).

Figure 8.3   Synectic Problem-Solving Example

Interestingly enough, one set of responses for how to avoid these problems was as follows:

1. Educational reputation can be hurt by bad satellite programs, both credit and noncredit: Avoid by meeting accreditation and any state certification standards. Create advisory boards by content area, utilizing program alumni from main campus, if possible. (Educational reputations can also be hurt

by poor main campus programs, too.)

2. Only adults able to afford tuition costs might have access to programs: Avoid by giving out financial aid and tuition assistance information at all information or briefing sessions. Solicit contract groups of courses from local corporations and agencies for employer-sponsored courses.

3. The expense to the university might be too great: Avoid by reminding the university that self-sufficient continuing and distance education cost centers can return 30% to 50% of revenue to the general fund within 5 years.

4. The education programs might not meet the market requests or the local community needs: Avoid by careful market research and environmental scans to help ensure the "fit" with the region. Advertising for the centers also helps.

This group exercise might last over more than one session, as group members research additional responses. Meeting the challenges of leadership in continuing and distance education can clearly be facilitated by accessing the thinking of a group. Optimally, the group represents a variety of points of view and different stakeholders. Brainstorming around just one of the "minuses" might be very productive, for instance for market requests.

INDIVIDUAL TECHNIQUES

Processing some of the ideas generated with group techniques can logically be done individually. Many individual creative techniques listed here can also be used for group problem solving. A leader can "walk through" the technique alone first, or gather group ideas first. Individual analytical techniques are quite familiar.

Individual Analytical Techniques

Checklists are a familiar problem-solving aid, as is the listing of "pros" and "cons" for a specific decision or problem solution that is basically analytical. Weighing ideas on a checklist of pros and cons on a scale of 1 to 10 (that is, marking them +1 to +10 or -1 to -10) according to one's feelings or some particular criteria also helps clarify priorities and is an individual analytical technique. An attribute list, which is described in the next section, can also be an analytical technique. The decision tree described in Chapter 5 is also analytical and can be used by individuals or by a group.

Another individual analytical technique could be called the "six-question approach." To demonstrate this, let us use the example of a need to purchase a new piece of computer equipment. The first step is to gather catalogues (or other reference materials appropriate to the problem). These resource materials help warm up the group and provide a springboard to discussion. Then ask these six questions:

1. What is it?
2. What must it do?
3. What *does* it do?
4. What did it cost?
5. What else might do the job?
6. What will that cost?

Thinking through each of these questions sharpens one's thinking and clarifies the issues involved.

Computer-Aided Problem Solving

Another aid to individual decision making and analytical problem solving is planning made possible by one of the (few) computer software systems designed specifically for continuing education management. Three types of software that are useful for continuing education aid in planning (projections, long-range plans, cash flow and budgets), communications and printing, and record keeping. The planning program can also be used for simulations as a director develops the five possible plans discussed in Chapter 3: for things as expected, for situations that are a little better, a little worse, much better, and much worse. Simulating the numbers, budgets, and other factors in a 1-year, 5-year and 10-year plan allow a dean or director to make a "dry run" or a pilot program view of a likely scenario. These are subject to error, as the future *is* uncertain and computers are famous for only projecting the known or linear possibilities that have been entered into the computer. However, uncovering hidden possibilities or problems that can be predicted is worth the effort involved (Senge, 1990).

Individual Creative Techniques

Morphological Analysis
Morphological analysis is an example of a technique that can be done individually or with a group. Morphological analysis is a comprehensive way of listing and examining all of the possible combinations for solutions to a problem. The steps are:

1. Define the problem broadly.
2. List the interdependent variables.

Variables	Old Population	Some New Population	New Population
Old Product	Existing continuing education center	Advertise a variety of off-campus sites in high schools or corporations	New continuing education center across town
Some New Product	Offer new master's degree programs (not offered off campus before) along with established degrees and programs	Advertise to new populations such as teachers, engineers, or corporate business employees, if one of these new groups had not been reached recently	Advertise *only* to new population, e.g., employees of a government agency or a corporation.
New Product	Offer all new master's degree programs; rotate existing ones to a new center	Offer mostly new master's degrees to old and new populations; add Saturday and noncredit computer classes	Offer all new programs at an all new center location across town.

Figure 8.4 Morphological Analysis—How to Expand Services to Increase Revenue

3. Enter the variables on the horizontal axis of a chart.
4. Select the most promising alternatives and list them on the vertical axis of the chart.

The object is to review all possible combinations, as shown in Figure 8.4, where the broad problem was: how to expand services in order to increase income.

A gradual progression can be made through Figure 8.4 with goals and objectives for future years. Floor space and expertise might be problems in this example. Acquiring the space and building solid relationships with a less active (or new) academic department might take some time. By building on old strengths of either the population served at present or the product (the program for adult students under discussion), an organization doesn't go too far out on a limb in trying new things. It has been found that to *start* with a new service for a new population is the least feasible of these alternatives (Shore, 1997). It is easier to start with a familiar service to a new population or a new service to a familiar population. For instance, if the institution hasn't been providing engineering programs at a distant location, it shouldn't open a new center (new population) with two-thirds new engineering programs. Each discipline has its own parameters and market, so a familiar academic content area, such as providing teacher education or information systems courses should make up more than half of the new center's array of programs.

Morphological analysis can also be done with a group in a brainstorming session to gain more ideas and add details to concepts already suggested. A staff training session might be greatly enlivened by such an exercise. In general, the whole process is designed to generate ideas. The combining and recombining of functions and possible alternatives give numerous opportunities to look at a problem and come up with fresh, novel solutions rather than looking along old lines with old habits.

Attribute Lists

A specialized form of morphological analysis is the *attribute list.* By listing attributes of the functions desired (or not desired) on one side of a matrix and possible forms across the other side of a matrix, form and function are separated and new insights emerge. Each function can be considered as it would appear in each form. Also, elements within the function can be considered.

An example of an attribute list of this type used to better understand a difficult administrative personnel problem involving a grievance filed is shown in Figure 8.5. This problem was resolved when the person took 3 months medical leave without pay and actually took a new job. It was found

Dimensions of the Problem	Elements within the Dimension
Rudeness	Of administrative assistant to professionals, faculty, visitors
Incompetence	Late work, lost work, surliness about complaints
Programs threatened	Income and prestige loss, relationship with community threatened
Wants all requests to be made in writing	Delays work, creates rigidity, violates norms of integrity
Sexism, racism, grievance filed by person with attributes listed above (citing sexism and racism as reasons for the behavior described above)	Involves legal language and delays, learning about parameters involved, can work to the benefit of managment or the employee

Figure 8.5   Attribute List for Personnel Grievance

that her references had not been checked when she was hired and that she had shown this behavior in the past. Her grievances against a large number of people in the organization (seventeen out of twenty three) were found to be unsubstantiated.

Attribute lists are also intended to generate ideas about a service, situation, or product. First, the list is generated and then analyzed for which items would improve the situation, service, or whatever is produced (satisfied, competent students in the case of continuing higher education programs).

For example, an individual or a group (staff or faculty) may want to improve offerings from an academic department to better fit the market requests. A list of attributes or features can be developed (Figure 8.6). Checklists can be developed under these items and then forced relationships developed next or later. When doing this as a group, the leader or facilitator can introduce a new word or words and then the group can brainstorm new ideas around it, before coming back to the main task. In the case of "New Uses of Computers" or "New Software" brainstorming might generate thoughts of introducing laptops with projection panels for all the instructors at off-campus sites to facilitate courses that have no computer lab available to them. Students are then required to have access to a computer at home or at work. Other analogies for other lists, such as lists of why this program is

Possible Content	Market Fit	Market Requests
Project Management	X	X
Information Systems	X	X
Construction Management	X	X (certain areas)
Artificial Intelligence	X	O
Manufacturing Managment	X	"Production" Mgt. requested. Ask can this word be substituted?
Organizational Behavior	X	X
Reengineering the Business Process	X	X
Total Quality Management	O	X
Industrial Statistics	X	O
Management for Scientists	O	X
Entrepreneurship	O	X
Finance and Economic Analysis	X	X
Calculus	X	O

Figure 8.6 Attribute List for Market Fit and Market Requests

"convenient" (like a shopping center with parking signs), or why it eases access for "academic red tape" (like on-line registration), can enhance this problem-solving method as an interim step in the main problem-solving task. A word like "Computer" causes forced relationships and new ideas in one direction. Words like "Mission and goals in re-engineering the business process" bring in a whole new group of relationships and ideas in another direction. Access, convenience, and education (A-C-E) are three key things for which adult students look.

Problem Redefinition
In creative problem solving, whether done by an individual or a group, *redefinition of the problem* may be needed. There are many redefinitional techniques, only a few of which will be reviewed in this chapter. Because staff persons in programs for adult students are usually quite creative, applying these skills to administration can be very useful. The book *Applied Imagination* by Alex Osborne (1960) is filled with additional ideas.

Questioning is always a favorite technique:

> What would happen if I made it (the center, the program, etc.) larger? If I made it smaller? What would happen if we turned it upside down? (e.g., ran it all weekend instead of all week? Put it on top floor instead of the bottom floor?) (These are "Reversals".) Rearrange it in another way? What would happen if we made it larger, so it would be more useful? (Reach towns within 100 miles instead of 50 miles with a combination of alternate or monthly weekend classes, audio tapes and e-mail?)

Restating the problem with key beginning phrases is helpful too:

> What would I do if I had three wishes?
> You could also define the problem as . . .
> The main point of the problem is . . .
> The problem, put in another way is like . . .
> Another, even stranger way of looking at it, is . . .
> The worst thing that could happen is . . . (another reversal approach)

Another question approach that is creative is the "List Ten Ways This Can Be Done" approach (or Ten Ways This Might Look, or similar phrasing for ten aspects of a problem). One can also ask, "How is it done in nature?"—sometimes called the bionic approach. An example would be: If a mighty oak grows from a little acorn, maybe a system of higher education centers can be grown from an acorn of an idea.

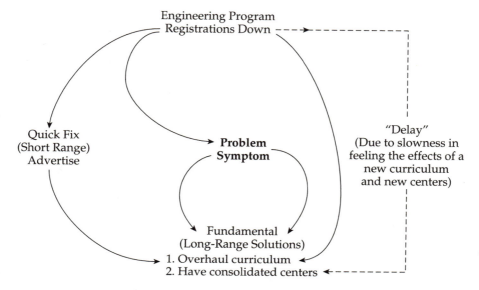

Figure 8.7   Long and Short-Term Planning

Systems Thinking and "Shifting the Burden"

In redefining problems it is important to worry about "quick fixes" that work, as they can postpone the need for a fundamental solution. One university, for example, had a problem with their Engineering graduate registration being low. A quick fix was to advertise more and to wider audiences, but the fundamental solution of overhauling and updating the curriculum (and the title) plus offering the program in consolidated off-campus education centers had been put into place (Figure 8.7). Basic solutions often are slow to show an effect; there is a results delay. A fresh spurt of direct mail and advertising might then "take up the slack" until the refreshed course content and new locations can "catch on" and reach into and pass the "awareness state."

With a fundamental solution the problem will go away. The fundamental solution is not likely to be the quick fix, in which the problem keeps reappearing. In fact, the reappearance of a problem is usually an indicator that a more fundamental solution is needed. In systems thinking, being "glad that the hole in your boat isn't in the end you're sitting in" is shown up as being a short-term gladness.

The fishbone thinking tool is often useful in understanding and redefining problems. In discussing whether information systems courses required computer labs at a distant site, the fishbone in Figure 8.8 was helpful.

Boundary Examinations

Boundary examinations, another creative technique, begin by first writing the problem out. Then one underlines the adjectives and nouns and with a dictionary finds three substitutes for each adjective and noun. Alternatives for verbs, though not shown here, can also be used. This process produces new ways to see what the problem is and thus can yield new solutions. For example:

Problem: <u>Angry</u>   <u>students</u> take up too much of the   <u>secretary's</u>
        • <u>upset</u>   • <u>adults</u>   • <u>counselors</u>
        • <u>frustrated</u>   • <u>customers</u>   • <u>directors,</u>
                                                       • <u>deans</u>

                 <u>time</u> at the beginning of   <u>evening</u> class times.
                 • hours   • mid-morning
                 • minutes   • lunch time
                 • attention   • evening

    Solutions that pop up from this boundary examination include finding out *all* the reasons students are angry or frustrated, and having time for students at lunch time or evening information sessions to offer admission requirements and logistics information and to help them with frustrations in enrolling and attending classes. These frustrations might include parking and library assistance or strategies for their degree applications, as well as understanding conflicts with their jobs or families.

Wishful Thinking

Wishful thinking, another creative technique, can be valuable in formal problem solving. To begin, one can complete the sentence "If I could break all the constraints I would . . ." For example, in budgeting seminars the advice is always given to design an ideal budget for what is really needed and wanted, and then work backward to what can be afforded, rather than to start with the present dollar amount available. Often one of the dreams may be the hottest topic for corporate grants or contract courses. One leader posted a long sheet of shelf paper on the door inside his office. As people had good ideas, they jotted them on this "wish list." When requests for education or training proposals came out from the state or federal government, they checked the list to find the topics that matched. One year, Human Resources Management degrees options at universities with ROTC (Reserve [military] Officer Training Corps) programs came out. Another year, Environmental Engineering as a degree option in ROTC programs was featured, as this was a specific new need for the U.S. Department of Defense. (Another request might be for Management Information Systems in graduate, undergraduate, and noncredit formats for ROTC programs.)

Wishful thinking can ignore restraints. The size of the building, the salary of workers, or the education or training budget are only a few examples. This device sets up new thinking patterns. The next phase is to return to the practical with statements such as "I can't really do that, but I can . . ."

Analogies and Metaphors

Devices often found in children's storybooks, analogies, and metaphors can also be used in leadership in continuing and distance education. An analogy is a direct comparison with a similar thing, object, or idea. In contrast, a metaphor is a reference to one thing, object, or idea to suggest a reference to another such as "the ship of state" or referring to old age as "the evening of life." Both are useful in problem solving to generate data and to produce ideas or solutions about a problem. Metaphors are more powerful because they demand a greater change of perspective, but both help participants see

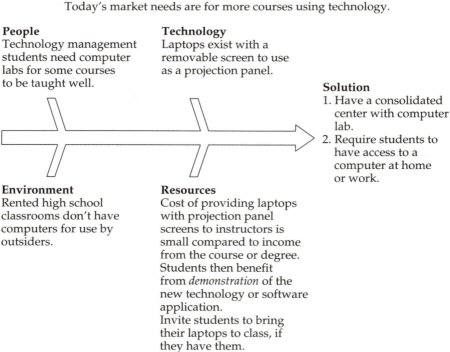

Problem:
Today's market needs are for more courses using technology.

People
Technology management students need computer labs for some courses to be taught well.

Technology
Laptops exist with a removable screen to use as a projection panel.

Solution
1. Have a consolidated center with computer lab.
2. Require students to have access to a computer at home or work.

Environment
Rented high school classrooms don't have computers for use by outsiders.

Resources
Cost of providing laptops with projection panel screens to instructors is small compared to income from the course or degree. Students then benefit from *demonstration* of the new technology or software application.
Invite students to bring their laptops to class, if they have them.

Figure 8.8 Using the Fishbone Tool to Make Decision about Computer Labs

new principles. For example, in the evening (as in the "evening of life") the light softens, the birds sing, and things quiet down. Other metaphors include "quiet leadership," "bear hug," "paper shuffler," or even "brainstorming."

Discussion involving analogies can be a useful lead-in to a group creative problem solving session using brainstorming or synectics. For example a discussion using analogies in adult education may revolve around the concept that continuing education serves as a support system in helping the faculty develop the student according to the student's goals. An architect also designs according to the client's goals. An opposing view is that of the continuing education staff member as a lackey, fetching and carrying as requested. Both analogies bring in a whole new cluster of concepts and make a good springboard for discussion at either a staff or faculty meeting, as to what role an education center supports. Another analogy is that the dean or director is like a "supportive parent," as both director and faculty members are concerned with the growth of those for whom they have responsibility. Direct analogy can use "as if." For example, staff may be encouraged to think of rude faculty members "as if" they had a terrible tragedy in the past. This builds compassion and patience before the faculty members even start talking. A metaphor that small business owners use frequently to describe their feelings about their enterprises is that of "having a child and watching it grow." They mention the great joy of creating something where there had been nothing.

Drawing a Model
Several approaches suggest *drawing a model* of the problem showing the relationships involved, drawn out in boxes or circles, much like the models for scenarios in Chapter 4 on planning. One can then add to this systematic outline of the problem or situation boxes connected by broken lines showing what lies outside the problem but is closely related to it. This can uncover possible causes of a problem and encourage decision making or planning (Figure 8.9).

SOME LAST TIPS ON PROBLEM SOLVING

Several analytical approaches can be used in the prediction of success. These can include: (1) asking "What will guarantee success?" and "What will guarantee failure?"; (2) listing in two columns "Our Expectations" and "Our Concerns" to facilitate analysis; and (3) listing "Anticipated Risks" and "Ways of Overcoming Risks" in two columns in a device similar to synectics. It would be ignoring the "real world" not to think through some of the negative questions that are likely to be asked, so sharpening the issues and

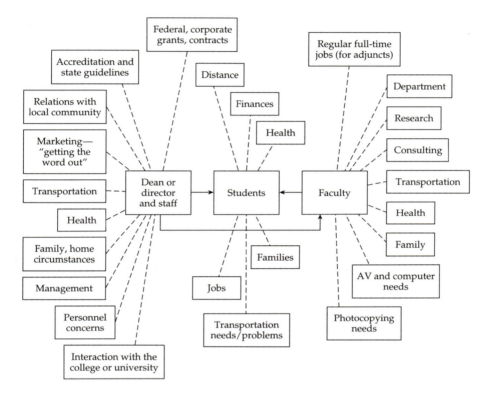

Figure 8.9   Factors Outside the Situation Model

facilitating the analysis with questions such as these, helps prepare the leader and/or staff for their new, optimal stage or plan.

Some last do's and don'ts might include:

- Try to identify the real problem, not just symptoms of the problem.
- Identify the "owner" of the problem if possible. If the wrong group is asked to solve the problem, it can produce resentment, non-cooperation, and even charges of meddling.
- Try to identify all the possible alternatives, as high quality problem solving and decision making require a good look at the choices.
- Develop a written plan for implementation. No solution is better than the plan to activate it. This means getting consensus on who does what, how, and when.
- Monitor the implementation. Appoint a monitor, coordinator or trouble-shooter who can use time and staffing charts developed jointly. These

can be developed roughly with flip charts at consensus meetings or a retreat and later refined. This avoids bottlenecks, frustrations, finger-pointing and slippages.

SUMMARY

Since problem solving is a continuing component of leading and managing programs for adult students, using creativity as applied to problem solving can give one a lift as well as uncover new ideas. Educators (and hopefully, leaders) know that creativity builds self-esteem. It also builds adults' self-esteem and feelings of competence. Reading through this chapter and trying some of the ideas, starting with a small sphere of influence, perhaps before branching on to a larger sphere, can give one that extra supply of energy that is needed in work with people.

Decision making, as opposed to problem solving, is usually future oriented and concerned with future consequences and the probability of success. Peter Drucker (1977) sees problem solving as often looking back. That is, when a problem is solved, a decision is no longer needed as things are restored to "normal" or a "steady state." Decisions, however, lead to change and changed circumstances, so that problem solving is again needed. As deans and directors see change as opportunity, and practice problem solving techniques alone and with their groups ahead of time or on small problems, they are better equipped to make decisions that focus on the future and a new optimal stage for their continuing higher education division and centers.

Both creative and analytical problem solving are needed by leaders in continuing higher education. These can be done either individually (mostly) or in a group, but a combination of the two is the most productive.

Creative approaches such as redefining the problem, reversals, morphological analysis, boundary examinations, drawing a model, wishful thinking, and using analogies and metaphors can be done, either individually or in a group setting. Brainstorming and synectics can be fitted into these approaches in a group setting or used independently. Conversely, these approaches can be fitted into brainstorming and even into synectics.

Analytic approaches have been more the norm in continuing education with the analyzing of registration and program trends, especially with the aid of computers. Checklists are used frequently, but attribute lists, decision trees and a "six question" approach are a few new ways of thinking (of many) that can be added to expand horizons in the analytical problem-solving arena.

The best problem solving supports and facilitates decision making, and helps programs move to a more optimal stage or condition. Using problem solving techniques helps the Dean or Director and the group move through each of the stages: idea generation, decision, course of action, alternatives, planning, implementation, operation, and evaluation. A trained facilitator can even be brought in for help with big problems or big decisions affecting a large percent of the program's resources.

Distance education and non-credit education are two interesting new approaches in higher education and will be discussed in the next two chapters.

BIBLIOGRAPHY

Ackoff, Russell L. (1988). *The Art of Problem Solving.* New York: Wiley.

Blake, Robert R., and Jane S. Mouton (1969). *Building a Dynamic Corporation through Grid Organization Development.* Reading, MA: Addison-Wesley.

Cartwright, Dorwin, and Alvin Zander (1960). *Group Dynamics.* New York: Harper & Row.

Chase, Stuart, and Marion Tyler Chase (1980). *Roads to Agreement.* New York: Harper & Row.

Cummings, Paul W. (1980). *Open Management.* New York: American Management Associations.

Drucker, Peter F. (1954). *The Practice of Management.* New York: Harper & Row.

Drucker, Peter F. (1977). "Peter Drucker on the Manager and the Organization." *Bulletin on Training,* March-April, p. 4.

Dyer, William G. (1978). "When Is a Problem a Problem?" *The Personnel Administrator,* pp. 66–71.

Eitington, J. E. (1984). *The Winning Trainer.* Houston, TX: Gulf.

Fisher, B. Aubrey (1974). *Small Group Decision Making: Communication and the Group Process.* New York: McGraw-Hill.

Gannon, Martin J. (1978). *Management: An Organizational Perspective.* Boston: Little, Brown.

Harrison, E. Frank (1975). *The Managerial Decision-Making Process.* Boston: Houghton Mifflin.

Lee, Irving J. (1952). *How to Talk with People.* New York: Harper & Row.

Marrow, Alfred J. (1972). *The Failure of Success.* New York: American Management Association.

Miller, David, and Martin Starr (1968). *The Structure of Human Decisions.* Englewood Cliffs, NJ: Prentice-Hall.

Murnighan, J. Keith (1981). "Group Decision Making: What Strategies Should You Use?" *Management Review,* February, pp. 55–62.

Osborn, Alex (1960). *Applied Imagination.* New York: Scribner.

Parnes, S. J., R. B. Noller, and A. M. Biondi (1977). *Guide to Creative Action and Creative Actionbook.* New York: Scribner.

Rawlinson, J. Geffrey (1981). *Creative Thinking and Brainstorming.* New York: Wiley.

Senge, Peter (1990). *The Fifth Discipline: The Art and Practice of the Learning Organization.* New York: Doubleday.

Simon, Herbert (1976). *Administrative Behavior.* New York: The Free Press.

Shore, David (1997). "Best Practices in Marketing to Adult Students" in OALS Satellite Downlink. Alexandria, VA: PBS Live Satellite Events.

Ulschak, Francis L., L. Nathanson and P. G. Gillan (1981). *Small Group Problem Solving: An Aid to Organizational Effectiveness.* Reading, MA: Addison-Wesley.

VanDersal, William R. (1974). *The Successful Supervisor in Government and Business.* New York: Harper & Row.

Walker, D. E. (1979). *The Effective Administrator: A Practical Approach to Problem Solving, Decision Making and Campus Leadership.* San Francisco: Jossey-Bass.

▶ 9

Leadership in Distance Learning

Augmenting learning with technology is especially appropriate for adults who are continuing their education. As leaders in institutions of higher education are reviewing their missions and considering the role of adult students in their particular situations, they may feel the need to rethink or "re-engineer" some processes to incorporate the benefits of technology in providing education and services to students in the Information Age. Enhancing the traditional mission of higher education of teaching (and learning), service, and research can be accomplished in many ways and expanded through able leadership and the use of modern technology.

DISTANCE EDUCATION CLASSES

The general concepts of a traditional educational system and of the teaching-learning paradigm are changing across the United States and internationally, as the power of the classroom on the "information highway" is explored. By removing artificial boundaries of time and space of the defined, sometimes rigid, "traditional" classroom, distance education via technology greatly enhances the ability to communicate, which is actually the foundation of any educational experience (Teletechnet, 1995). A third of higher education institutions offered distance education courses in fall, 1995. Of all institutions offering distance education, 62% of public 4-year colleges, 12% of private 4-year colleges, and 58% of public 2-year colleges offered distance education. One fourth of these institutions offered full degree programs that could be taken at a distance. A total of 25,730 distance education courses were offered in the academic year 1994-95 (National Center for Education Statistics, October 1997).

Leadership, as defined in Chapter 3, can be using new processes to reach old or new goals, so directors in distance education *are* in leadership roles, whether chosen or not, as this is a "new" process for higher education. However, this new process focuses a spotlight on the goal of higher education. Is the goal to educate students? To do more research? To serve the community? Or to render enough free time to the faculty to do consulting? Assuming that educating students is a top (or near the top) goal, the discussion can proceed.

Definitions of Distance Education

Definitions of distance education vary somewhat. Three descriptions that are useful come from those already active in the field:

> The term distance education represents a variety of educational models that have in common the physical separation of the faculty member and some or all of the students. (University of Maryland System for Distance Education)

> At its most basic level, distance education takes place a when teacher and student(s) are separated by physical distance, and technology (i.e. voice, video, data, and print), often in concert with face-to-face communication, is used to bridge the instructional gap. (Engineering Outreach staff at the University of Idaho)

> Distance education is instructional delivery that does not constrain the student to be physically present in the same location as the instructor. Historically, distance education meant correspondence study. Today, audio, video, and computer technologies are more common delivery modes. (Virginia Steiner, The Distance Learning Resource Network)

Accessing the vast array of global information, facilitating student-to-student and student-to-faculty communication, and using groupware applications are just a few of the enhancements possible with distance education. Perhaps it would be valuable to review a few sample programs and offerings at this point to get a sense of the variety of structures operating and available today. (More descriptions of structures and specific programs—including "virtual universities"—are given in Appendix G, Distance Education Organizations Worldwide.)

Examples of Distance Education Programs

Some large and growing distance education systems include the Central Florida Consortium of Higher Education Distance Learning Programs, University of Louisville (Kentucky), the Utah System of Higher Education Distance Education Network, the University of Maryland System Institute for Distance Education, and a number of others listed on the Internet (see Appendix G).

Virginia's Teletechnet

The Teletechnet network in Virginia has provided more than eighty upper-division undergraduate courses to students beyond the traditional community college's 2 years of undergraduate study. Students receive lectures via satellite video. They interact with faculty during class sessions through interactive audio and outside of class through e-mail and voice mail. Students complete homework assignments, search library holdings, and participate in classroom discussions through specific computer software. A valuable by-product of this system has been the increased communication between the community college system and the university (Old Dominion) sponsoring the upper-level courses. In 1995 the program was offered at sixteen sites around the state, with funding in place for an increased number of sites. Funding was also received from the National Science Foundation to study models of faculty training needed for appropriate use of this technology. Student evaluations showed that students achieved as well, if not better, than their on-campus counterparts. Graduates of the Teletechnet programs are being offered new jobs and are being promoted by their present employers, student surveys show. In 1995 there were 500 users in the program, and by 1998 the programs were predicted to be offered to nearly 12,000 students in over twenty degree programs (Teletechnet, 1995).

Indiana University

Since 1912, Indiana University, using the "old" definition of distance education, has enrolled more than 400,000 students in independent study courses taken by correspondence. In the late 1990s they are one of the many institutions nationwide making higher education available through distance learning technologies. Their new MultiCampus Technology Project (MCTP) aims to provide educational opportunities throughout Indiana on each of Indiana University's eight campuses. They are connected by a high-speed network that provides audio, video, and computer based communication tools for instruction. Students and instructors can interact with each other across campuses. It is projected that off-campus sites will eventually be able to participate in on-campus programs. The IU Independent Study program today serves 18,000 students worldwide in 50 states and 30 countries with 240 university courses. While these are still mostly correspondence courses, course syllabi and learning guides for many courses are available by e-mail. Indiana's experience with individual study is serving the institution's leaders well as they seek to reach more students with technology. They are moving forward rapidly with centralized leadership from a large state system.

Western Interstate Commission for Higher Education

The Western Interstate Commission for Higher Education (WICHE) was created in 1953 to provide for interstate sharing of resources in higher education, originally for joint purchasing. Today the 1,000 postsecondary institutions in the fifteen WICHE states are looking to telecommunications to deliver and support new and more accessible kinds of education to students, wherever they are located, to meet future growth projections. A 50% or greater increase in the number of high school graduates is predicted by the year 2009 in four large western states. The WICHE Cooperative for Educational Telecommunications is the name of the information exchange and policy advocate group for the member institutions. About 8,000 students each year have participated in all of the undergraduate, graduate and professional levels of exchange education from the member schools. Distance education is being looked to for matching up degree programs with students in rural and underserved areas and for offering "competency" programs through Western Governors University. WICHE has also produced a series called "Principles of Good Practice" that sets forth quality standards for electronically offered academic programs. The leadership for this group is, of course, decentralized and consensus-based, which may allow for more "institutionalizing" of new concepts but is also slower.

The University of Phoenix On-Line

The University of Phoenix On-Line "campus" was created solely for the purpose of distributing quality education to working adults regardless of where (in the world) or what time of day they are able to participate. These students might not otherwise be able to continue their education because of distance from the university, scheduling problems or physical immobility. Students who must travel frequently for business can connect from airports or hotels via their laptop computers. Students with place immobility who are physically disabled or who must care for young children or the aged can participate in class from home. Students who transfer to another geographic area can continue their education without transferring to another institution and possibly losing credits or repeating courses (University of Phoenix, 1995).

A complete and autonomous branch campus is devoted to serving the university's distance students. This branch provides textbooks and materials; enrollment, academic, and financial aid counseling; technical support and training; learning resources; registration; and even a live, on-site graduation ceremony.

Each course has been designed especially for on-line delivery and contains the same objectives and expected course outcomes as traditional classes. Students receive an annotated curriculum guide with assignments, outcomes, goals, and readings, plus textbooks and instruction from faculty. Students use public phone lines, Internet, or CompuServe® to connect. The program has been in operation since 1990. It has been entirely self-supporting since 1992 and in 1997 had 40,000 users at more than 1,100 sites. Degree programs are structured to lead to degree completion over a specified period of time, and in 1995 the programs boasted a course completion rate of 98%, with 300 students having graduated with bachelor's or master's degrees. The university forecasts continued high usage of their program and others like it as 50% of those attending college today in the United States are adults in the workforce (University of Phoenix, 1995; Bronner, 1997).

The Virtual Classroom

The Virtual Classroom™ (Hiltz and Turoff, 1995) features "learning without limits via computer networks" and is a joint project between the New Jersey Institute of Technology (NJIT), the Corporation for Public Broadcasting and the Alfred P. Sloan Foundation. More than 3,000 users engage in for-credit courses, offered by NJIT and a number of other colleges and universities, from personal computers at home or at work. Students represent Europe, Asia, and South America as well as North America. An entire degree, the B.A. in Information Systems, is currently being offered.

The Virtual Classroom™ is a teaching and learning environment constructed in software. The core of the learning environment is a series of conferences set up for each class, with plenary sessions, electronic lecture modules, and discussion questions interspersed between modules. Students may access the classroom 24 hours a day, 7 days a week. One special feature is a software program that can require that students give their own answers before seeing the responses of others which can be attached to communication items.

Enrollment in these courses has grown steadily with many repeat enrollments. Increased participation in a course and improved access to the professor are reported by the students as positive benefits. Students with English as a second language report that they have an enhanced learning experience as the "classroom" can be set at their own reading and writing pace.

Naval Postgraduate School

The Naval Postgraduate School (NPS) has introduced a pilot program in interactive video teletraining (known as VTT) to enable active-duty helicopter pilots to take courses in systems management at their home bases or afloat. The philosophy behind this and the NPS's Distance Learning program, initiated in July 1994, is "If you can't bring the officer to the (Navy's) University, bring the University to the officer" (Honegger, 1996). Since 1994 over 350 students in Aeronautics and Astronautics, Electrical and Computer Engineering, Computer Science, and Systems Engineering departments have taken credit courses using this new technology. One interviewee urged the Navy to make the NPS its "Distance Education University."

The minimal job interference and major savings on travel and housing costs, plus the ability to instantly apply what is learned to the missions and the jobs in the field, make this approach an attractive possibility for the military and other government entities. For the cost of supporting one full-time student plus housing, the Naval University can equip an entire "distant site" classroom, capable of reaching large numbers of students.

Resistance to Distance Learning

One of the greatest barriers to full support of distance learning is the unwarranted fear that it will displace traditional teaching methods, or even make the traditional campus obsolete (Honegger, 1996). Many supporters of distance education feel that this attitude is analogous to the movie industry fighting to hold back VCRs and video movie distribution, whereas in actuality the years lost cost the movie industry millions of dollars in potential revenues (Peters, 1994). Distance education administrators tend to agree that the traditional classroom won't go away, but that the technology makes the education *more* personal and customized, to balance the "mass education" now found in many large classrooms and large universities. The future of distance learning is customization and personalization of instruction, not mass education (Honegger, 1996).

To thrive, universities may need to become two schools: one traditional and one electronic. Distance learning students would pay the same tuition as on-site students, with personalized programs that vary in the handling of on-site classes and thesis requirements by individual and by program.

Other Existing Distance Learning Programs

Maricopa Community College in Arizona has developed an "internal" model of distance learning by wiring all ten of their campuses, five of which are in Phoenix, so that any course may be taken at any campus. The course is given "live" at one campus and electronically at the other nine. This is the second-largest college system in the nation, with year-round enrollments of approximately 160,000. They offer 6,213 credit course offerings with three variations of the Associates degree. The backbone for this electronic course availability was put into place in 1996.

The Rochester Institute of Technology in New York State has another well-developed system for offering fifty or more courses electronically. By downloading particular software from the Internet and then inputting their user name and password, students can access the courses for which they are registered. In reviewing the available list of courses, prospective students may click on a course number to go to any Web pages that are available for that course, or click on the name of a faculty member to go to the instructor's Web page. An information telephone line is available at 1-800-CALL-RIT.

Diversity University, is a joint effort that seeks to reach students who are disabled or geographically isolated through the Internet and other distributed computing systems (McWhorter, 1995). It provides facilities for real-time on-line courses and meetings and puts out several virtual education journals. More than 4,000 registered users and many visitors "show up," some daily. Accessibility has always been the philosophy of the program.

Mind Extension University, sponsored by Jones Intercable, includes a mixture of readings, interactions with CD-ROMs or Web sites, and e-mail chat groups with its satellite courses to teach "more than a lecturer in a classroom" (Pelton, 1996, p. 19). Students can learn faster and better at their own pace.

Stanford University has taken up tele-education and offers its courses via satellite in the United States. National Technological University, widely available in the United States, has received financing to expand across the Pacific Ocean by satellite. Rennselaer Polytechnic Institute, California Polytechnic State University, and the Teleuniversité of Quebec are offering multimedia-based classes on and off campus. CD-ROMs allow students to learn at their own pace and in their own area and are considered cost-effective (Pelton, 1996).

International distance learning programs are also available and are developing rapidly, according to the International Conference on Distance Education held in Russia in 1996. Norway has the Norwegian Executive Board for Distance Education at the University and College Level, and other countries' efforts can be accessed through the Association for International Education.

The International Space University (ISU), based in Illkirch, France, has nearly thirty interactive or satellite campuses electronically interconnected around the world. The students and faculty of ISU work in teams and conduct interdisciplinary studies. The philosophy of this innovative university is that if individuals cannot know everything in the Information Age, then teams of interactive people can seek to do so (Pelton, 1996).

In May 1994 an international electronic workshop was held to improve quality in university distance education. College and university faculty participated—at a distance—from Chile, Argentina, Venezuela, Mexico, Canada, Hong Kong, and the United States. Each week, participants downloaded lecture notes, discussed them on-line, completed assignments and sent in comments when appropriate. Those planning the next series hope to incorporate replication in Spanish (Dirr, 1995). A single university could adopt this format—perhaps even for faculty staff development for distance learning, or for other needs. Faculty support enhancement is but one possible use; many institutions of higher education have a wide variety of technological enhancements for other administrative and support services.

NEEDED STEPS FOR AN INSTITUTION TO SET UP DISTANCE EDUCATION

According to Ted Christiansen, Assistant Vice President for G. W. Television at George Washington University in Washington, D. C., four components are needed to set up and maintain distance education programs.

1. The administrative management structure has to be set up for the programs, including: registration, records, fees and billing procedures, text book ordering, and national marketing (in addition to the Internet and Web page marketing inherent in the program's existence). Many of these are listed in the next section.

2. There needs to be a Faculty Coaching Group that works with the faculty to support translating the course content to distance education. Software is available for doing this, and Windows 95™ (and above) with "save to HTML" menu choices is a simpler option, for the technical end of this task. However, concerns such as where to stand, where to look, how to wear the microphone, whether to use slides, magazine pictures, audio or video clips, and more need some advice and guidance. Some institutions have a Faculty Teaching Center that could be enlisted to help with some of these tasks.

3. A Media Production Group is needed with more people needed for web and multimedia production. Mr. Christiansen's staff of 24 needs 4 to 5 more people for the latter two, and supports two studios.

4. A Research and Development (ongoing) Task Force or small group is needed for the updating of equipment and uses of new technology. This group could be self supporting, with research grants and contracts from corporations (Christiansen, 1997).

See details of the full master's degree program in Educational Technology Leadership at G. W. University in Appendix H, "Teaching with Technology at One Institution of Higher Education."

ADMINISTRATIVE AND SUPPORT SERVICES ENHANCEMENTS

Some of the early technological enhancements that have become routine in many institutions include those for administration, finance, student services, and registration functions. Library functions have also enjoyed extensive improvements, with on-line search services; access for students at home and at work; access for handicapped students; and numerous other innovations for finding, obtaining, and manipulating information (North Carolina State University Libraries, 1995). Less standard, but fast developing, are Internet home pages that many universities and colleges now have.

Registration functions can be speeded by telephone registration, which can help reduce the enormous costs associated with course registration. One system (Lucent, 1996) does the following:

- Students call in by telephone to register, providing their student number and date of birth for security reasons.
- The system verifies the student's eligibility and can "flag-out" students if they haven't met appropriate requirements.
- Students can add or drop courses using the telephone keypad.
- The system provides immediate feedback on class availability, verifies the class and section selected, and can fax a printout of the student's schedule at any time after registering.
- The system can interface with the university billing system to total fees and send a bill or to allow students to pay by credit card.
- When a course approaches its enrollment limit, the system dials the appropriate department chair. Administrators spend less time monitoring registration and more time making appropriate decisions, such as to add a section or close the course.
- With the system, students can preregister for a subsequent semester. A summary report of this information helps department heads plan ahead.
- Management software allows the institution to better control and monitor the automation of student registration, in order to measure the effectiveness of system requirements as presently written.

The benefits of this and similar telephone registration systems are that they provide registration anywhere, in minutes rather than hours; improve student satisfaction, particularly for nontraditional students; eliminate the need for temporary registration staff; and enable department chairpersons to better meet student course needs. Furthermore, students can gain quick access to the information they need, eliminating the need for a staff to provide this mostly standard data (Lucent, 1996). Web-based registration is a further possibility, as is networking the bookstore into class registration numbers to enhance text ordering and availability.

Evidence of the increasing use of the Internet for informal "distance learning" is the proliferation of "home pages" put out by institutions of higher education describing their campuses, their offerings, and even giving photographic campus tours. In an informal survey of these home page listings, the Cornell University home page listed more than 439 Web pages. These electronic "drop-in" sites often include maps of the campus, floor plans of buildings (a boon to the handicapped student seeking access); and general "one-stop shopping" information about procedures, regulations, course materials, library resources, infrastructure, and even research results (Sherwood, 1995). They give details of all their departments, program offerings, fraternities and sororities, clubs, and many other kinds of organizations. As mentioned before, almost all institutions are using this electronic tool for public relations and information in order to answer standard questions and to allow would-be students to connect with various link-ups. Site audits of competitor institutions' home pages are almost a must in the fast-paced world of adult enrollments. Look for those with on-line registration possibilities as higher education takes up electronic commerce.

EDUCATIONAL INTERACTIONS

Interesting outreach activities and interaction with other educational facilities are also a part of the enhancement of learning via technology. Lane Education Network in Oregon, which extends to the University of Oregon, Lane Community College, local school districts, health care providers, and government, is one example of this. Language instruction, physics instruction, and desktop-to-desktop noncredit training in industry are also provided on the network (University of Oregon, 1995).

College students help public school students with their homework via the Purdue Connection, a service through IDEANET from the Indiana State Department of Public Instruction. College students who are majoring in secondary teaching thus have early contact with the age group of students they might teach. An unexpected benefit is the chance for spontaneous conversations on careers and other choices arising in the teenagers' lives. The Purdue students use a dedicated computer in the School of Education, networked to the public schools, to connect (Caldwell 1995).

George Mason University (GMU) in Virginia set up "Center for the New Engineer" tutorial modules from its School of Information Technology and Engineering (Denning, 1995), an interesting learning enhancement. This bold new approach to enhancing the education of engineers and scientists is being accessed at the rate of 3,500 times a week, with 60% of accesses coming from within GMU and the rest external to the institution, including from seven foreign countries. Internet (only) visitors were measured at 1,400 per week in 1995. The facility can be browsed and used via the GMU home page. Four initial projects (Denning, 1995) sought to:

- Open the path from research to the curriculum
- Open the path from businesses to the curriculum
- Create communications between the university and regional K–12 schools
- Improve internal communications and collaborative work groups

Many community colleges have developed extensive distance educational enhancements, like Honolulu Community College's World Wide Web Campus Wide Information Service. Students, faculty, staff, and administrators are assigned individual accounts and have full access to the Internet via logon to the campus network. Leaders of this community college in the middle of the Pacific Ocean looked for ways to enhance their educational mission with information technology. They now use the Web to distribute forms and information about the campus, offer supplemental instructional support, deliver distance learning, and access library databases. *Using* the technology is the key to benefiting from it, they believe, and they found that getting individual departments and users involved in creating and maintaining their portion of the information system also helped the acceptance rate of the system (Honolulu Community College, 1995).

Noncredit distance training is rapidly being embraced by business and government alike, as will be discussed in the next chapter. The delivery of courses by nontraditional, cost-efficient methods such as satellite broadcast, video self-study with local small group interaction, and compressed video teletraining will soon be the norm rather than the exception in the noncredit realm, many believe. The U.S. International Revenue Service designed such training for approximately 800 full-time trainers and several thousand part-time educators and trainers, starting with a satellite course for approximately 100 trainers nationwide to "train the trainers" (Training Officers Conference, 1996). Many examples of such training use, and course offerings for noncredit are available via the Internet.

SUPPORT FOR DISTANCE LEARNING INFRASTRUCTURES

A number of distance learning resources and organizations have become available. These include some interesting distance education Web sites such as:

- Distance Education Clearinghouse (University of Wisconsin—Extension)
- AT&T/Lucent Technologies, Center for Excellence in Distance Learning
- Commonwealth of Learning
- Education First
- Indiana University Distance Learning

In addition to these web sites, more distance learning resources are listed in Figure 9.1.

Two of the professional associations that support administrators in higher education who develop telecommunications systems (including local area networks and wide area networks) and information management systems are the Association for College and University Telecommunication Administrators (ACUTA) and the Association for Managing and Using

---

About ISTE (International Society for Technology in Education)
ACSDE (American Center for the Study of Distance Education)
Academic Outreach—University of Michigan
AERES (Australian Educational Resources)—Distance Education, Open Learning and Flexible Delivery
Ameritech Distance Learning
AT&T Learning Network
Bell Atlantic Distance Learning
The Distance Education and Training Council
DEOS-L(Discussion Forum for Distance Education Learning)
Department of Distance Education Homepage (Western Michigan)
Distance Ed (University of Colorado at Denver, School of Education)
Distance Education Subject Guide (University of Alberta)
Distance Learning Resources (provided by Arlington Courseware)
Distance Learning Sites (provided by Bell Atlantic)
Distance Learning at Ohio State
Distance Learning in Medicine (National Institutes of Health)
EDUCOM Home Page
General Information (Distance Education) from Okanagan University, British Columbia
Issues in Distance Learning (University of Colorado at Denver)
New Media Education at Emerson College
NCSU Distance Learning, North Carolina State University
NDLC Home Page (National Distance Learning Center)
New Media Centers Home Page
Ohio State Distance Learning Project
The Pacific Advanced Communication Consortium
SFU Centre for Distance Education (Simon Fraser University)
USDLA Home Page (United States Distance Learning Association)
The World Lecture Hall at the University of Texas

Figure 9.1   Distance Learning Resources

Information Resources in Higher Education, known as CAUSE. These two, plus the EDUCOM and AAHE roundtable discussions on technology and other, smaller regional and local groups share the knowledge and information needed to further the missions of their institutions. The mission of ACUTA is "enabling colleges and university telecommunications professionals to contribute to the achievement of their institution's mission through: (1)the development of leadership, management, and technical capabilities; (2) peer networking; (3) the exploration of key issues, and (4) access to quality information" (ACUTA Home Page, 1996).

Five goals have been developed for ACUTA:

Goal I (Members). Telecommunications departments will be recognized and respected by their institutions for professional expertise and technological leadership in support of the institutions' mission.

Goal II (Association). ACUTA will be viewed as the organization of choice, and advocate for college and university telecommunications professionals.

Goal III (Access to Market-Driven Programs and Services). Members will have easy access to quality information, programs, services, and peer networking opportunities designed to meet their changing needs.

Goal IV. ACUTA programs and services will:

- Be responsive to changing trends in technology and its application to higher education.
- Relate the broad spectrum of telecommunications technologies to the higher education environment.
- Incorporate leading-edge ideas and applications.
- Address various experience levels.
- Respond to the common interests and needs of members.
- Address needs of various sizes of institutions.
- Educate telecommunications professionals in telecommunications managerial and technical skills.

Goal V (Industry Relations). ACUTA will be recognized by vendors as an influential and effective facilitator of collaboration and information exchange to develop and/or implement the effective application of telecommunications technology in partnership with educational institutions. (ACUTA Home Page, 1996)

CAUSE has a large number of member universities and colleges and offers information about their management institutes through the Internet. Many of the member institutions list the CAUSE logo and the names and phone, fax numbers, and e-mail addresses of their CAUSE members under their institutional headings.

These organizations accomplish their goals by sponsoring conferences, seminars, workshops, newsletters, and home page and directory services. For instance, a workshop at a recent ACUTA conference was entitled "New Learning Models and Their Effect on Telecommunication." Panelists described how schools utilized various media to enhance distance learning, how current technology is changing learning models, and how this affects telecommunications systems.

Distance education facilities around the world demonstrate a great variety of sizes, shapes, and relationships with their governments, businesses ,and other organizations. There is also variability in the relationships with the learners themselves. A more complete listing of distance education departments within conventional institutions, open and distance learning institutions, virtual campuses, and distance learning networks can be found in Appendix G, Distance Education Organizations—Worldwide.

SUMMARY

The accumulated information of our world has increased an estimated ten million times since the period of ancient Greece. It is likely to increase another ten million times in the next century (Pelton, 1996). The power and economics of global networking, global business, and worldwide education will be hard to comprehend or deny. Recent U.N. studies reveal that there will be more people to educate in the next 30 years than have been educated in all history (Pelton, 1996). Socrates, Plato, and Aristotle had their golden age 2,500 years ago, but students today are still put in a classroom with an authority figure lecturing. The challenge of reforming, improving, and extending education to the entire population is large, but various modes of distance education can help. Powerful new technologies now available for educating people (around the world) suggest that the task can and will be accomplished. These technologies can help educate more people more effectively at less cost. This is yet another challenge to the field of higher education.

Human beings will always have an edge (over machines) in reasoning, judgment, critical analysis, and making connections, so even as learning is redefined to include more teamwork, critical thinking, and continual learning by students, rigorous and challenging multidisciplinary and interdisciplinary studies will be needed. Training by rote and repetition without providing a basic understanding is not the goal. It is seen as a danger to democratic processes and to self-esteem, as well as to long term commitment of students (Pelton, 1996).

Augmenting educational processes with distance technology may become increasingly popular due to its cost-effectiveness. The elimination of time and space constraints allows for larger class sizes, divided into sections, without escalating variable costs (very much). As state and private funding for institutions of higher education becomes increasingly scarce, while at the same time the demand for highly skilled workers increases exponentially, maximizing use of the Internet, user-friendly software packages, and multimedia learning environments is a way to find practical solutions to the shrinkage of educational resources. Distance education issues will remain in the areas of cost, allocation of resources, accessibility, reliability, and quality. Challenges will continue in resource allocation, training, maintenance and the training needed for it, accessibility, continued funding, and maintaining distance education as a priority and a mission focus. Lastly, service requirements for technical assistance and alternative delivery options will continue.

Intelligence is no longer viewed as static. One-time-only education at ages 18 to 22 is no longer viewed as appropriate for a lifetime in the workplace, and many adult students have considerable place and time constraints. Tuition can rise only so far before people are priced out of the market, so cutting costs has never been more important if the United States is to have an educated workforce. Denying people the education they need to earn a living is not a part of the American dream or of any "generic" higher education mission statement. In the Information Age, rethinking new processes to achieve old and continuing goals is especially appropriate. Releasing the learning capacity of every person and benefitting from the power of team learning and interactive critical thinking can be done for less money than is being spent now, using a variety of new and distance technologies (Pelton, 1996). Leadership, planning, decision making, teamwork, and marketing will be needed, as discussed in previous chapters. However, distance education can (and should) be included in noncredit planning, marketing, finances, and proposal writing efforts, as discussed in subsequent chapters. These are all elements of leadership skills, built upon knowledge, in continuing education and distance education.

BIBLIOGRAPHY

Bronner, Ethan (1997). "University for Working Adults Shatters Mold." The New York Times, Oct. 15, pp. A1, A22.

Caldwell, D. S. (1995). "Purdue Connection." in National Information Infrastructure Awards Campaign. West Lafayette, IN: Purdue School of Education.

Christiansen, Ted (1997). Personal interview. November 20, Washington, D. D., George Washington University.

Denning, Peter J. (1995). "Center for the New Engineer (CNE) at School of Information Technology and Engineering of George Mason University." National Information Infrastructure Awards Campaign. Reston, VA: Morino Institute.

Dirr, Peter J. (1995). "International Electronic Workshop to Improve Quality in University Distance Education." National Information Infrastructure Awards Campaign. University Park: Pennsylvania State University, CREAD.

Hiltz, R, and M. Turoff (1995). "The Virtual Classroom.™ Learning Without Limits via Computer Networks." National Information Infrastructure Awards Campaign. Newark, NJ: New Jersey Institute of Technology.

Honegger, Barbara (1996). "Distance Learning: NPS Brings 'Electronic Classrooms' to the Fleet." In *The Graduate*, Monterey, CA: Naval Postgraduate School.

Honolulu Community College (1995). "HCCINFO—Honolulu Community College's World Wide Web Campus Wide Information System." National Information Infrastructure Awards Campaign. Honolulu, HI: Author.

Lucent Technologies (1996). Lucent Technologies Business Communications Systems. Http://www.lucent.com.

McWhorter, Jeanne (1995). "Diversity University: an Educational Text-based Virtual Reality Environment." National Information Infrastructure Awards Campaign. Wheeling: West Virginia Northern Community College.

National Center for Education Statistics (1997). "Distance Education in Higher Education Institutions." Released October 6. Washington, DC: Author.

North Carolina State University Libraries (1995). "NCSU Libraries: Creating the Research Library of the Future" National Information Infrastructure Awards Campaign. Chapel Hill, NC: Author.

Pelton, Joseph N. (1996). "Cyberlearning vs. the University: An Irresistible Force Meets an Immovable Object." *The Futurist*, 30 (6), 17–20.

Peters, Tom (1994). *The Seminar*. New York: Bantam Books.

Sherwood, K. D. (1995). "University of Illinois at Urbana-Champaign Web." National Information Infrastructure Awards Campaign. Urbana: University of Illinois at Urbana-Champaign.

Teletechnet (1995). Virginia Community College System. Norfolk, VA: Old Dominion University.

Training Officers Conference (1996). Distinguished Service Awards in "Training Design" presented to the Internal Revenue Service, June 11.

University of Oregon (1995). "The Lane Education Network." National Information Infrastructure Awards Campaign. Eugene, OR: Author.

University of Phoenix (1995). "University of Phoenix Learning Resource Center." National Information Infrastructure Awards Campaign. Phoenix, AZ: Author.

Western Interstate Commission for Higher Education (WICHE) (1996). *Wiche in the West: 1996 Overview*. Wiche Home Page www.wiche.edu:Author.

► 10

Planning, Implementing, and Evaluating Noncredit Programs

Noncredit programs are traditionally more flexible, more market-responsive, and sometimes more relevant than credit programs. They can be seen as part of the mission of an institution of higher education, in extending its reputation and credibility to provide high-quality, relevant courses as outreach and service to the surrounding population. By empowering alumni in the adult community with lifelong learning opportunities, such institutions extend the learning community and the intellectual capital of the region (and of further regions if they are reached by distance learning). Preparing citizens, empowering them and enhancing their lives, links the institution to the community and balances other initiatives as a service to the community.

A university can be seen as not just a *place* with buildings only, with a distinction between the central campus and satellite or remote "outposts," but as a resource that distributes to locations and at times that best match the needs and interests of able students. The traditional "yak in the box" (Peters, 1994, p. 184) is continuously being redesigned and reinvented to the benefit of students. Lecture only, in a classroom setting, is being outpaced by creative organizational structures for learning, including learning at a distance as discussed in Chapter 9. Educational services are indeed expanding in the "knowledge age."

Furthermore, noncredit programs can certainly be profitable on the whole, and many institutions of higher education have added noncredit or training divisions in one guise or another to the education services they provide. The variety of titles of those in charge of continuing education, whether for credit, noncredit, or for both combined under one director, is interesting to note. The titles demonstrate a wide spectrum of perceptions: Dean, Director, Associate Vice Chancellor for Extended Studies and Public Service, and even Vice President for Student Services and Economic Development. These titles appear to show the rising importance of planning and administering programs for adults.

Changes in demographics, in the economy, and in the nature of work are altering the way public and private sector organizations provide training, and also the ways in which higher education delivers its programs and services to business and industry. The education and training of adults have become highly important, according to the U.S. Department of Labor and the American Society for Training and Development, as population trends are creating democratic changes in the composition of the work force. Workers will change careers three to five times and jobs five to eight times in their lifetimes. Two-thirds of the people working in 1998 will be working in 5 years (Wee, 1996). Over half of the new jobs of the future will require postsecondary education and training. An emerging service economy will provide jobs for 88% of the work force in the next 5 years. Over the next 10 years, 75% of the work force will need significant retraining. These and other trends of change are announced frequently in the media and in research (Wee, 1996).

How much institutions of higher education want to play a significant role in the area of work force development varies, but this is an area high in possibilities and opportunities especially in the noncredit arena. Some institutions divide their noncredit programs for ease of administration into various categories such as: (1) Management and Technology, such as computer courses and small business and management courses; (2) Work preparation, such as real estate licensure, nurse aide training, or apprenticeship or other contract programs developed in partnership with local industry; (3) Lifelong Learning, such as oil painting, music appreciation, or languages. Some of the first two program categories offer "pre-employment" preparation as well as on-the-job training. Many institutions have also found that "Alumni Universities" filled with the third category of short, 1-week summer classes are profitable for all ages of alumni, including senior citizens. An active and well-run children's program is often partnered with these alumni "college camps."

Certificate programs of five to eight courses in an organized format are also a viable noncredit option. These can range from financial planner certification to landscape design to publication specialist. Information systems, complex software, and client/server requirements lend themselves to training courses of this type. Training opportunities for mid-level professionals continue to be an unmet need appropriate for higher education, noncredit courses. Some have even been called "graduate level noncredit" courses.

ADULT LEARNERS

No discussion of noncredit education or training would be complete without considering the contribution of Malcom Knowles (1980, 1984, 1989). His concern that the needs, skills, abilities, and talents of adults differ to quite a degree from those of the 18- to 22-year-old population undergirds much of his writing. He developed a framework for learning situations in which complexity of the learning task was placed on the vertical axis of a graph and the level of the learners' learning ability on the horizontal level of the same graph. Level of learning ability included previous exposure to the subject matter, readiness to learn, motivation, general intelligence, and other factors. He then placed learning theorists on a continuum along the graph, with *behavioral teaching* methods for the lower levels of task and ability at one end. If the learning task was complex, such as gaining knowledge and understanding of the theory behind applications, then the *cognitive theorists'* teaching approach was appropriate. For a highly complex task and a high level of learning ability (as in management classes), *self-directed learning* and *projects* and the *humanistic theorists'* approach are appropriate. Knowles explained this framework in his book *The Adult Learner: A Neglected Species* (1984). Adult learners, with their myriad experiences and varied backgrounds, make a real contribution to the classroom, and this group had indeed been neglected. Knowles developed a number of corollaries to his framework, including the concept that people feel a commitment to a decision in proportion to the extent that they feel they have participated in it, that creative leaders stimulate and reward creativity, that creative leaders are committed to a process of continuous change and are skillful in managing change, and that creative leaders encourage people to be self-directing. Some of these theories are foundational to other chapters in this book that discuss administration of continuing education in ways that can release human energy and group synergism for those planning programs for adult students.

Applying these concepts to adult learning creates additional insights. Learning takes place when the student perceives the subject matter as relevant to his or her own purposes, when the student is responsible for participation in the learning process, and when self-evaluation is primary and evaluation by others is of secondary importance. Continual learning and an openness to experience and change, Knowles believes, are the most socially useful things to learn in the modern world (1989). Some adjunct and full-time faculty staff development in these and other aspects of adult learning may be necessary to undergird a new continuing education program in an institution of higher education.

LONG-RANGE FORECASTS, GOALS, OBJECTIVES, AND ACTIVITIES

As colleges and universities review their roles and philosophies in relation to noncredit programming, it becomes apparent that noncredit programs are a viable option for additional income-producing activities that also provide much needed educational services to a particular geographic area. Long-range forecasts taken from major trends, such as those discussed in Chapter 1, can be spelled out with implications for a noncredit unit of an institution. (For one example of a long-range forecast see Appendix B.) As a follow-up, goals and then more specific objectives and activities can be developed. For example, because an increased demand for service and technical professions and occupations is an anticipated trend, an increase in career and job-related education might be one goal. Work-related needs for the following levels can help expand an institution's noncredit role:

- Entry-level training
- Retraining
- Cross-training
- Upgrading
- Job transitioning

If the population in an institution's surrounding geographic area (for a publicly supported institution) or in a wider area for other institutions is mobile, then education and reeducation about the noncredit division's or unit's programs and services will be needed. This can also be called marketing. A marketing plan needs to be developed and implemented (as discussed in chapter 11) to complement the institution's overall marketing or public relations plan. The noncredit unit must establish additional relationships with employers in surrounding industries and businesses concerning the education and training needs of their personnel. This can be done at greater distances if distance or satellite learning is an option for noncredit and off-campus credit courses. One institution even had audiotaped courses with Internet discussion groups for students on several continents.

If the citizenry in the area is well educated and interested in education, utilizing the talents and expertise of members of the community to enhance the noncredit education program is always a good idea. All of the planning should be done against a backdrop of continuing assessment of the educational needs of the population served. Once-a-year planning, with more frequent adaptations, is a must for keeping offerings current and relevant. The service area might be a county for a community college and a metropolitan area or the nation for a larger, 4-year institution.

Another major long-range forecast based on a trend might be that the potential student population will be more diverse and embrace a broad expanse of ages, races, ethnic origins, languages, and entry-level skills. Implications would be that the unit must then assess the needs of its changing population, identify available resources, and implement, where feasible, offerings to meet those needs. Activities might include ESL classes, test preparation classes, more activities and classes for senior citizens, and even alumni discounts for senior citizens, to name a few of the hundreds of options possible. The unit may focus on these special needs but must maintain a comprehensive program to attract all students and to aid them in fulfilling their educational needs. Ongoing examination and evaluation of program, services, and staff plus revision when appropriate will be needed to meet the changing student population requirements. This may mean broadening the base of instructional programs and the expertise of faculty members so that the unit can respond to changing student demands for noncredit curricula.

Accessibility to the division's instructional sites for potential adult students becomes more important, as do alternative types of scheduling and planning that consume less commuter time and energy These are goals that need to be developed for part-time students (both credit and noncredit). With career mobility as a current trend, students may place more emphasis on course content as opposed to degree preparation as reasons for enrolling in programs. Furthermore, alternative methods of instructional delivery will continue to need development as the technology matures, such as cable TV, ISDN lines, and satellite delivery for noncredit as well as credit programs.

Increased competition for enrollments is also a trend, both for credit and for noncredit students. The more than fifty-billion-dollar training industry attests to this competition in the noncredit arena, but as institutions shorten their response time from initial request to course delivery (for many years, slow response was a main complaint from industry), institutions of higher education's noncredit units have an edge on the competition with higher quality. Noncredit courses, of course, should pay for themselves or should be discontinued.

Private entrepreneurial vendors of educational services have quite often drawn consultants directly from the ranks of college and university professors, which has profound long-range implications for educational institutions (Cross and McCartan, 1984). The impact on faculty time and commitment to the institution, in addition to the loss of money, can be partly attributed to industry's not wanting to deal with complicated procedures and the delays of academic decision making. An additional factor in companies turning to the training industry is the added expense of college overhead (Cross and McCartan, 1984). Occasionally noncredit offerings by the same professors compete with an institution's offerings for either credit or noncredit.

Computer technology, interest in information technology, and management implications in the work environment for re-engineering business processes with information technology will continue to develop rapidly. As more individuals own their own computers and the management of whole enterprises becomes more streamlined, short courses at all levels will be welcome. Implications will be for new courses, computer labs, and courses requiring laptops. Many additional implications for institutions can be developed from the forecasts and trends in the arena of computers and information technology.

While the preceding forecasts are external, that is, outside the institution of higher education, internal forecasts and their implications can also be developed on a 1-, 2-, or 3-year planning cycle. For example, internal predictions or forecasts about new technology being used, new education centers being opened, and new marketing plans being developed will all be useful when followed by spelling out the implications and the activities needed. This can be done as a group or by individuals. The ongoing planning, implementing, operating, and evaluating of noncredit courses and programs keeps them fresh and relevant—and also income-producing for the host institution. A marketing plan will be needed. The plan also:

- Identifies marketing opportunities
- Stimulates thinking to make new uses of the institution's resources
- Assigns responsibilities and schedules work
- Coordinates and unifies efforts
- Facilitates control and evaluation of results of all activities
- Creates awareness of obstacles to overcome
- Provides a valid marketing information source for current and future reference
- Facilitates progressive advancement toward the unit's or division's goals

The marketing plan, based on long-range forecasts and goals, should be *simple, clear, practical, flexible* (i.e., adaptable to change), *complete*, and *workable*.

DISTANCE LEARNING AND NONCREDIT COURSES

Many state universities that have developed a distance learning network have included noncredit courses as well as credit courses. The Education Network of Maine is the distance learning network of the University of Maine system. This system extends access to education and training (noncredit), and also dispenses information to more than a hundred rural communities. Courses are also available through local cable channels, and by 1995, courses were available in 80,000 homes through cable systems (University of Maine, 1995). The Iowa Communications Network brings distance learning and communication to all Iowans of all ages including higher education courses that are for credit and not for credit (Iowa Public Television, 1995).

Another example of technology enriching noncredit learning is educational partnerships with commercial cable companies: Cox Cable's "Exclusive Cable Educational Credit and Non Credit Courses" can be accessed through the local community college, Cuyahoga Community College, in Parma, Ohio. Students interact with the instructor through modem or telephone, just as they do on the Iowa Network. Interaction is also enhanced through use of computers. This service in Ohio reaches ten communities and 64,000 homes in the Cleveland area. Cuyahoga Community College has an extensive Internet home page and listings under distance learning (Hammaker and Mason, 1995). These are but a few samples of the access to learning in the noncredit arena provided by distance education technology. The developers of these services feel that growth is definitely likely in the future for themselves and others.

CONTRACT COURSES

Contract courses or on-site courses that are noncredit allow employers to pay for a group of students on one billing, often at a group discount. The closed enrollment course(s) can then be somewhat tailored for the employer's need or a new course can even be designed. Figure 10.1 shows a time line for an elaborate, year-long contract program run in several locations. Such a plan would also be appropriate for a credit contract program of course.

Special employer needs can be addressed in other ways also, such as an open-enrollment certificate program in Basic Literacy, or any number of other topics, with the courses that make up the certificate selected by the employer or the military service. Some employers host a "graduation" at which certificates are presented and some do not.

More contract courses may be called for in the future as there is a new emphasis on learning in organizations. Two causes of this new emphasis are (1) the rate of change with new technology, global competition, and social trends; and (2) the changing nature of work itself (Weisbord, 1989; Dixon, 1993). Management and training development initiatives must change along with the broader changes in the world of work. Learning can be differentiated from development: Learning often involves new techniques to operate more effectively within an existing framework, and development may mean

| | Months | | | | | | | | | | | |
I. Planning	1	2	3	4	5	6	7	8	9	10	11	12
1. Negotiate services	X											
2. Sign letter of agreement	X											
3. Mid-semester and semester-end reports			+		+		+		+		+	+
4. Send survey letter	+											
II. Implementation												
1. Flyers, advertising, e-mail out, direct mail if appropriate		O	+		X	X			O	O	+	
2. Briefings held on site or in satellite center		X	X			X	X			X	X	
III. Operation												
1. Registration	X				X				X			
2. Books delivered (if any)	X				X				X			
3. Classes start	X				X				X			
4. Train staff, as needed	← – →											
5. Weekly coordination with field representatives	X	X	X	X	X	X	X	X	X	X	X	X
IV. Evaluation												
1. Evaluation forms distributed at end of classes				X					X			X
2. Start planning next briefings and advertising			X				X			X		
3. Renegotiate, if yearly contract											+	+
4. Annual report on the program											+	+

O = approvals; X = key event; + = deliverables.
* This example assumes three semesters, with a new cohort every fall or spring. The time line is also appropriate for credit contract programs.

Figure 10.1   Time Line Example: Year-Long Contract

moving from one framework to another. Ascertaining the goals for a contract course or program in this context will be important. Are organization employees to be taught techniques for functioning in a framework that is inconsistent with their existing framework? If the corporate culture is at cross-purposes with the new learning, then deeper (or higher level) changes may need to be sought (Broad and Newstrom, 1992). Noncredit (and credit) course developers and planners can help their surrounding corporate community by being aware of these distinctions and helping to explore them. Development occurs when employees attempt to deal with real problems that they care about.

Situating learning in the workplace, where it can be an effective help, is potentially a real service of institutions of higher education. Whether employees are learning from an expert, from each other in their interactions, or from reflection together on their actions, they are becoming a "learning organization," in more alignment with the mission and goals of their organizations (Senge, 1990). Learning only from an expert may not fit the twenty-first–century management approach of empowering teams and working (and developing solutions) together. Other instructional approaches will be needed, with work-related projects interspersed with the learning and development needed for a new framework to be adopted. Helping people to perceive the world through more than the lens of past experience—by looking at future trends to help understand present reality—is especially useful in contract courses. It is also useful in open enrollment courses, both noncredit and for credit, of course. Examples of learning-plus-development programs that have been offered for noncredit follow.

One company with a pressing business issue, but that also wanted to train employees in global teamwork and global marketing, divided classes up into teams. Each team worked on problems identified by senior management, such as "How to do Low-Cost Production" or "How to Manage Global Human Resources." The projects selected for a team were carefully assigned to be outside the team members' expertise. This produced a "think tank" atmosphere in the class and also developed collaboration across organizational boundaries. Seminars on cross-cultural issues were interspersed with team fact finding missions. Team members were encouraged to negotiate with others (outside the class) for help.

At the end of several months the "final project presentations" of the solutions the teams developed were presented to the class and to senior management. Many of the solutions were acted upon.

Another contract program interacted with the offering institution more by having one to three interns from the university department help employee students with their projects. Again, senior-level executives were invited to be present for final presentations.

A third example, also using teams, divided "course" time between project work and seminars. Problems for the projects were selected according to certain criteria, such as being of strategic importance, being global but with regional implications, offering the possibility of risk taking, and offering a "payoff" that could be quantified. Each problem had a client (see synectics discussion in Chapter 8) who owned the problem. Teams analyzed their problems and were allowed to redefine them as necessary. Seminars on change, finance, and human resources were interspersed with the project work. The workable solutions produced launched a dialogue between participants and top management about strategic issues.

A leadership development contract program at another site included precourse readings on topics of self-assessment and current work situations and postcourse follow-up projects on implementation of plans developed in the course. Many organizations are moving toward manager follow-up of changes due to employee training after 3-month, 6-month, and 12-month intervals; this plan, with half-day follow-up sessions at the same intervals, fits into the organizational cycle and goals.

The challenge for contract courses, in addition to providing what is specifically requested, is to broaden the meaning of learning in organizations to create and include such experiences. Numerous topics would allow for this, such as "Managing Planned Organizational Change" or "Leadership in Complex Organizations."

QUALITY CONCERNS

While noncredit programs are often more flexible, market-responsive, and often more "current" than credit programs, the maintaining of high-quality content must be a first concern. Without the "quality engine" of academic departments and curriculum review committees the issue of quality must be addressed directly. Having a board of advisors (formal or informal) by topic area helps temper this concern somewhat, and regular course evaluations are vital.

The concern for quality and authentic assessment can be seen in the Western Governors' University approach for "competency" (noncredit) courses to have assessment criteria set up by panels of experts in each field. They see this as a subset to the accreditation procedures that might be useful for the three regional accrediting associations with which they interact (AAHE Conference, Washington, D C, April 1997). Other new initiatives in assessment requirements appear to be building on the "portfolio assessment" experiences of the K–12 education community. Some school systems have found this approach to be valid but expensive.

SUMMARY

Completion of noncredit courses or of longer noncredit multicourse certificate programs can raise the quality of an individual's work life and can increase the individual's professional ability to contribute to his or her field and to the community at large (Smith, 1991). Helping individuals prepare themselves for rapid success in their efforts to enter, upgrade, or transition in the workplace through noncredit programs seems to have a very bright future for institutions of higher education, as this is another quite "do-able" form of educational service.

Noncredit continuing education can also provide a useful service to an institution of higher education by bringing in important potential student market needs and pilot testing some of them. Units that provide noncredit services also often develop a welcome surplus of funds for the general fund of the institution, but this always should be done against the backdrop of the following ten activities:

1. Assessing needs
2. Planning
3. Organizing
4. Developing cooperative relationships
5. Marketing/Promoting
6. Implementing
7. Evaluating
8. Reporting
9. Projecting
10. Budgeting

As horizons open for high-quality institutions to provide education services, both credit and noncredit, to those who need it (and can afford it or find funding for this "investment"), the mission of teaching, service, and even research will also expand for these institutions of higher education. Much has been written about noncredit programs, especially in the training area, so the discussion here has been brief, as the focus of this book is more on for-credit programs in continuing education, a more neglected topic. The landscape of opportunities for educational services is changing. Additional resources for adult, career, and vocational education can be found in the ERIC Clearinghouse on Education. Many resources focus on helping all workers have the opportunity to acquire the knowledge and skills needed to adapt to constantly emerging new technologies, new work methods, and new markets. This is being done through public and private vocational, technical, workplace, and higher education placement of many noncredit (and credit) programs. The focus of these programs is on factors contributing to the purposeful learning of adults in many different life situations related to adult roles.

Research on the adult life cycle gives greater knowledge of the issues and tasks of adult lives and an awareness of the function of education in career and life changes. A reconceptualization of programs and institutional strategy for identifying and serving adults may be needed. The expectancy that adults change and develop leads to the creation of resources within the educational system that adults can use in their change process. Replacing a lockstep, one-chance educational system with a system with many entry points and methods allows for the pursuit of many goals, whether career-related or life-enhancing (or both). Looking at adults, asking whom the institution serves and what adult students need, may create a need to write proposals for funding or contract programs as described in the next chapter.

BIBLIOGRAPHY

Apps, J. W. (1981). *The Adult Learner on Campus.* Chicago: Follett.

Arends, R. I. and J. H. Arends (1977). *Systems Change Strategies in Educational Settings.* New York: Herman Science Press.

Boone, E. J., R. W. Shearon, E. E. White and Associates (1980). *Serving Personal and Community Needs through Adult Education.* San Francisco: Jossey-Bass.

Broad, M. and J. Newstrom (1992). *Transfer of Training: Action-Packed Strategies to Ensure High Payoff from Training Investment.* Reading, MA: Addison-Wesley.

Brookfield, S. D. (1986). *Understanding and Facilitating Adult Learning.* San Francisco: Jossey-Bass.

Cross, K. P. (1978). The *Missing Link: Connecting Adult Learners to Learning Resources.* New York: The College Board. ED 163 177.

Cross, K. P. (1981). *Adults as Learners.* San Francisco: Jossey-Bass.

Cross, K. P., and A. McCartan (1984). *Adult Learning: State Policies and Institutional Practices.* ASHE/ERIC: Washington DC.

Cross, K. P., and Ami Zusman (1979). "The Needs of Nontraditional Learners and the Responses of Nontraditional Programs." In Charles Stalford (Ed.), *An Evaluative Look at Nontraditional Postsecondary Education.* Washington, DC: National institute of Education.

Dixon, N. M. (1993). "Developing Managers for the Learning Organization." *Human Resource Management Review, 3* (3), 243–254.

Garrison, Don C. (1980). "Community Colleges and Industry: A Stronger Partnership for Human Resources Development." In Robert Yarrington (Ed.), *Employee Training for Productivity.* Washington, DC: American Association for community and Junior Colleges. ED 190 188.

Gold, G. G. (1981). "Toward Business–Higher Education Alliances." In G. G. Gold (Ed.), *Business and Higher Education: Toward New Alliances.* New Directions for Experiential Learning No. 13. San Francisco: Jossey-Bass.

Goldstein, I. L., and P. Gilliam (1990). "Training Issues in the Year 2000." *American Psychologist 45* (2), 134–143.

Gross, R. (1977). *The Lifelong Learner.* New York: Simon & Schuster.

Gross, R. (1982). *Invitation to Lifelong Learning.* Chicago: Follett.

Hilton, William J. (1983) *Reaching out to Adult Learners: The Why and How of Lifelong Learning.* Denver: CO: Education Commission of the States/Kellogg Foundation Lifelong Learning Project.

Hammaker, R. and J. A. Mason (1995). *Smart TV™ Exclusive Cable Educational Credit and Non-Credit Courses.* Parma, OH: Cuyahoga Community College.

Iowa Public Television (1995) *Iowa Communications Network.* Johnston, Iowa: Author.

Knowles, Malcolm S. (1980). *The Modern Practice of Adult Education* (rev. ed.). New York: Cambridge.

Knowles, M. S. (1984). *The Adult Learner: A Neglected Species.* Houston, TX: Gulf.

Knowles, M. S. (1989). *The Making of an Adult Educator.* San Francisco: Jossey-Bass.

Knox, A. B. (1986). *Helping Adults Learn.* San Francisco: Jossey-Bass.

Lopos, G. , M. E. Holt, R. E. Bohlander and J. H. Wells (Eds.) (1988). *Peterson's Guide to Certificate Programs at American Colleges and Universities.* Princeton, NJ: Peterson's Guides.

Lynton, Ernest A. (1982). "Improving Cooperation between Colleges and Corporations." *Educational Record, 63,* 20–23

Marcus, L. R., A. O. Leone, and E. D. Goldberg (1983). *The Path to Excellence: Quality Assurance in Higher Education.* ASHE-ERIC Higher Education Research Report No. 1. Washington, DC: Association for the Study of Higher Education. ED 235 697.

Maryland State Board for Community Colleges (1978). *Continuing Education Manual.* Annapolis, MD: Author. ED 154 899.

Ohio Board of Regents (1982). *A Report on Non-Credit Continuing Education Activities in Ohio: 1980-81.* Columbus, OH: Author.

Parnell, Dale (1983). "Labor/Industry/College Partnership Breaks New Ground." *Community and Junior College Journal, 53,* 16–20.

Peters, Tom (1994). *The Seminar.* New York: Bantam Books.

Senge, P. M. (1990). *The Fifth Discipline: The Art and Practice of the Learning Organization.* New York: Doubleday.

Smith, A.O. (1991). "An Institutional History of Certificate Programs at George Washington University." In *Perspectives on Educational Certificate Programs: New Directions for Adult and Continuing Education.* No 52. San Francisco: Jossey-Bass.

Smith, R. M. (1982). *Learning How to Learn.* Chicago: Follett.

University of Maine System (1995). *Education Network of Maine.* Bangor, ME: Author.

U.S. Dept. of Health, Education and Welfare (1978). *Life-Long Learning and Public Policy.* Washington, DC: Lifelong Learning Project.

Weinstein, L. M. (1982). "Labor Unions." In R. E. Anderson and E. S. Kasl (Eds.), *The Costs and Financing of Adult Education and Training.* Lexington, MA: Lexington Books.

Weisbord, M. R. (1989). *Productive Workplaces.* San Francisco: Jossey-Bass.

Young, Robert B. (1981). "The Evaluation of Community Education in Community and Junior Colleges." In Holly M. Jellison (Ed.), *A Look to Future Years: Prospects Regarding the Scope and Process of Community Organization,* Monograph No. 4, Center for Community Education. Washington, DC: American Association for Community and Junior Colleges. ED 206 365.

▶ Section III

Marketing and Finances in Continuing Education

Operational issues are ongoing and require leadership, planning, decision making, teamwork, motivation, and problem solving. However, two areas that affect all of continuing education in any framework, whether credit or noncredit programs, are marketing, including the dissemination of information about the programs, and finances.

A well-done marketing campaign leads prospective students from awareness to observing, trying, persuading, and enrolling. Many institutions of higher education have found pervasive overall benefits from showcasing their name and superior programs, courses, and degrees via their continuing education divisions. Individual characteristics and style of institutions should dominate, but a wide range of choices is available in the marketing and finance areas.

Finances, including the forecasting of return on marketing expenses, are foundational to most continuing education divisions. Most institutions have their own reporting styles and requirements, so specific recommendations cannot be made for these. A discussion of proposal writing is included in Chapter 12, because both the private sector and the public sector respond to proposals in education.

Recognition for a job well done is rare in many job situations. Continuing education can look to clear numbers of people attending information sessions and enrolling in response to marketing efforts as measures of success. However, praise is always well received by participants in a group effort that results in providing more educational services to students and a productive return to the institution. As in a family of children with one child prodigy, a continuing education department can cost more in preparation (in terms of marketing and advertising), but also can yield great returns both financially and in educational services provided. These can have a large impact on the population as the society moves into the Information Age. Calling on satisfied "adult student alumni" for future financial and verbal support should not be overlooked. Alumni contributions and continuous learning registrations will help the programs continue to grow and build. Many colleges and universities see their under age 25 students as beginning a lifelong relationship with their institutions.

► 11

Marketing, Diffusion of Innovations, and Direct Mail Processes

Marketing relates to an exchange between two parties (exchanging something of value), and the exchange must be seen as a process, not as an event. Good marketing tries to build up long-term, trusting relationships with valued student/customers. Institutions of higher education have accomplished this for many years by promising and delivering high-quality service and fair prices to their students over time.

MARKETING CONCEPTS

Many institutions of higher learning have subsidized tuition in many ways to keep "prices" fair and education accessible to all, which could be called part of "marketing." *Relationship marketing,* as relating to the student/customer is called, cuts down on the costs of transactions in both time and money, as interactions become routinized rather than negotiated each time (Kotler, 1994). That is, once a student enrolls in a degree program there is a routine for registering and paying for each course. This savings in time and expense long has been taken for granted by institutions of higher education. In times of scarce dollars, further cutting into this "pared down," yet traditional approach to "routinized relational" marketing (meaning routine relationships) will do more harm than good to revenues. In fact, *spending* some budget dollars on improved registration and accounts payable systems will yield dividends.

The concept of exchange leads to a broader concept of the "market" of potential students. A new definition would be "all potential students sharing a particular need or want who might be willing and able to engage in [classes] to satisfy that need or want" (Kotler, 1994, p. 11). This doesn't mention *where* the students are (are satellite courses an option?); *how old* the students are (traditional students or working adults or seniors?); or other variables such as time of classes (evening, weekend?) that have traditionally been included in the view of institutions of higher education as to how, why, and where they provide education services. In a time of declining outside financial supports, broader thinking about potential students can begin to bridge the gap appearing in the budgets of many institutions of higher education.

The marketing concept most useful to institutions of higher education (IHE) is that diagrammed in the top of Figure 11.1 This might be contrasted with the old "industrial" selling concept diagrammed at the bottom of the figure. Many institutions of higher education have long eschewed marketing concepts as "too commercial," but this way of thinking (or not thinking) about student/customer satisfaction could positively affect some large institutions of higher education, including community colleges or state universities.

If the previously mentioned customer/student-focused approach seems attractive, it is important to understand what the customers/students need. In marketing terms, they may have stated needs, real needs, unstated needs, "delight" needs, and secret needs (Kotler, 1994). Being aware of the complexity of the human psyche means that institutions of higher education will want to select aspects of their courses and education services that have the most relevance for the students and to help students see how to get what they want. This is especially important for small, private institutions with little or no public funding. Student counseling at intake and even career counseling have long been part of the tradition of most higher education institutions, but the concept has further implications for getting to know about potential students: their likes, needs, dislikes, and past behavior. A variety of measures can be surveyed in a present group of students in a field such as telecommunications, and the results can be used in direct mail pieces to potential students. An annual survey that will clean up the mailing list while asking such questions as "What magazines do you read?" and "What professional associations do you belong to?" amasses data. Such data can suggest what mailing lists from journals or professional associations for that particular discipline's potential students should be purchased.

Coordinated marketing may mean a new "student/customer" orientation for the whole institution, as this concept is becoming the norm for businesses and much of higher education nationwide. Students, especially adult students, expect the same courtesy and ease in making a purchase (paying tuition) from a college that they expect in paying for any transaction of over a hundred dollars or more.

	Starting Point	**Focus**	**Means**	**Ends**
IHE	Target market	Customer needs	Coordinated marketing	Profits/Surplus through student/customer satisfaction and return
Industry	Factory	Products	Selling and promoting	Surplus/Profits through Sales volume

FIGURE 11.1   Marketing Concepts for IHE Compared to Concepts for Industry

Many organizations do not grasp the customer service/marketing concept until they see a "sales" decline: slow growth, change in buying (enrollment) patterns, increasing competition, or increasing marketing expenses without notable improvement.

ORGANIZATIONAL RESISTANCE

Many institutions of higher education, not unlike other institutions and bureaucracies, have shown resistance to and slow learning of (followed by fast forgetting after a success) concepts of marketing, especially at departmental levels (Kotler, 1994). As shown in Figure 11.2, marketing can be seen as a less-than-equal function of the institution as in A, or as related to the student (of any age) as the controlling variable as in B, or as the integrative function around the student as the central orientation of the institution of higher education as in C. Other models with marketing as the largest or even the central function of the institution are almost never seen in institutions of higher education, although they exist in the marketing literature. However marketing is viewed—and these models only scratch the surface—most institutions of higher education and organizations manage to get some marketing going. The leaders may attend seminars or hire outside marketing talent and introduce marketing planning and control systems. However, in the wake of marketing success, there is a strong tendency to forget the marketing principles of continuing to know the target markets/potential students, communicating with the market (adult students) in many ways, and responding better to the market's (the adult students') wants and needs (Kotler and Fox, 1985).

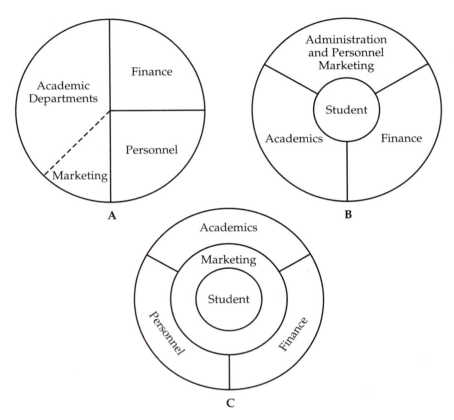

Figure 11.2   Marketing as a Function of the Institution

COMMUNICATION AND CHANGE

"Communication is essential for social change," according to writers in the communications field. Communicating about innovations draws on long traditions of diffusion, from anthropology, from early and rural sociology, and up through communication and marketing today (Rogers and Shoemaker, 1971). When individuals or the society changes, there are three sequential steps: (1) The invention or innovation (e.g., in higher education this might be new courses or degree programs related to knowledge needed for the Information Age), (2) the diffusion of information about it (today called communication and marketing), and (3) the consequences (better jobs for graduates, better processes for organizations and corporations perhaps using information technology, etc.). Sociologists and anthropologists have long held that change occurs when a new idea is used (or not used), and that social change is therefore an effect of communication (Rogers and Shoemaker, 1971). While it is not the purpose of this book to discuss all the larger societal ramifications of this concept, it does give a firm foundation to the goals and budgets for marketing in continuing education in colleges and universities.

DIFFUSION OF INNOVATIONS

The diffusion process, often the title for marketing in nonprofit and health organizations, includes four steps that are also found in marketing:

1. Awareness
2. Knowledge
3. Persuasion
4. Adoption

These four steps are applied to continuing education as *awareness* of programs; enough *knowledge* about the programs (often through direct mail brochures) to enroll; *persuasion* opportunities, such as attending information sessions and counseling telephone calls or interviews; and *adoption* or enrollment in courses (see Figure 4.3 in Chapter 4).

In discussing innovations, which could be descriptions of new courses or refreshed old-course content as well as new degree formats and new location sites, there are five attributes to consider:

Relative advantages
Compatibility
Complexity
"Trial-ability"
Observability

Relative advantages of innovations are much like the features and benefits listed in marketing texts and might include convenience, attractiveness of format, smallness of classes, superiority of faculty, and quotes from distinguished alumni. These are much the same as possible features and benefits of all higher education. These advantages as compared to or related to short-term, noncredit training might be stressed, as noncredit often competes with credit courses in some disciplines.

Compatibility refers to how evening and satellite programs fit into the lives of their students; obviously the rise in enrollments in such programs is related to their timing and location being more appropriate and convenient for adult students. Anything that describes compatibility in terms of existing values or activities of the targeted student population will help. This might include nearness to public transportation, accessible and free parking, Saturday classes, or Saturday computer lab hours, and, of course, distance education to be received at home.

The *complexity* of how to begin higher education programs needs to be reviewed and simplified. Do students stand in line for 2 hours in the snow to register, or do they have touch-tone telephone registration hours from 6:00 a.m. to 9:00 p.m., or something in between? Do students have to wait in long lines at the book store; or can books be ordered by phone, charged to a credit card, and delivered to their home by parcel service? Needlessly complex registration activities can be simplified, which will enhance adult enrollments and thus income and also the service provided. The students' use of libraries and of the Internet and search services can be enhanced by giving out for free (or for a low charge) the software needed for Internet access from home or workplace personal computers.

"Trial-ability" of a new degree program can be greatly increased by allowing two or three courses to be taken by students in a "nondegree" or "nonmatriculated" (trial) status. Individual school faculties within a university may allow transfer in of a variety of nondegree (but for credit) courses from their own programs or from other institutions (two or three at the most for the graduate level, of course). Faculty cultural norms will determine how these courses are to be viewed: as important evidence of work done or as unimportant evidence (as graduate enrollees traditionally receive high grades) or varying views in between these two extremes (such as assess the total applicant, or look only at the undergraduate GPA).

Observability means that inquiring students can observe something about the degree and center location, possibly by attending information sessions or briefings on upcoming semesters held *in* the center or class location. Observability gives students a chance to see other potential students and ask questions about how they would handle and enjoy being in a class. Furthermore, they see other students in classes and are reminded that as adults they look familiar (compatible) to them.

ADOPTER CATEGORIES

Adopter categories, a term used in communications and in marketing, follow the bell curve (see Figure 11.3). At the leading edge are the "Innovators" (2.5%), who are venturesome people, eager to try new ideas, especially modern ones, and are willing to try something first in their circle of friends. The "Early

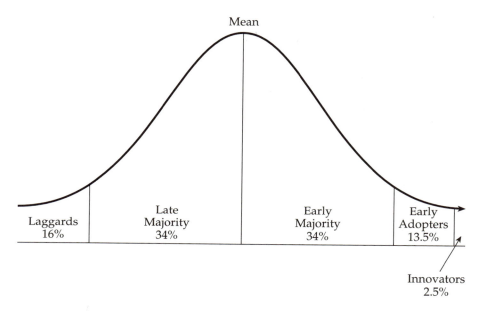

Figure 11.3   Adopter Categories on the Innovativeness Continuum

Adopters" follow. This group (13.5%) often includes opinion leaders. The "Early Majority" are more deliberate thinkers and represent 34% of the adopter group. They may deliberate for some time before they start a course or program. (Rogers and Shoemaker, 1971).

The "Late Majority" follows, another large group (also 34%) who are people who won't try something unless a friend has tried it and reports back. They are skeptical types and probably won't start unless economic necessity or increasing social pressure requires it. Last are the "Laggards," the last 16%, who really do not try new things (such as college courses) unless nearly all their friends have enrolled already. Communication research generalizes about these types and summarizes the findings under socioeconomic status, personality variables, and communication behavior. Obviously a different part of the marketing strategy for a discipline can be aimed at each adopter group. For example, the phrase or slogan "Be the first in your group to try . . ." would reach innovators but would not reach the same group as "The information age is here *now*—now is the time to tune up your skills," which might reach the Early or Late majority, depending on the locale.

DIRECT MARKETING

Direct marketing and public relations are tools of growing importance in marketing planning of all kinds and are especially useful in continuing education in higher education. Direct marketing is an interactive system of marketing that uses one or more media such as direct mail, catalogs or schedules, telemarketing, electronic Web sites and shopping, and more, to create a measurable response. In continuing education the measure might be of the number of responses or inquiries generated by a direct mail campaign or an Internet home page. The advantages of direct marketing are selectivity, personalization, better timing, continuity, high readability, testability and privacy (Kotler, 1994). Higher education markets to those who are interested in getting a college degree or an advanced degree and also to those possible adult students who want quite a bit of information before making an expensive investment. Information might include course descriptions for a particular discipline and the degree structure and schedule and format considerations. Direct mail is an ideal vehicle with which to convey this information, and, of course, there is no competition within the same direct mail piece. Newspaper and radio advertising enhance the impact of a direct mail campaign by a factor of four (Elliott, 1982), but these media do run ads from competing colleges and universities, and they cannot convey the amount of information that a direct mail piece can. They are useful for "reminders" about information sessions and registration dates or other short pieces of information. (Note ads that appear *before* a direct mail campaign don't have this enhancement effect and do poorly. Timing is very important.)

A "VIP" letter (for "Very Important Persons" or opinion leaders) sent to opinion leaders and heads of corporations in a particular field in advance of a direct mail campaign, can further enhance the impact of a direct mail campaign. While the cost per thousand people reached in a direct mail campaign is higher than in a mass media campaign, the higher target-market selectivity reaches much better prospects for a particular student population match to a program. Some research shows that 85% of marketing through direct mail is the correct percent for the higher education "marketing mix" of approaches. This is due to the narrowness of the target markets and also because of the amount of information that can be sent in a direct mail piece (Elliott, 1982).

Because effective direct mail campaigns are costly, higher education continuing education administrators need access to good advice, marketing textbooks, and perhaps membership in the Direct Marketing Association, so as to have continuing input of new ideas and applications or use of direct mail pieces. Hiring a marketing firm or individual can be useful but the "style" of the university must be represented properly and not down-graded, which can cause internal repercussions.

The response rate to direct mail advertising (normally 2% to 3% is considered "good"), understates the long-term impact of the campaign. This is especially true in higher education and can be more easily understood when reviewed against the time lag for the adopter categories. Colleges and Universities always have another semester. Regardless of problems, late schedules, snow and ice, students KNOW this educational service will continue and be there for them when they decide to go (except perhaps in the case of very small, poor, private colleges, as some of those may be closing.) Direct mail has a high readership thus producing a high awareness of the content of a program or programs over time. A percentage of readers form an intention-to-buy-at-a-later date, which should not be underestimated, especially in higher education.

Direct Mail Strategy

Continuing educators need to analyze the characteristics of present students and potential students in a particular discipline. Who would be the most able, willing, and ready to enroll in the future? Who would benefit greatly and improve their career path with this program or degree? A once-a-year "audit survey" of addresses, tastes, employment, and even books and magazines read or professional or organizational memberships is very useful and also keeps the in-house mailing list current. In addition to surveys, student comments, personal interviews, and employee enrollees' comments also help planners learn more about potential adult students. This is called the "target market." Once it is defined, perhaps by sending the audit questionnaire to current students, the list acquisition and management steps can proceed from a better knowledge base about future students. The list compiled in-house by the continuing education staff of current students, current inquiries, and opinion leaders is typically the best list (Kotler, 1994). Additional lists can be purchased from list brokers (more in the following section), but small segments of these lists should be pilot tested before a large mass mailing is done, to assess their worth. An expensive list with a 35% return might be a better buy than an inexpensive list with a 3% return.

What is sent in a direct mail campaign is of key importance. Five components in a direct mail piece are: (1) the *envelope*, which could be the regular, dignified institution of higher education's usual logo and style; (2) the *letter* enclosed, which should include the how, what, why, when, and where and some narrative about what benefits the receiver will gain from attending an information session and/or taking this course or degree (a relevant "P.S." on the letter increases response rate); (3) a *circular*, flyer, or brochure, in color, and a (4) *response coupon*, which together should give details, course descriptions, the degree structure when appropriate, and even testimonials

from students and opinion leaders; and, finally, (5) a *postage-free reply envelope* or the coupon already mentioned, which boosts response rates.

A great advantage of direct mail is that it allows early testing in the real,
prospective adult student population market of the elements of the mailing
piece involved, and this can save costly mistakes. Those testing the direct
mail pieces should watch for differences produced by copy, features and
benefits listed, tuition prices, the media used, and mailing lists selected.
These are best observed when only one major component is changed per
mailing, such as using the same brochure design and mailing list, when
there is a new tuition rate.

By adding up the planned direct mail campaign costs and expecting a
conservative 2% return, the administrator can figure out in advance the
break-even rate needed to advance a given program when balanced against
projected tuition income for this 2% enrolling. In this analysis it is important
to figure the additional future enrollments needed to finish a degree program (but decreased somewhat for attrition) into the response rate numbers
and income. These future enrollments are called "customer lifetime value,"
and this value is usually high in higher education. Projected income for a
campaign can be: (1) conservatively based on last year's similar initiative; (2)
somewhat more aggressively based on last year's enrollment numbers plus
a percentage of new students, or (3) aggressively based on all-new-student
projected return.

Eventually integrated direct mail processes and "database marketing"
will be key in all higher education institutions willing to be involved in continuing education, according to marketing companies. The time line in Figure 11.4 shows a possible sequencing of a VIP letter plus direct mail campaign for a new semester of adult continuing education. The sequence is a
10-week cycle leading up to a 12- 14-week semester. A VIP letter-with-one-
circular mailing is followed in 2 to 4 weeks by an extensive direct mailing
featuring dates for information sessions in letters and brochures describing
courses and degrees. Radio, newspaper, and Internet/on-line services and
advertisements can further reinforce the dates in readers' minds. Follow-up
phone calls (or group "blast" facsimiles or e-mails), can be made to remind
students of acceptances for briefing dates and to do advance counseling for
the program(s), if appropriate.

Next, as depicted on the time line in Figure 11.4, information sessions are
held with opportunities for program chairs, lead professors, or deans to
describe course content, faculty and student characteristics, and admissions
procedures and to answer questions from the group. Evaluation forms with
a name and address block are turned in after each session. Registration by
telephone or mail follows, the semester begins and ends, and the all-important course evaluations are done. Insights from these evaluations, in addition
to improving the courses and programs, can be used in future advertising.

Week	1	2	3	4	5	6	7	8	9	10	11	12-14
1. Send VIP letters and brochures to opinion leaders and to newspapers, radio, and TV (for public service announcements—PSAs)	X											
2. Send direct mail and brochures to identified target lists	- -	- -	✕	►X								
3. PSA spots or radio ads running						X						
4. Information sessions held, reminder and counseling telephone calls made	- -	- -	- -	- -	- -	- -	X	X	X			
5. Registration										X	X	
6. Statistical analysis is done, comparing direct mail factors and information session attendance with number of enrollees											X	
7. End of term— students get degrees, certificates and do final assessment												X

- - - ► = preparation time

Figure 11.4   Time Table for Direct Marketing

Evaluating the Institution's "User-Friendliness"

Questions adapted from the Malcolm Baldrige National Quality Awards are useful criteria for addressing customer (in this case student) focus and satisfaction. This category in the awards accounts for 25% of the points. Much of the information needed for understanding the market (of adult students) must come from measuring results and tracking trends. Expensive marketing without this analysis and input can be far less effective (Hodlin, 1996). Adult student satisfaction is one of the best indicators of an institution's prosperity. "User-friendliness" promotes student satisfaction, reduces frustrations, and can be uncovered (partly) with evaluations.

Questions to ask about the evaluation process are:

How does the institution evaluate and improve its processes for determining adult student requirements and expectations?

What are the institution's processes for determining current and near term requirements and expectations of adult students?

How does the institution provide effective management of its responses and follow-ups with adult students (or any students)?

How does the institution provide easy access for students specifically for the purposes of seeking information or assistance and/or to comment or complain?

How does the institution ensure prompt and effective resolution of complaints, including recovery of student confidence?

How does the institution learn from complaints and ensure that students receive information needed to eliminate the causes of complaints?

How does the institution follow up with students on courses, services, and recent transactions to determine satisfaction, resolve problems, build relationships, and gather information for improvement?

How does the institution evaluate and improve its overall adult student relationship management?

How does the institution determine adult student satisfaction and satisfaction relative to competitor institutions?

Mailing Lists

Analyzing revenue means many things to many people, and in continuing education it can include everything from figuring the return on a mailing list that returns 3.5% versus another list that returns 4% to noting and mapping the zip codes that enrollees list as home addresses. In the case of lists, the cost of the mailing list itself must be figured into the equation for the possible return, and a clear answer will emerge as to which list to use. For example, the costs of mailing to 3,000 names on four lists of varying price and efficacy (with $700 being the new students' tuition) are compared in Figure 11.5.

The benefit of maintaining even a relatively small in-house list, which includes important opinion leaders that can further boost distribution, is that with local effort from the continuing education division professional staff the response rate can be taken from 1% to 3% or 4% fairly easily. Maintenance is essential, but with the current availability of powerful desktop computers this should not be too cumbersome for even a minimum-salary employee. Using a proven in-house list that is updated regularly can produce a better response rate, even if it costs $50 per 1,000 to keep the list updated. The success of an in-house list will vary with the following (Elliott, 1982):

- Quality of names
- Mailing lead time
- Course price
- Quality of promotional literature
- Promotional copy and layout
- Course location
- Choices of programs offered
- Ease of registration
- Frequency of use of a given set of names
- Geographical spread of the names used
- The use of title versus the use of names
- The state of the economy
- The size of training budgets
- The particular time or season of the year
- The financial strength of a targeted industry or occupation
- Unknown factors

Building an in-house list usually is done through a combination of (1) names of previous enrollees; (2) names of those who have made inquiries; (3) a VIP list of opinion leaders, decision makers, and immediate superiors

---

List 1 (purchased for $60 per 1000 names; 3.5% return):
    3 X $60 = $180; 3000 X 3.5% = 105 enrollees
    105 X $700 = $73,500
    $73,500 - $180 = $73,320 revenue

List 2 (purchased for $40 per 1000 names; 3% return):
    3 X $40 = $120; 3000 X 3% = 90 enrollees
    90 X $700 = $63,000
    $63,000 - $120 = $62,880 revenue

List 3 (in-house; $50 cost to maintain; 4% return):
    3 X $50 = $150; 3000 X 4% = 120 enrollees
    120 X $700 = $84,000
    $84,000 - $150 = $83,850 revenue

List 4 (in-house; not maintained; 1% return):
    3 X $0 = $0; 3000 X 1% = 30 enrollees
    30 X $700 = $21,000 revenue

FIGURE 11.5   Mailing List Response Rates for Mailing to 3,000 Names, with $700 Tuition

who approved funding of previous enrollees; and (4) compilations from logical published lists. Names written into evaluations of other persons interested from a student's workplace, whether superiors or colleagues, can be a valuable addition to an in-house list.

In the case of noting and using zip codes, one cross-hatches on a map (by hand or computer) the areas producing the heaviest response rate. The pattern gives the viewer immediate insight into which local (and inexpensive) newspapers to put additional ads into or which targeted regional mailing lists to buy. It also sections out a target market for specific market surveys about new program offerings or other questions the division might have.

Mailing list selection should be part of the annual marketing plan for each program. All too often this is considered *after* the planning process. Reliable relationships with one or two list brokers should be maintained. However recommendations from two or three brokers should be considered for selection, especially if their recommendations conflict, as brokers tend to have their specialties. The program specialists who talk frequently with students should meet with several brokers in order to familiarize them with particulars of the program's marketing needs.

As one very successful director of a professional continuing education program said:

> With services of several brokers, combined with the commitment of his or her staff and a thorough understanding of these concepts . . ., a director should be well prepared to improve the mailing list response rate on any continuing education activity. Even though a high-quality mailing list is not a sufficient condition for a continuing education office to be successful, it is certainly a necessary condition. (Elliott, 1982, p. 24)

THE "FOUR P'S" OF MARKETING

Product, price, place, and packaging are the famous "four P's" of marketing taught in business schools. Higher education continuing education is able to impact *place* and *packaging* (including format and advertising) more easily than *price* (tuition set by the board of trustees) or *product* (course content). Having said that, creativity in the areas of impact can lead to enormously attractive innovations and therefore increased enrollments. Would a summer condensed "institute" of two, four, or six courses be possible for a highly distinctive topic or degree? Would a weekend or Saturday program be attractive?

Place refers to the site of your courses—off campus, at contract sites, in your own facilities, or in rented space. Care should be taken in establishing long-term arrangements with new sites, for example, in high schools or government agencies. For a large set of programs, building or renovating space for classrooms provides the greatest long-term benefit and the least possibility of unwanted disruption.

Price, as already indicated, usually refers to the tuition set by the board of trustees, but variations for contract course group rates or a percentage off for distant locations can usually be arranged. Many schools provide a discount rate for teachers or other special groups.

Product, which is course content and quality in this discussion, is the most important element and should always receive priority in logistical concerns. Providing instructional materials and equipment to enable high-quality teaching and learning is important, as this is the core benefit or essential service for which the student is paying tuition. The generic or expected attributes of any college-level course or degree program are the absolute minimum of service that can be provided.

Packaging and format can include variety in class scheduling, which helps adult students and multiplies the use of existing classroom space. Other factors that can be included in "packaging," beyond the obvious advertising decisions, include self-service, such as registration by telephone, on-line access to libraries, or telephone ordering of books by course number.

Other areas of impact to increase effectiveness of marketing might include consideration of consumer affluence, which can mean that students are willing to pay more for convenience, dependability, and prestige; *name and image* recognition for the total institution of higher education; and *innovation opportunity,* which means stressing in advertising and direct mail the large benefits to the student of this location, this schedule, this format, this topic or degree program, or other opportunities this innovation is creating for them in today's knowledge-based economy. Students need to learn about the aspects of the program that will mean the most to them. Messages should have meaning and relevance to them. Students also need to be shown how to get what they want, which requires the staff to know as much as possible about the students' (and potential students') wants and needs: their likes, needs, dislikes and past behavior. All of this shows "caring" and helps to reduce the usual five or six contacts needed (via mail, advertising, or personal contact) to create an actual registration or any purchase over $100.00.

It can be tempting to "coast" on a monopoly situation (as the only institution of higher education in the area, due to state or federal funding) that can be a short-lived "niche" of safety. Distance learning, new satellite centers opened by competing institutions, and of course the giant training industry have made serious inroads on the market for the provision of education to adult students. However, with the Information Age ever requiring new skills and more substantial knowledge information backgrounds, the "augmented" offerings of additional services and benefits that institutions of higher education can offer and the "potential" offerings of possible new features and services that might eventually be added (Kotler, 1994) add up to a very large possibility for prosperity and community service for higher education.

Figure 11.6 shows how the four P's of marketing can be adapted in planning for two alternative education centers with similar but different educational needs. These needs determine the product. Packaging and format— whether evening, daytime, or weekend—and price factors are given in the boxes in the figure. The "right angle" problem-solving device is used to show that the thinking done for one center can be a springboard for ideas for another.

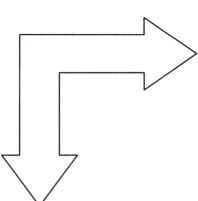

Site B Market Needs and Product

Telecommunications
Management (Human Resource
  Management on Saturdays)
Information Systems
Higher Education
Education K–12 (Weeknights and
  Saturdays)
Noncredit courses

Price
All offerings at preset off-campus
tuition rates

Packaging (Format)
Weekday evenings, except where
noted

Site A Market Needs and Product

Telecommunications Policy, M.A.
EE/CS (Electrical Engineering/Computer Science)
Engineering Management
Human Resource Management
  (government agency contract on weekdays)
Noncredit courses

FIGURE 11.6   Right-Angle Transfer of Start-Up Planning (and Marketing) Site A to Site B: Product, Place, Price, Packaging

SUMMARY

Marketing, especially through direct mail, and diffusion of innovation strategies is vital to institutions of higher education. When marketing is seen as an *exchange* of information between the institution of higher education and the student, the concept of potential students can be widened considerably. The more each knows about the other, the more likely it is that a favorable match-up (or enrollment) can be made. Organizational resistance to marketing is not limited only to institutions of higher education but can be found in many organizations and bureaucracies. Arguments that have proven effective for the use of marketing in higher education include:

The university or college's assets are of little use without students.

The key task of institutions of higher education is to attract and retain students (although research and service will remain part of the mission).

Student satisfaction is affected by the performance of a variety of other departments.

Marketing needs to influence these other departments (e.g., library, student accounts, registration, etc.) to cooperate in delivering student satisfaction.

Education traditionally increases enrollments during a recession. As the global society moves into the twenty-first century, appropriate communication and integrated marketing of the opportunities provided by institutions of higher education should help to ensure their continuing prosperity, when coupled with good management. Institutions will have to adapt the marketing approaches described in this chapter to suit their needs, whether they be direct mail, advertising, public relations outreach, or (the preferred approach) a combination of all three. Marketing principles well used for the academic culture are the path to building life-long relationships with student-customers who will come back again and again. A focus on the external customers or students needs to be deployed internally through the layers and departments of the institution, no matter how loosely coupled. Otherwise, the internal needs that receive focus may not be in phase with student needs and may create added work that is not of value to the institution. Student satisfaction is one of the best indicators of the institution's prosperity. When higher education employees are empowered to help students, they became involved and committed. They are capable of helping students only when provided with right information. This requires teamwork. Successful leaders (in any type of organization) provide resources their people need to serve the customers (students) well.

BIBLIOGRAPHY

Abraham, Magid M., and Leonard M. Lodish (1990). "Getting the Most out of Advertising and Promotion." *Harvard Business Review,* May-June, pp. 50–60.

Akao, Yoji (1990). *Quality Function Deployment: Integrating Customer Requirements into Product Design.* Cambridge, MA: Productivity Press.

Blattberg, Robert C., and John Deighton (1991). "Interactive Marketing: Exploiting the Age of Addressability." *Sloan Management Review,* Fall, pp. 5–14.

Bossert, James L. (1991). *Quality Function Deployment: A Practitioner's Approach.* New York: ASQC Quality Press, Dekker.

Dutka, Alan (1994). *AMA Handbook for Customer Satisfaction.* Lincolnwood, IL: NTC Business Books.

Elliott, Ralph D. (1982). *How to Build and Maintain a High Quality Mailing List.* Manhattan, KA: Learning Resources Network.

George, S., and J. Weimerskirch (1994). *Total Quality Management.* New York: Wiley.

Hayes, Bob E. (1992). *Measuring Customer Satisfaction.* Milwaukee, WI.: ASQC Quality Press.

Hodlin, Steven F. (1996). "Stay Customer Focused to Ensure Long-Term Success." Presentation given at the Quality Network Seminar, Suburban Maryland High Technology Education Council, May 15, Rockville, MD.

Hopkins, Tom (1982). *How to Master the Art of Selling.* New York: Warner Books.

Houston, Franklin S. (1986). "The Marketing Concept: What It Is and What It Is Not." *Journal of Marketing,* April, pp. 81–87.

Juran, J. M. (1989). *Juran on Leadership for Quality.* New York: The Free Press.

Kotler, Philip (1994). *Marketing Management: Analysis, Planning, Implementation and Control.* Englewood Cliffs, NJ: Prentice-Hall.

Kotler, Philip, and Alan R. Andreasen (1991). *Strategic Marketing for Nonprofit Organizations* (4th ed.). Englewood Cliffs, NJ: Prentice-Hall.

Kotler, P. and K. Fox (1985). *Strategic Marketing for Educational Institutions.* Englewood Cliffs, NJ: Prentice-Hall.

Nash, Edward (1986). *Direct Marketing.* New York: McGraw Hill.

National Institute of Standards and Technology (1996). *Malcolm Baldrige Quality Award Criteria.* Gaithersburg, MD: Author.

Ogilvy, David (1988). *Confessions of an Advertising Man.* New York: Atheneum.

Pride, W. M., and O. C. Ferrell (1987). *Marketing: Basic Concepts and Decisions.* Boston: Houghton Mifflin.

Rogers, E. M., and F. F. Shoemaker (1971). *Communication of Innovations.* New York: Macmillan.

Sarbanes, Paul S. (1996). *U.S. Senate Productivity Award.* Washington, DC: U.S. Senate.

Schaffir, Kurt H., and H. George Trenton (1973). *Marketing Information Systems.* New York: Amacom.

Stone, Robert (1993). *Successful Direct Marketing Methods.* Chicago: NTC Books.

Whiteley, Richard C. (1991). *The Customer Driven Company: Moving from Talk to Action.* Boston: Addison-Wesley.

► 12

Finances and Proposal Writing for Unique Institutions

Running a continuing education division in higher education and keeping it economically feasible requires good management practice. Attention must be paid to the financial aspects of the education centers, the record-keeping processes, and planning for future income, which may necessitate proposal writing. Because education is essentially a service, personnel is key, and attention needs to be given to the vision for goals and objectives and to training. Budgets and records need to be kept. All these tasks need to be done well by a person hired especially for these skills. To aid in understanding the foundation for the financial part of a profit center approach for education operations, this chapter includes a start-up plan. Education centers that are already in operation within a continuing education division can "fill in" from the following activities as seems appropriate.

DAY-TO-DAY OPERATIONAL BUDGETS

Good management practice must prevail in day-to-day operational budgets, as well as throughout the finances of continuing education. While there is an entrepreneurial atmosphere and a stronger marketing and advertising presence in the competitive and crowded area of continuing education, the end does *not* justify the means, as institutions of higher education are "in it for the long haul." The "long haul" is longer than ever with life-long learning, and so truth in advertising is a must. Institutions have credibility and reliability at stake, and the reputation of the enterprise must not be tarnished by poorly thought out advertising or budgeting. Worthy ends do not justify unworthy means in this or any other initiative.

Comments made by an Ivy League university president at a recent graduation could also be applied to a philosophy on finance and budgeting at institutions. The choice of what to believe and what to reject, what to do or not do, ultimately falls to the leader. Not all views or options are equally praiseworthy. The real world, like the campus, is full of seductive nonsense, and nonsense cloaked in high-sounding scholarly language is still nonsense.

Continuing education and distance education leaders have learned to make choices by evaluating options, to set goals by thinking through their implications and consequences—often with the help of the group—and to function within the realm of reason. Absolute single-mindedness can block out creativity and the multiple interfaces so needed at all levels and in all directions in adult continuing education.

The categories of the day-to-day operational budget often show the current thinking of the organization. One set of expense categories might look like this:

A. Income
B. Expense

       Salary, nonacademic full- and part-time
       Hourly wage, temporary workers
       Work study students' hourly wage
       Fringe benefit allocation
       Conference/seminar expense
       Domestic travel
       Special events/business relations
       Advertising
       Miscellaneous office expense
       Office furniture expense
       Office equipment
       Postage
       Freight in/out
       Telephone expense
       Office supplies
       Instructional supplies
       External printing expense
       Contract services
       Computer equipment over $600
       Printing and graphics (fee for service—internal)

C. Surplus or Deficit

In this budget, contract services might include hotel meeting rooms for information sessions, computer lab services, a mailing list service fee, or a number of other miscellaneous costs, some of which might eventually have their own budget lines.

Preparing for the Unexpected

Beware of cutting expenses too much when launching a new program, as the institution will be unprepared for the unexpected when it happens. In one example an institution had put a lot of effort into establishing a new master's degree at a fairly distant location, even changing the topic slightly to adapt to local needs. After approvals from the state and a local sponsoring group, information sessions were to be held 2 and 3 months prior to the start-up of fall classes. When the ads in the inexpensive local papers were to run, the person in charge "forgot" to send the ads in. Brochures, flyers, and e-mail had been distributed, so the first two information sessions had to be held. There was still time to place the ads again for the next two sessions.

However, in the meantime a large, well-known competitor institution mailed postcards to every post office address in that county (about 15,000), plus radio advertising, and subsequently held an information session for 150 attendees for several courses to be offered (not even a whole degree). The lack of awareness of competition and its effects greatly impacted the low-cost, forgetful marketing approach of the institution with the year of lead time and "front-end" effort. This was felt in the end result and a great deal more money was spent in a "catch-up" effort.

Calculating Return on Investment

Some of the realities of funding traditional education at a distance have been described in previous chapters. The realities of funding initial expenses for distance education technology will mean pro-rating such an expense over a 5-year (or, optimally, a ten-year) period with the institution, rather than funding it within a budget such as the one listed above for one year.

When budgeting for the expenses of distance education, one needs to provide a detailed summary of the nominated system's investment costs (including up-front development expenses and annual maintenance charges). Also needed are estimates of returns on this investment, including increased surplus revenue, reduced costs, and indirect cost avoidance. By including the indirect cost avoidance figures for not building new spaces with new overhead (janitorial services, furniture and equipment), and being able to demonstrate reduced costs even as the numbers of students increase, the budgeter makes the logic behind distance education become even more appealing. Estimates of costs and returns should be made per annum over a

5-year period. This data will help a distance education proposal make it past the first round of decision making. The final "clincher" may be the estimates of surplus revenue stemming from using new technologies to provide new learning opportunities in new locations.

The changing profile of university budgets and the seemingly constant redefinition of what is fundable and not fundable will affect this purchase of distance technology, but this purchase can be a window of opportunity for a continuing education unit that can return 30% to 50% of revenue to the university. Open and clear budgets also leave any organization in a better position when audit time arrives. Furthermore, clear income and expense records can place a unit in a much stronger position when it comes to requesting additional funds for such new initiatives. Pro-rating of these requests over a longer than 1-year period, perhaps 5 or even 10 years, adds to the likelihood of agreement.

STARTING UP: DEVELOPING A MANAGEMENT PLAN

Developing a management plan is a good first step in developing any new entity, especially one that is supposed to become self-supporting. Because most institutions have some sort of adult or evening program (84% had these by 1982 [Cross, 1984]), this discussion will focus on the context of opening satellite centers. One recommendation is to allow at least 6 to 12 months for planning a start-up. This gives time to do a needs survey in the geographical area and to meet with interested community opinion leaders and with faculty who are willing to offer programs there.

External Review

Any start-up plan should carefully review at least three other continuing education centers, if possible, and place them on a matrix like that shown in Figure 12.1. Rank each item for each competitor as better or worse than your plan. Take note of good ideas or new possibilities that this exercise yields.

Setting Goals and a Time Line

Other important parts to a start-up plan should include:

- A time line for beginning and ending tasks
- Measurable goals and subgoals
- An action plan
- Allowance for obstacles
- Provision for review and resetting of goals

Location	Floor Plan	Staff Competence and Attitudes	Equipment
Continuing Education Center A			
Continuing Education Center B			
Satellite Center C			
Our Center			

Figure 12.1   Competition Chart

The time line for the year before opening day is similar for most centers. The year before that, spent in getting university approvals, would vary with the area and with zoning and other regulations that must be met.

Income Issues

Much of a unit's or center's success in staying viable will depend on how well the organization plans the program, the marketing, and the income. If the cost per student is figured so low that the margin (of income over expense) does not even cover expenses, the center will not be able to build up a surplus (of credibility as well as dollars) for future growth or to cover emergencies. If the income from the students is set too high, enrollment will fail to meet projections.

It is best if the tuition and other sources of income are decided upon before the center opens—so that the "general cost per student average level" or for "program average level of income" that one is expected to maintain is clear, with adjustments for inflation as needed. Is this institution of higher education expensive, medium priced, or almost totally publicly supported? From where does the institution draw its students? These factors will help to decide the choice of location and the area and to pinpoint corporate personnel offices to which to disseminate information, flyers, fact sheets, and brochures. They will also determine to some extent the quality of services to be offered, within approved accreditation ranges. Extra programs in management or a Saturday computer lab program may not be desirable for some areas but very appropriate for others. Such determinations can be developed with the exercises in the chapter on problem solving (Chapter 8).

Additional income from federal, state, local, or corporate grants should be planned at this point, always remembering the basic rule of don't put all your eggs in one basket—or not to rely on only one or on too few grants.

Grants do need to be renewed and they do get canceled, so having several funding sources is always wise. A section on proposal writing is included in this chapter. Proposals to corporations to pick up on the trend of educational partnerships are also useful. The outline presented here will give a thorough presentation format for decision makers to develop into a contract or a memorandum of understanding (MOU) for a contract program that is to be housed within an agency or a corporation.

Educational costs to adult students can also be reduced through employer incentives, or postponed through individual federally guaranteed student loans for those under the limit of the IRS adjusted gross income (which at the time of this writing is $75,000 a year). Incentives could be given through corporations that retrain employees who are in obsolete jobs. Further support has been given to some state-supported institutions by allowing them to charge full cost for on-site workplace contract courses. Other states review courses and allow state funding for vocational and technical education, for other courses, after review, on a course-by-course basis (Maryland State Board of Community Colleges, 1978). Inadequate financial aid has been an impediment to serving adult students over time, as education for the non– 18-to 22-year-old population was considered to have nuances of serving the cultural interests of the leisured classes (Cross, 1978, 1979).

After establishing an income policy that is synchronized with the program's philosophy and overall program goals, the director must look at the amount of income and enrollments needed to cover expenses and the building of surplus. This surplus may need to be in addition to paying off advances from the institution of higher education provided to start the center (Minnesota Higher Education Coordinating Board). Partnerships with business and industry, whether through grants, tax regulations, or loans, are an important part of the work force's path to the twenty-first century.

If the education center has been operating for a year or longer, one can analyze past records and find out the percentage for operating expenses and net surplus. A surplus is a necessity for unexpected raises in supply prices, for adding classrooms or staff or lengthening hours, or for building or renting more centers.

If the center has just opened, one will have to estimate the costs and income carefully. A good rule of thumb is always to figure enrollments at 10% to 50% less than the maximum possible. This overage in planning will allow planning for a surplus and give coverage in case of a sudden drop in enrollment. Costs for administration, bookkeeping, and publicity dissemination costs (i.e., all of the overhead) should already have been figured into the cost per program on a percentage basis. This will help the director know how many student slots will need to be filled for the program to stay in the black.

Not all academic programs need to have the same overhead percentage attached to them. A sliding scale is possible when it is allowed that some programs may have a higher percentage and some a lower percentage for overhead, due to how new they are and how well established they are in their field. An example of applying this differential would be an MBA program versus an infant special education program. (The MBA program is obviously a better known entity.) A limited new program benefit in terms of lower overhead percentage might also be used and serve as an incentive to departments to offer programs. Revenue sharing might allow a department and a dean to share a percentage of the revenue surplus—in a percentage negotiated between the two of them.

If income is figured too low, the resulting additional students may cost more than the center can support in terms of additional faculty, educational materials, or computers needed. Other centers' tuitions should be considered if the center does not have substantial outside grants. One should keep in mind the overall "mark-up" for tuition and above-cost percentage that is needed to pay for overhead and to build a surplus, in addition to knowledge of regional competing continuing education centers' tuitions.

FINANCES AND PROPOSAL WRITING

For efficient operation one needs information from financial records for watching trends and making reports. Furthermore, one should also use records to plan. A plan that is well thought out strengthens the chances for success. A record to show the statistics of the plan is the budget. Working up a budget helps one determine just how much increase in surplus is reasonably within reach. The budget will answer such questions as: What income will be needed to achieve the desired surplus? What fixed expenses will be necessary to support this income? What variable expenses will be incurred? A budget enables one to set a goal and determine what to do in order to reach it.

Of course, one should compare the budget periodically with actual operations. Using contingency planning and responsiveness planning as described in Chapter 3 at least quarterly or every 6 months is also a good idea. Efficient record keeping allows one to make these comparisons. Then, when discrepancies show up, corrective action can be taken before it is too late. The right decisions for the right corrective action will depend upon knowledge of management techniques in buying, marketing, selecting and training personnel, and handling other management problems as described throughout the chapters. The Budget Priorities Draft worksheet in Figure 12.2 can be a useful staff workshop/orientation or mid-spring yearly planning tool for integration of good ideas and developing goals.

Since presenting proposals for many reasons (funding, grants, support) is frequently asked of nonprofit and service organizations the following section may be useful as an outline. A positive attitude and careful attention to detail are two key ingredients for proposal writing.

PARTS OF AN EFFECTIVE PROPOSAL

A well written proposal describing an idea that will help one's division of center improve and/or serve more students can be written with a few guidelines. The first step is making a personal call and/or writing a letter introducing the idea. Most groups or foundations usually only want a two-

---

Please list what you would like, what you see as helping the division, and what you need. This is not a promise of getting all of these, but your lists will help us set priorities. Thank you.

Item and Your Priority for It	Price

Figure 12.2   199_ to 199_ Budget Priorities Draft

to-four page letter introducing an idea as a first submission. This should cover all of the areas of concern which will be addressed at greater length in a later, larger version; other funding sources require both a very brief summary such as this and the proposal or application.

For either length document, the following main points must be covered, at a minimum:

1. Why the project should be undertaken (Why should this organization be funded to do it?)
2. How you will carry it out—what steps it will entail, how they will be organized
3. How it will be managed—what is the staffing, what are their qualifications, how will they be managed, how will the time line be followed to ensure all intended activities take place
4. What are the institution's qualifications for doing it (how the project would fit into what the organization is already doing, showing where other ongoing program activities would make for a better project result by serving as no-cost resources [This is a way of underscoring the parenthetical question in 1, above.])

The presentation of each of these main points is discussed at length in the following subsections.

In addition to these documents, of course, is the budget for this proposal. It must be treated separately because of the many different situations of grantees and grantors. Suffice it to say here that it should indeed be included and should match the document: With a three-page letter a half-page of budget breakout should be enough to give the reader the general categories of expenditure envisioned, the total amount involved, and some sense of whether the estimates seem reasonable; with a longer proposal substantially more detail will probably be required.

Understanding of the Problem.

Why should the project be undertaken? (Why should *this* organization be funded to carry it out?) (We can do it better than anyone else—whatever it is)

Regardless of how much is known about the potential funding source's interest areas, whether through an explicit statement in application guidelines or other means, one must lay some general groundwork for establishing the value of the proposed work. This section also introduces the institution making the proposal. By stating awareness of the context in which one operates, one lets the reader assess one's credibility and also, therefore, the project's. This section is often called "Understanding of the Problem." This means understanding the problem or need and establishes that it needs to be mutually understood. This section further describes the situation that the project would address. Sometimes it's called "Background Statement" or even "Introduction."

At this point one can cite statistics on the number of potential adult students in the city, the number needing reeducation for the work force, and other facts that in concert establish the need for continued provision of the services to be offered (including mention of recent cutbacks in adult public programs). If the project proposed involves any improvements in the way services are provided now, note here the existing problems that the project would resolve (e. g., more accessible locations, more management information systems courses offered, etc.).

It is necessary to describe the institution somewhat in this section, to show what its role has been in services to date. This is the first opportunity to show the reader how important the institution's services have been and thus how important it is that they continue and expand. Note that this is different than the *description* of the organization, which comes later. Some institutions include catalogs and other publications to augment this section.

To conclude this section in a way that effectively leads the reader to the next section describing the project, end on a note that brings together the problem described and the institution's ability to address it now. The point to get across (although the language here is too strong) is: "And thus it is clear that our institution of higher education is ideally situated to address this pressing need." Then the final sentence in this section carries the eager reader into the proposal: "The following section describes exactly how we will carry out this important project."

Description of the Project

How will the project be carried out? What steps will it entail? How will they be organized?

This section establishes in the reader's mind the answer to whether the applicant *should* be allowed to carry out this project. Is the planning sound? Does the project really address the need identified earlier? Has the project been thought through, step by step, and described in enough detail to make it clear that the applicant already has some idea of how to cope with problems that arise? Writing this section actually gives one a chance to do this very planning. While the idea of the project should be clear before one starts writing, the level of detail in this part of the proposal must make it clear to the reader that the applicant can manage the project and that the project makes sense. This is accomplished by the following components: (1) an introductory section that briefly states what the project is and, if appropriate, describes the theory behind the project;(2) the "nuts-and-bolts" section, which shows how this applicant will *do* the project—teach the classes, help the graduates, and so on; (3) identification of the elements of the project, which are left for more detailed descriptions in the Management Plan section; and (4) a list of measurable outcomes you expect to see.

There are two ways to present "how you will *do* the project," and they can be used separately or together. Both require that one present some sort of time line for the project—how long is the time period, what important steps happen at what points in the time line, when can results (such as reports) be expected, and so forth. (Some idea of this time line should go in the introduction to this section as well.) The two techniques are organizing the time line by (1) job function (e. g., staff positions) or by (2) task or activity. The choice depends on the nature of the project.

If one is seeking funds for ongoing operations, with no major events occurring during the time period, a description of staff activities can outline the project. It is important that the work be *quantified* in this section—number of students served by each faculty and staff member per month, number of computer lab hours scheduled or used, number of handouts distributed — whatever the project concerns. This permits the reader to get a "feel" for the project and its impact relative to the size of the problem.

The other technique for describing activities is basically chronological—what will happen first, what will happen next, and so forth. This is useful when there are activities that cannot begin until earlier project steps have been completed, like selection of teaching/testing materials, outreach to seek enrollments, and so forth. Planning like this will help the applicant foresee potential problems if things don't get done in time for other things to start and to develop approaches around them. It also can help one adjust the project plan at a problem stage to modify one's thinking so that these problems will never arise again (or, if they do, one will be prepared for them). This element alone does more than any other part of the proposal to convince the reader that the applicant knows what he or she is talking about and that the funding group can have confidence that the organization funded will spend their money wisely. That is why, even if the "function" method of describing the project is chosen, one should give examples of possible situations that may arise or demonstrate how the different staff functions will interrelate—outreach and faculty member visiting the same employer at the same time, meetings and student counseling occurring in a certain sequence, and the like.

If the project is designed to continue to provide the same services as at present but on an expanded scale, the writer should probably use the chronological approach, to demonstrate how each new capacity required will be put in place before services are needed—materials or lab preparation, space, hiring of staff or faculty, buying materials, upgrading record keeping. Expanding might include adding more enrollment openings, offering senior citizen noncredit classes, adding computers or more facilities for handicapped students, adding a satellite continuing education center in a geographic area previously unserved or distance learning, or opening a second center across town. Establishing the reader's confidence in one's planning ability increases the overall chances of the proposal's being accepted. This section also underscores the organization's value in furthering the funding organization's own objectives by noting past projects that have related activities or that demonstrate similar management requirements as now being proposed. One is thus saying to the reader, "We will do this well because we have a record of doing such things well and will continue to do so in the future, whether with your funding or not." This tells the reader again, that this is an institution of merit and stability (Cavenaugh, 1993).

Management Plan

How will the project be managed? How will the time line be followed?

Givers of grants need to have some sense of how the money is to be spent. A way that this can be presented that will reinforce both the plans for project activities and the detailed budget is in the form of discussion of management controls. This need not be pages of detailed charts and graphs, but should contain the following:

1. A section on staffing, with an organization chart for the project; a brief statement as to how the project fits into the larger organization administratively; and, for each staff position, a description of the duties of the position and, for professional staff, a description of the person who is proposed to fill the position. Résumés should also be appended to the end of this section.

2. A project time line (if appropriate). Here a chart can be helpful, with months across the top and activities down the side, using horizontal lines of appropriate length to indicate when each activity occurs and how long it lasts (see Figure 9.3).

3. An additional section on staffing that describes when different staff positions begin and end (if different from the start and end of the project period) and which are part-time and which full-time. This staffing also can be shown in a chart, with months across the top and positions down the side, with a horizontal line depicting when each position is active. Such charting can also be useful in acknowledging short-term services, such as testing or technology consultants, and can, in conjunction with the project activities time line, give one an idea of which will be the project's busiest months. (At this point one can begin saying, "Oh, that falls too close to the

mid-winter holiday break—let's change it" and making other adjustments in light of how the project fits into the world going on around it.)

Institutional Qualifications

What are the institution's qualifications for doing the project? How would the project fit into what the institution is already doing?

The last section presents a fuller description of the applicant's institution, being less specifically oriented around the particular project being proposed than any other section. Here one might give a brief history of the institution, citing the growth in amount of services provided since it was formed; mentioning significant qualifications of faculty other than those who will be working on this project directly, pointing out their value as resources to the project; describing other areas of work the institution is involved in, whether related to the proposed project or not; and listing some specific past undertakings, including where appropriate the funding agency and the name and phone number of the person there who documented the work. Depending on the institution's size and scope this could be a lengthy list; it need not be exhaustive but should provide several different references that can be contacted independently—three to eight sources on more recent projects are sufficient.

Conclusion

If the application covers all four areas, one will have given the potential supporter a good idea of who one is, what one wants to do, why it should be done, and how one will do it. If one had to compress all of this into a three-page letter (with the all-important budget—the heart of the matter) the only thing one could say after this is, "We await your early reply and are eager to begin this important project. Thank you for your consideration. Sincerely Yours," . . . This format's content and sequence lead to that ending note almost automatically, with or without the final reminder.

In planning to prepare an application for funding, one should allow enough time (working backward from the date it is due to when one should start and when one *must* start) to cover all of the necessary points. Very few funding applications are successful. Most of the failures are rejected for lack of completeness. There is no reason for a proposal to suffer this fate, especially considering the investment required even to prepare the application, in the writer's time away from other duties and responsibilities.

A shorthand way of keeping all of these sections in mind, and remembering that one is competing for money against others so one must make a strong case, is the following:

1. Understanding of the Problem: We know all about this.
2. Description of the Project: We'll do this exactly like successful ones should be done, only better because we know so much about the problem (see 1).
3. Management Plan: We'll plan; we'll manage.
4. Institutional Qualifications: We've been doing this for years (see 1).

Of these summaries, only the comment for No. 3 should be taken as tongue in cheek: It seems to say, "We'll get by," and foundations and agencies certainly don't want to fund that sort of casualness! Instead, it stands as a reminder that there *must* be planning and management control evident in and discussed in one's application.

The process of making decisions as a group with one's staff and faculty and then writing them up (preferably also with a group) with a time line is a useful planning device even if no funding source is involved. Many of the ideas in the scenario section in Chapter 4 would generate income on their own. If there are national, state, or community funding sources that would be interested in the project or part of it, add Steps 1 and 4 for a more complete document. A Proposal Drafting Guide is offered next as a further aid. Both sets of guidelines were developed by persons who have separately been awarded several million dollars for their institutions in education and human services fields. The following is taken from materials developed and shared by Austine Fowler (1982).

PROPOSAL DRAFTING GUIDE

This guide has been prepared to assist in preparing technically valid, fundable proposals.

Answer all questions that apply to the program.

Include all supportive and illustrative materials available.

Anyone who reads the proposal should clearly understand the program purpose, the plan to operate, what objectives are, and what will occur on a day-to-day basis.

A. TITLE

Name of the program.

B. SPONSOR
1. Name of the sponsoring institution, division, or unit.
2. Name and title of responsible person.

3. Brief outline of sponsor's background as to type of institution, division, or unit; include any activities sponsor may now participate in or programs currently operated by sponsor.

C. BACKGROUND AND OVERVIEW (including needs assessment)

Support the request for funds for the program being applied for.

D. CHARACTERISTICS OF POPULATION TO BE SERVED

1. Who is this program expected to reach?
2. Outline eligibility requirements (if any).
3. How many persons will be served during the first year of operation?

E. PROGRAM MISSION (PURPOSE)

What is the purpose of the program?

F. STATEMENT OF THE PROBLEM

Why is the program needed? Be sure to state specific problems and statistics involved.

G. PROGRAM OBJECTIVES (planned activities to fulfill mission)

What are the specific objectives of the program? (What is it you are trying to do?)

H. LOCATION (include map)

1. What are the geographical boundaries of the total area to be served?
2. Indicate the census tracts if appropriate to show age and educational attainment of the area population.
3. Indicate on a map prospective site(s) where program is expected to operate (include addresses when possible).

I. PROGRAM OPERATION

Describe in detail how the program will operate. The following questions will assist you.

How will the program operate?
How is the operation related to the objectives of the program?
How will the program work in relation to staff members?
How will the program work for the population to be served?
How will the program work in relation to the other activities of the sponsor?

J. RESIDENT PARTICIPATION

1. What part do residents of the area play in the operation of your present institution? Students? Faculty or student residents?

2. What part did residents have in developing the plans for this program? If the institution is publicly funded, "what will be the service to the citizen?"
3. Describe other ways in which local residents will be involved (subcommittees, local corporations, etc.).

K. ADMINISTRATION

1. How is this program administered?
   Briefly describe the staff structure and the role of the policy-making and advisory boards (if any) involved in running the program.
2. How will the program be connected to other community programs operated in the same region?
3. Include two organization charts, each of which clearly illustrates the supervisory relationships: (a) of the staff and (b) of the policy-making and advisory or alumni boards.

L. PERSONNEL

1. List each staff position and furnish a detailed job description for each job title (include nonprofessionals, etc.). Be as specific and complete as possible.

   One can follow this sample outline:
   a. Job Title:
   b. Reports to:
   c. Supervises:
   d. Duties and responsibilities:
   e. She/He would work closely with:
   f. Qualifications necessary for the job:

2. Guidelines for Training:
   In preparing proposals for programs to be funded, you should be aware that most proposal readers, in reviewing requests for funding, will consider whether an adequate program of staff training will be conducted during the grant period.

   Therefore, include in proposals a brief outline of plans for an in-service training program. This training program should be designed to:
   a. Improve the ability of staff to relate
   b. Increase the technical skills needed by staff to work at maximum capacity

   As part of the process of developing an in-service training program, an in-service training committee should be established. This committee should be broadly representative of staff, including both professional and nonprofessional employees. Adjunct faculty training in working with adult students, improving teaching skills, and translating courses for distance learning is highly desirable.

In the proposal, training plans for the following three groups should be discussed separately:

a. Office and clerical workers
b. Non-professional employees
c. Professional staff and faculty

Indicate also the resources on which you plan to rely for training (e.g., your own professional staff, consultants, courses, etc.).

Training plans consisting only of routine supervision or weekly staff meetings will not be acceptable. Training time need not necessarily be extended evenly throughout the grant period. If desirable, it may be concentrated within a relatively short period, for example, daily for several weeks. College courses and requirements for taking them can be listed in this section.

M. BUDGET

Use a categorized worksheet in preparing the budget for this program. Special things to look for are the following:

1. In "Personnel," *fringe benefits* should be computed. Break down percentages of fringe components (Social Security, health insurance, etc.).
2. In "Travel," local travel should be based on actual *need*; any out-of-town travel must be justified in a budgetary footnote.
3. In "Space costs and rentals," write in the actual cost and actual square footage wherever possible.
4. In "Consumable supplies":
    a. *Office supplies:* budget on a per-person, per-annum formula based on actual cost.
    b. *Postage.*
    c. *Publications.*
    d. *Nonfederal share* (for federal funding): The amount of nonfederal share to support the proposed program must be at least 20% of the total program cost. This 20% may be in the form of cash (to pay for some specific budget item, i.e., personnel, equipment, consultant services, etc.) or donations of free use of space, equipment, etc. All nonfederal share items must be itemized in the budget and become a part of the total program costs. This is also true for "in-kind contributions" in the private sector.
5. In "Equipment," determine on the basis of anticipated need:
    a. What equipment is owned;
    b. What equipment is rented, the monthly rental, and the feasibility of purchasing
    c. Estimated cost of servicing machines

6. In "Other costs":
   a. *Telephone*: Cost should be estimated on a per-person formula based on actual cost experience.
   b. *Web site costs,* if any can go here.

N. EVALUATION
   1. How will this program be evaluated?
   2. Who will conduct the evaluation?
   3. What type of information will be gathered? Outcomes must be measurable.
   4. How do you expect program evaluation to affect program operation?

O. PLANS FOR NEXT YEAR (usually used for re-funding)
   1. What modifications will be made in the present programming and operation?
   2. What new methods, approaches, or components will be added to help achieve program objectives? (Distance education fits nicely here.)
   3. What old methods, approaches, or components will be discontinued? Why?
   4. What staff changes, if any, will be needed because of program change or modification?

SUMMARY

Most institutions of higher education have particular budget systems and reporting requirements that a continuing education division or unit must fit into, so this chapter focused more on income issues and proposals. However, during times of economic stress the external resources most needed by colleges and universities are financial. Whether budgeting within the institution is usually political or rational, the rational link between budget decisions and the needs of an institution may be stronger in times of financial stress (Hackman, 1991).

Proposals to develop income can be written for support grants or for contract courses and degree programs. The adult education market for credit or noncredit courses is volatile and follows external trends more than the traditional undergraduate enrollment indicators. Therefore, care needs to be given to both market needs assessment and planning for projected income as well as for budgeting and reporting of expenses. Many institutions of higher education have public funding sources and have found less enthusiasm from their public sources (such as the state legislature) for educating adult students. Grants and contract group rates from employers and agencies or foundations concerned with the retraining of the American work force for the Information Age are one answer to this persistent problem. Moving from one age into another is an educational problem, as it was at the turn of the nineteenth century moving into the Industrial Age. Like then, more provision and improvement for continuous, lifelong learning are needed. With creativity and the synergy that can be established by group problem solving, institutions of higher education of all types can play a vital role in educating and reeducating the adult population, leading the way and not obstructing the path into the Information Age.

BIBLIOGRAPHY

Bowen, Howard R. (1977). *Investment in Learning: The Individual and Social Value of American Higher Education.* San Francisco: Jossey-Bass.

Bryce, H. J. (1987). *Financial and Strategic Management for Nonprofit Organizations.* Englewood Cliffs, NJ: Prentice-Hall.

Caruthers, J. Kent, and Melvin D. Orwig (1979). *Budgeting in Higher Education.* Washington, DC: AAHE-ERIC.

Cavenaugh, David N. (1993). Personal Interview. National Association of Community Health Centers. Washington, DC.

Coley, S. M., and C. A. Scheinberg (1990). *Proposal Writing.* Newbury Park, CA: Sage.

Conrad, D. L. (1980). *The Quick Proposal Workbook.* San Francisco: Public Management Institute.

Cross, K. P., and A. M. McCartan (1984). *Adult Learning: State Policies and Institutional Practices.* Washington, DC: ASHE-ERIC Higher Education Reports.

Cross, K. P., and A. Zusman (1979). "The Needs of Nontraditional Learners and the Responses of Nontraditional Programs." In Charles Stalford (Ed.), *An Evaluative Look at Nontraditional Postsecondary Education.* Washington, DC: National Institute of Education.

Cross, K. Patricia (1978). *The Missing Link: Connecting Adult Learners to Learning Resources.* New York: The College Board. ED 163 177.

Cross, K. Patricia, and Hilton, William, J.(1983). *Enhancing the State Role in Lifelong Learning: A Summary Report of a Project.* Denver, CO: Education Commission of the States. ED 235 390.

Floyd, Carol E. (1982). *State Planning, Budgeting, and Accountability: Approaches for Higher Education,* AAHE-ERIC Higher Education Research Report No. 7. Washington, DC: American Association for Higher Education. ED 224 452.

Fowler, Austine (1982). "How to Write a Proposal." Speech given at Administering Day Care and Preschool Seminar, July 14, Trinity College, Washington, DC.

Hackman, Judith, D. (1991). "Power and Centrality in the Allocation of Resources in Colleges and Universities." In Marvin W. Peterson (Ed.) *ASHE Reader on Organization and Governance in Higher Education.* (4th ed.). New York: Simon & Schuster.

Hall, M. (1988). *Getting Funded: A Complete Guide to Proposal Writing* (3rd ed.). Portland, OR: Continuing Education Publications.

Highlights from Council on Foundations Convention (1988). *The Grantsmanship Center Whole Nonprofit Catalog.* Los Angeles: Grantsmanship Center.

Hills, Frederick S., and Thomas A. Mahoney (1978). "University Budgets and Organizational Decision Making." *Administrative Science Quarterly, 19,* 22–44.

Kiritz, N. J. (1980). *Program Planning and Proposal Writing.* Los Angeles: Grantsmanship Center.

Kurland, Norman D., Robert L. Purga, and William J. Hilton (1982). *Financing Adult Learning: Spotlight on the States.* Denver, CO: Education Commission of the States/Lifelong Learning Project. ED 235 387.

Lefferts, R. (1982). *Getting a Grant in the 1980's* (2nd ed.). Englewood Cliffs, NJ: Prentice-Hall.

Levin, Henry M., and Russell N. Rumberger (1983). *The Educational Implications of High Technology.* Palo Alto, CA: Institute for Research on Educational Finance and Governance, Stanford University School of Education. ED 229 879.

Maryland State Board for Community Colleges (1978). Continuing Education Manual. Annapolis, MD: Author. ED 154 899.

McPherson, Michael (1982). "Higher Education: Investment or Expense?" In John J. Hoy and Melvin H. Bernstein (Eds.), *Financing Higher Education: The Public Investment.* Boston: Auburn House.

Metcalfe, W. O. (1973). *Starting and Managing a Small Business.* In Starting and Managing Series, Vol. I. Washington, DC: U.S. Small Business Administration.

Minnesota Higher Education Coordinating Board (1981). *Post Secondary Education for Part-Time and Returning Students.* Minneapolis, MN: Author.

Morris, L. L., and C. T. Fitz-Gibbon (1978). *How to Measure Program Implementation.* Beverly Hills, CA: Sage.

Morris, L. L., and C. T. Fitz-Gibbon (1978). *How to Design a Program Evaluation.* Beverly Hills, CA: Sage.

Pfeffer, Jeffrey, and Gerald R. Salancik (1974). "Organizational Decision Making as a Political Process: The Case of a University Budget." *Administrative Science Quarterly, 19,* 135–151.

Shoemaker, C. J. (1995). *Administration and Management of Programs.* Englewood Cliffs, NJ: Prentice-Hall.

Tringo, J. (1982). "Learning from Failure: Resubmitting Your Rejected Proposal." *Grants Magazine 5,* (1), 18–22.

Vinter, R. D., and R. K. Kish (1984). *Budgeting for Non-profit Organizations.* Atlanta, GA: Georgia State University.

Wacht, R. F. (1984). *Financial Management in Non-profit Organizations.* Atlanta, GA: Georgia State University.

Whitelaw, W. (Ed.) (1982-1983). "The Economy and the College Student." In Mary Ann Rehnke (Ed.), *Liberal Learning and Career Preparation,* Current Issues in Higher Education No. 2. Washington, DC: American Association for Higher Education.

Appendix A

Sample Mission
Statement for
Off-Campus Programs

The University's graduate and professional degree programs are designed to accommodate working professionals who wish to continue their development through part-time study. Such programs constitute a sizable portion of the University's offerings on campus. In addition, the University offers degree programs identical in quality to the on-campus programs at off-campus centers. Noncredit courses, seminars, conferences, and institutes offered by the various academic units of the University also meet the needs of working professionals for continuing education.

The University's location is critical to the character of the institution. This city offers unique intellectual and cultural resources for study and extracurricular activity. The University seeks to relate these rich resources to its academic activities and to include among its offerings curricula and opportunities for research and public service specifically related to the metropolitan, national, and international aspects of the city.

Sample Market Plan
Development Questionnaire

EXCELLENCE UNIVERSITY MARKETING PLAN
OVERVIEW FOR OFF-CAMPUS PROGRAMS

Objective: To strengthen Off-Campus Programs (OCP) financially and intangibly within the University and within the metropolitan area.

1. Executive Summary: Main Goals and Recommendations

A. Review of existing capabilities and programs and determination of effectiveness against goals (objectives).

A goal of 10% improvement or 200 registrations over the 2000 base of Fall registrations is possible.

Most programs are strong, with some further adjustment needed for the Engineering tracks, new tracks, and locations at which they are offered. However, with 1/3 of callers judging a product by the first telephone call, according to the literature, the telemarketing center, as presently configured, will continue to cause a loss.

B. Survey Metropolitan area institutions of higher education to identify significant potential opportunities.

The County and the Suburban Technology Council continue to ask for EU's EE/CS Telecommunications degree and promise extensive support for it at Site A and Site B. It is not offered or does not exist at other centers or universities. The region continues to show strong interest in EU's teacher certification and Education programs as well as in the Arts and Sciences and Information Systems programs.

2. *Objectives and Goals*

   To restate or support the goal of being a leader in the metropolitan area for contracts and graduate education in quantifiable terms, e.g., increase revenue $100,000, decrease costs $50,000, increase enrollment from 12,000 to 18,000, or whatever.

   Three-year goal: Increase to 3,000 registrations per semester, up 1,000 from Fall (2,000). One-year goal: Increase registrations 10%–15% (200 to 300).

3. *Situation Analysis*

   A. **Background. Trying to be specific on the existing/potential for the continuing "base" business EU has.**

   EU OCP has a good history and a good base of credibility with the students.

   B. **Normal Forecast. (Spell out opportunities we expect—or if we can't, refer to "contract with X opportunities to meet goals." Be specific on the amount of business and the areas we hope to get it from.)**

   C. **Opportunities and Threats. (Here we can be less specific and use words like "Area employers communicate a substantial need for: graduate programs in the northern region, MIS programs all over, Security Management. We believe we can position ourselves to meet those needs. Threats are: telemarketing center, change in style for EU service, competition, and economy." (End with a positive statement.)**

   Demographics are such that continuing education should do well in the region. EU has better courses and more of them, and a structure (OCP) for new formats and locations.

   D. **Strengths and Weaknesses. (List SUCCESSES. What we have learned from failures: Be honest about weaknesses—discard, improve, or work around.)**

   Successes:
   1. New Engineering started in Fall at Site A.
   2. Site C program has stopped losing numbers.
   3. Information Systems has transitioned from one school to another.

4. Most Arts and Sciences programs are strong.
5. Teacher certification is strong.
6. Programs with populations that respond to newspaper advertising are doing well, e.g., Arts and Sciences.
7. Government agencies are coming "on-line" with more and more needs for MIS and TCom.

Weaknesses

1. Telemarketing center lost interview calls (20–40) for Engineering new starts.
2. Calls and messages after 5 p.m. are ignored. Perhaps credit programs need more careful attention.

4. *Marketing Strategy*

The marketing mix could continue to be:

a. 55% direct mail
b. 15% ads
c. 10% word of mouth and in-house newsletters
d. 20% associate director's calls and counseling

A. Target Markets. Be specific about general markets—name names. Optimally of actual needs we know about and—with support and luck—we think we could get.

B. Marketing Expenditure. Probably should be keyed to a percent of revenue.

5. *Action Program*

A three-part action program with activities for future students, inquiring students, and present students is needed. It should be noted that all programs are always presented personally to training directors or operations directors in specialized fields.

6. *Controls*

A. Cost Guidelines

B. Actual production of programs:

- Number of students vs. number of students last year vs. budget
- How much money planned for this year vs. plan, registrations, and budget for last year

C. Program's Successes:

- Evaluation—by the customer/student. All programs should use evaluation forms but many do not.
- Evaluation by OCP.

	Future Students	Inquiring Students	Present Students
January	Calls on training directors (ongoing)		
February	Inquiry calls Counseling (ongoing)		
March	VIP letters regarding briefings, also to association newsletters	Schedule mailout	Schedule mailout
April	Briefing ads	Briefing flyers mailout	
May	Registration	Registration	Registration
June	VIP letters regarding briefings, also to association newsletters Ads	Briefing flyer mailout Schedule mailout	Schedule mailout
July	Briefing		
August	Briefing		
September	Registration	Registration	Registration
October	VIP letters regarding briefings, also to association newsletters	Briefing flyer mailout	
November	Briefing ads	Schedule mailout	Schedule mailout
December	Registration	Registration	Registration

Opportunity Identification

Two charts are suggested: one generic, plotting the gross market potential (from the summary by subject and degree program; e.g., the number of teachers in an area is 7%–8% of the population) by year; and one plotting specific companies and their potential by year.

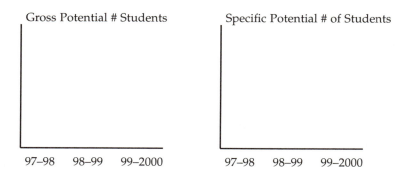

Appendix C

Sample External and Internal Planning: Unit Plans

UNIT PLAN FOR FISCAL YEAR ____

Administration or Campus	Department or Unit	Function	Unit Code
Central Administration			
[X]	Noncredit	Instructional	
☐			
☐			
☐			

Key Result Areas

Unit Name _____

List below the kinds of work that demand major portions of the time of the unit's personnel. (Please use gerunds—verbal nouns in the "ing" form.)

1. Assessing needs
2. Planning
3. Organizing
4. Developing cooperative relationships
5. Marketing/Promoting
6. Implementing
7. Evaluating
8. Reporting
9. Projecting
10. Budgeting

Long-Range Forecasts and Implications Relevant to Goals, Objectives, and Activities of Unit during FY 19 ___–___

UNIT_____—Internal

#	Forecasts Relevant to Unit	#	Implications of Forecasts for Work of Unit
			Forecasts External and Internal to Unit
1a	Computing Services support to the Unit will increase moderately.	1b	There will be a continued need to share information with Computing Services staff regarding the needs, functions, and responsibilities of this Unit.
2a	There will be more diverse programming with less program and support staff to meet the needs of the population.	2b	1. Increased enrollments per staff member will require a reassessment of the remaining staff to meet subsequent increased workload factors. 2. There will be a need for the remaining Programming staff not only to absorb courses that are cost-effective and popular from former Program Directors, but also to develop new markets. 3. *An aggressive marketing/ promotion plan will need to continue to develop and be implemented and evaluated* to create greater business and community awareness of offerings.
3a	*Effective management and budget methods will continue to be important to the businesslike management of the Unit.**	3b	Modifications of Computing Services programs will need to be undertaken to assist in the development of more cost-effective programming and marketing techniques. Additionally, financial models simulating various scenarios will become more frequent and yield better reports. There will be an increase in the number and variety of internal reports required.

*Italics are for that year's emphasis

Continued

Long-Range Forecasts and Implications—Internal/*Continued*

#	Forecasts Relevant to Unit	#	Implications of Forecasts for Work of Unit
	Forecasts External and Internal to Unit		
4a	Increase in traffic and mass transit costs will adversely affect the ability of the community to respond to educational offerings.	4b	1. There will be a need for alternative methods for registering students particularly the direct registration of students at many locations. There will also need to be an increase in the number of sites at a variety of locations used for programming. 2. There will be a need for computers, telephone hookups, and other appropriate equipment to accommodate off-campus registration.
5a	*As a result of the stabilizing function Community Services will contribute to the College, staff morale will rise and the workload will return to acceptable limits.*	5b	1. Staff communication training, human relations exercises, and continued opportunities for inter-staff input in decision making will need to be emphasized. 2. Staff grades and compensation must be examined to reflect more adequately the nature of responsibilities and expertise needed within the Unit.
6a	The College credit programs will increase and this will result in less classroom space for non-credit courses on the three campuses.	6b	1. The Unit will need flexible scheduling opportunities to use campus classrooms at peak as well as non-peak hours. The Unit will have to continue to plan more effective use of leased extension sites. 2. There will be a need to continue efforts to help other units of the College recognize the purpose, functions and activities of the Unit.
7a	There will be more use of office information technology.	7b	1. Time- and effort-saving techniques will need to be continued. Staff training and retraining will become more important. *It will become even more important to encourage a positive office environment.* 2. *As office information technology increases, steps should be taken to enhance its positive integration into the office environment.*

Continued

Long-Range Forecasts and Implications—Internal/*Continued*

#	Forecasts Relevant to Unit	#	Implications of Forecasts for Work of Unit
		Forecasts External and Internal to Unit	
8a	*Bridges with credit departments will become more and more important and will build on the current foundation.*	8b	1. The Unit must continue to exchange information with the credit faculty and the administration. 2. Efforts should be made to develop course offerings and activities with credit departments.
9a	Efforts to promote the three campuses and noncredit programs as a single institution will continue.	9b	1. The Unit must continue to exchange information with the credit faculty and the administration. Use of credit faculty where appropriate in noncredit offerings should be continued. 2. Staff knowledge of the credit programs and services will need to be emphasized. 3. Constant efforts to inform the other College units of this Unit's purpose and activities will need to be continued.
10a	Tuition and fees to the public will increase.	10b	The Unit must offer high-level (quality), cost-effective instruction to the public.
11a	There will be an increase in instructional services at currently leased sites.	11b	Increased security and maintenance measures will need to be undertaken.
12a	There will be a continuing need for College-wide staff development activities.	12b	The Unit should continue to provide College-wide staff development training.
13a	There will be a continuing need for Unit-wide staff and faculty development activities.	13b	The Unit should provide regular and appropriate training and learning opportunities for both staff and faculty.

Long-Range Forecasts and Implications Relevant to Goals, Objectives, and Activities of Unit during FY 19 ___–___

UNIT_____—External

#	Forecasts Relevant to Unit	#	Implications of Forecasts for Work of Unit
	Forecasts External and Internal to Unit		
1a	The potential student population will be more diverse and will embrace a broad expanse of age, race, ethnic origins, languages, and entry-level skills.	1b	1. The Unit must assess the needs of its changing population, identify available resources, and implement, where feasible, offerings to meet those needs. 2. The Unit must maintain a comprehensive program to attract students and aid them in fulfilling their educational needs. 3. The Unit must continue to examine and evaluate program, services, and staff and revise where necessary to reflect the needs of the student population. 4. The Unit should continue to develop a comprehensive public relations program.
2a	Enrollment of senior citizens will increase as the population ages.	2b	1. Tuition dollars per enrollment may go down, having a particularly significant effect on revenues for Community Services. 2. State laws will need to be examined to ensure that institutions are not being adversely impacted financially by providing needed services to senior citizens. 3. Local government support for enrollment of senior citizens may need to be provided to the College's noncredit program as it is to the Adult Education program of the public schools, since tuition cannot be charged to these persons.
3a	County population will remain relatively affluent, well educated, and/or interested in education.	3b	1. The Unit should continue to assess the educational needs of the County population. 2. The Unit should continue to utilize the talents and expertise of members of the community to enhance its noncredit educational program.

Continued

Long-Range Forecasts and Implications—External/*Continued*

#	Forecasts Relevant to Unit	#	Implications of Forecasts for Work of Unit
	Forecasts External and Internal to Unit		
4a	The population of the County will continue to be a mobile population.	4b	1. A program of education and reeducation of County residents about the Unit's programs and services should be continued. 2. The Unit's marketing plan needs to be developed and implemented in concert with the College's overall plan.
5a	An increased demand for service and technical occupations is anticipated in the County, with a resulting increase in job-related education at the College.	5b	1. The Unit must establish additional relationships with employers in surrounding industries and businesses concerning their education and training needs for their personnel. It must adapt programs and courses to meet these educational needs. Increased emphasis will be given to on-site instruction. 2. Job-related education will become an increasing part of the College's role including: a. Entry-level training b. Retraining c. Cross-training d. Upgrading e. Job transition 3. The Unit needs to broaden the base of instructional programs and the expertise of faculty members so that it can respond to changing student demands for curricula.
6a	The cost of transportation will have an increased impact on the educational programs.	6b	1. Alternative scheduling and planning to consume less time and energy will need to be developed. 2. Accessibility to the Unit's instructional sites for potential students will increase in some instances as METRO and County Ride-On become available in additional parts of the County.

Continued

Long-Range Forecasts and Implications—External/*Continued*

#	Forecasts Relevant to Unit	#	Implications of Forecasts for Work of Unit
			Forecasts External and Internal to Unit
7a	More people will come to the College for nondegree programs, and career mobility will become increasingly important. Students will place more emphasis on course content as opposed to degree preparation as reasons for enrolling in programs.	7b	1. The Unit must continue to develop offerings and course schedules that meet the needs of part-time students. 2. The Unit should investigate alternative methods of instructional delivery, e.g., cable TV. 3. The College needs to do a better job of convincing government officials of the value of noncredit educational training.
8a	There will be increased competition among organizations for noncredit enrollments.	8b	1. The College Office of Community Services should assume a leadership role in the coordination of County noncredit/continuing education courses and programs. 2. The County may scrutinize more carefully the College's noncredit offerings. 3. Given anticipated budget restraints affecting all levels of government, it can be anticipated that these courses and programs will need to become more self-funding. 4. The Unit needs to utilize the results of the CAP study with respect to the demand for noncredit courses and programs and develop strategies to deliver these courses and programs at prices acceptable to the market but adequate to cover costs.
9a	Computer technology, interest in computer technology, and application of computers in the work environment will continue to develop rapidly.	9b	1. More County residents will own a computer and will desire to take noncredit courses to aid them in understanding and using their computers. 2. Unit personnel must become increasingly sophisticated in the use of computers.

Continued

Long-Range Forecasts and Implications—External/*Continued*

#	Forecasts Relevant to Unit	#	Implications of Forecasts for Work of Unit

Forecasts External and Internal to Unit

#	Forecasts Relevant to Unit	#	Implications of Forecasts for Work of Unit
10a	Improved communications technology (ISDN, video, cable TV, telephone) will change instructional needs and methods and some noninstructional processes at the College.	10b	1. Technological advances in instructional processes will facilitate improvements in instructional delivery systems. 2. More efficient communication processes should reduce the need for meetings and should reduce travel between campuses. 3. Training of personnel in the use of communication technology is essential.
11a	Office technology will continue to develop and will change the way in which office processes are conducted.	11b	1. More staff with technological expertise will be needed. 2. Training for existing personnel is critical. 3. Jobs will need to be reviewed in terms of adequate compensation. 4. Short- and long-term planning for office technology is critical. 5. The Unit's continuing programs should assist community organizations and students to understand and utilize technology effectively. 6. Linking of word processing and data processing will be essential to efficient use of technological resources.
12a	Cooperation between the College and the County Public Schools will become increasingly important if County educational needs are to be met in the most efficient way possible.	12b	1. The College should lobby the State Legislature to permit some community college noncredit courses to count for credentialing of public school teachers. 2. Research data should be shared between the College and the County Public Schools to aid in understanding the nature and needs of students. 3. Outreach activities to the high schools should be well planned, well implemented, and coordinated.

Long-Range Forecasts and Implications Relevant to Goals, Objectives, and Activities of Unit during FY 19 ___–___

UNIT_____—Internal

#	Forecasts Relevant to Unit	#	Implications of Forecasts for Work of Unit
	Forecasts External and Internal to Unit		
1a	The College telephone system will not improve in efficiency or effectiveness.	1b	1. There will be a need for continual training of staff to deal with inquiries. 2. Possibly, budget for telephone answering devices.
2a	Computing Services support to the Unit will increase moderately.	2b	There will be a need for reeducation of Computing Services staff regarding both the functions and responsibilities of this Unit.
3a	There will be more diverse programming with less Programming and Support staff to meet the needs of the population.	3b	1. Increased enrollments per staff member will require a reassessment of the remaining staff to meet subsequent increased work load factors. 2. There will be a need for the remaining Programming staff not only to absorb courses that are cost-effective and popular from terminated Program Directors, but also to develop new markets. 3. An aggressive marketing/promotion plan will need to be developed and implemented to create greater business and community awareness of Community Services offerings.
4a	Effective management and budget constraints will continue to be of concern as the unit strives to reestablish the reserve fund to an acceptable level.	4b	Modifications of Computing Services programs will need to be undertaken to assist in the development of more cost-effective programming and marketing techniques. Additionally, financial models simulating various scenarios will become more frequent and yield better reports. There will be an increase in the number and variety of internal reports required.

Continued

Long-Range Forecasts and Implications—External/*Continued*

#	Forecasts Relevant to Unit	#	Implications of Forecasts for Work of Unit
	Forecasts External and Internal to Unit		
5a	Increase in traffic and mass transit costs will adversely affect the ability of the community to respond to educational offerings.	5b	1. There will be a need for alternative methods for registering students, particularly the direct registration of students at many locations. There will also need to be an increase in the number of sites at a variety of locations used for programming. 2. There will be a need for CRT terminals, telephone hookups, and other appropriate equipment to accommodate off-campus registration.
6a	Interstaff stress due to staff reduction and increased workload, some physical office crowdedness, and associated pressures will result from the expanded daytime and weekend programming efforts.	6b	1. Staff communication training, human relations exercises, and continued opportunities for interstaff input in decision making will need to be emphasized.
7a	The College credit programs will increase and this will result in less classroom space for non-credit courses on the three campuses. Perhaps credit outreach programs should be administered by the unit.	7b	1. The Unit will need flexible scheduling opportunities to use campus classrooms at peak as well as nonpeak hours. The Unit will have to continue to plan more effective use of leased extension sites. 2. There will be a need to continue efforts to help other units of the College recognize the purpose, functions, and activities of the Unit.
		8b	Time- and effort-saving techniques will need to be continued. Staff training and retraining will become more important.
8a	There will be more use of information technology equipment internally.		
		9b	The Unit must continue to exchange information with the credit faculty and the administration. Use of credit faculty where appropriate in noncredit offerings should be continued.
9a	Competition for funding of FTEs by both the Unit and the credit departments may cause		

Continued

Long-Range Forecasts and Implications—External/*Continued*

#	Forecasts Relevant to Unit	#	Implications of Forecasts for Work of Unit
			Forecasts External and Internal to Unit
10a	Efforts to promote the three campuses and Community Services as a single institution will continue.	10b	1. The Unit must continue to exchange information with the credit faculty and the administration. Use of credit faculty where appropriate in noncredit offerings should be continued. 2. Staff knowledge of the credit programs and services will need to be emphasized. 3. Efforts to constantly inform the other College units of this Unit's purpose and activities will need to be continued.
11a	Tuition and fees to the public will increase.	11b	The Unit must offer high-level (quality), cost-effective instruction to the public.
12a	There will be an increase in instructional services at currently leased sites.	12b	Increased security and maintenance measures will need to be undertaken.

Goals of Unit (Continuing, Not Time-Limited)

Include both management goals and technical goals.

UNIT_____

1. To operate responsively and cost-effectively to provide the described services without tax support.
2. To determine desired direction of the Unit by identifying the non-credit needs of the community.
3. To evaluate the implications of the high school student educational needs assessment.
4. To continue to develop vocational/technical programs to meet the needs of the business community.
5. To implement, as appropriate, the recommendations of the study of evening and weekend student characteristics and interests.
6. To continue a course pricing system that is fair, equitable, and cost-effective.
7. To continue the competency of staff and faculty to design and conduct courses and informational programming in support of the College cable TV channels and distance learning.
8. To continue to recruit faculty, students, and staff in keeping with the affirmative action goals of the College.
9. To develop and implement a marketing/promotion plan to increase business and community awareness of the Unit's courses and services.
10. To provide, in accordance with the recommendations of the high school/college connection program, joint programs for high school and College faculty on topics of interest.
11. To establish noncredit courses for business organizations on topics pertaining to new and emerging technologies and on other subjects of interest.
12. To implement changes to noncredit programs based upon the findings of the evaluation of the programs.
13. To expand the number of hours of course programming on cable TV.
14. To work with the Office of Economic Development to analyze and evaluate the Unit's ability to meet the educational needs of prospective employers moving to the County.
15. To implement effective methods of publicizing high technology and high technology–related noncredit offerings to businesses and industries and to the community.
16. To explore the feasibility of conducting follow-up studies of non-credit students to identify the career implications of enrollment in noncredit courses.

Current Status of Unit

UNIT_____

1. Strengths and Areas Requiring Improvement. List both strengths and areas requiring improvement of the Unit and of its programs/activities in terms that are relevant to its ability to meet needs of its service population(s).

Strengths (Short phrases rather than sentences are preferred.)

a. Competent and knowledgeable programming and support staff.
b. Sophisticated data collection systems and information management system.
c. Special function unit.
d. Supportive institutional environment.
e. Accessible, adult-oriented off-campus educational facilities.
f. Attractive and effective publications.
g. Highly flexible in response to business, organizational, and community needs.

Areas Requiring Improvement (Short phrases rather than sentences are preferred.)

a. Increased access to office and classroom space as well as instructional equipment on College campuses.
b. System of internal and external information reporting.
c. Profitability of various noncredit activities and programs.
d. Upward mobility potential for programming and support staff.
e. Computerized support system.
f. Long- and short-term financial planning models.
g. Marketing and promotion of courses and services.
h. Financial condition.
i. Staff morale.

2. Organization and Staffing. Describe the organization of the Unit (attach an organization chart); indicate the number of authorized positions by classification and whether those positions are filled, e.g., "3 full-time faculty members, 1 part-time member; 1 full-time clerk-typist—vacant."

The Office is headed by a Provost who reports to the Academic Vice President. The Unit has an authorized staffing level of 20.0 positions but uses temporary and part-time staff for several office and site support functions, particularly during peak periods. The Unit is organized into functions concerned respectively with programming and support services. The programming is supervised by the Provost and includes all program planning staff assigned to two campuses and one off-campus site and the support staff at those locations. Support services include internal accounting, word processing, and record keeping. These functions include support of the programming functions through word-processing services, certificate issuance, and maintenance concerns of the sites, as well as fiscal and budgeting activities. Support services staff is located at the North Campus.

Continued

Current Status of Unit/*Continued*

3. Facilities and Equipment. Briefly describe the physical facilities and major equipment items used by the Unit and indicate whether they are adequate for supporting the programs/activities of the Unit; e.g., number of sq. ft., number of work stations, sq. ft. per employee, audiovisual equipment, etc.

The facilities and equipment to support the Unit's programs are dispersed and varied. They include segments of space on two campuses, and at two leased sites. Occasional use is made of various institutional settings to conduct specific courses (i.e., public schools, churches, etc.). Since the latter sites are not under College control, they will not be addressed. However, it is important to point out that many of these sites are not effective for course programming, i.e., adult environment.

4. Concerns and Issues. List specific concerns, areas that require strengthening, and issues that must receive attention in the future in order to better meet the needs of those being served.

- Extension Centers A, B and C each must have a complete individual plan like this.
- Distance Education issues, costs and projections for each component need to be addressed.

Objectives, Performance Standards, and Associated Activities

UNIT_____

Objective # ___ / Related Goal # ___

Activities/Work Steps	Person Responsible*	Major Resource Needs

*If a manager from any other unit is responsible for any work steps, that manager must be so informed and asked to include an appropriate objective in his/her plan.

Performance Standards (What are the criteria of acceptable performance on the objective?)

Continue any section on extra pages if necessary.

Appendix D

Sample Continuing Education Department Annual Report

EXCELLENCE UNIVERSITY'S YEAR IN REVIEW (EXCERPTS)*

Evening Programs (EP) is the administrative unit responsible for marketing and supporting the University's seventeen graduate degree programs for adult students at eleven off-campus locations. While the University's expectations for EP remain in chronic flux, basic goals include: marketing graduate programs, providing administrative support services for off-campus programs and locations, identifying opportunities for new off-campus programs (open enrollment or under contract), proposing new sites to meet the needs and interests of adult students, and generating sizable surplus revenue for the University. EP has successfully fulfilled these goals in this academic year.

Strengths and Accomplishments

Student Recruitment
Operating within a geographic region that places high value on continuing education, EP has been able to recruit and retain qualified students at off-campus sites by administering a broad range of innovative programs. These

*Names have been changed to protect the privacy of the writer and the institution involved.

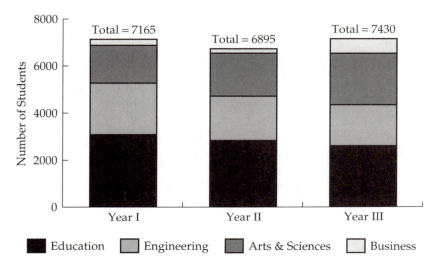

FIGURE D.1   **Excellence University's Off-Campus Enrollments by School**

programs offer excellence in classroom instruction, responsive adult student services, and coursework leading to highly valued EU graduate degrees. (See figure D.1.)

Budget Performance
The Division this year has reversed the precipitous downward trend in off-campus enrollment and increased the number of part-time, adult student enrollments by 7%. By increasing enrollment, hence tuition revenue, and by containing expenses, EP expects to meet gross revenue and net income targets for the year. (A full budget report will be prepared after the close of the fiscal year.) (See figures D.2 and D.3.)

Inter-University Relations
EP has restored positive relations with the University's academic units based upon a shared commitment to academic excellence in off-campus programming, administrative efficiency, fiscal responsibility, responsive student services, and decency in institutional relations.

EP Administration
The Evening Programs Division is blessed with a dedicated staff and is committed to strengthening its outreach to the community; serving new markets; providing rapid, solution-oriented responses to the needs of faculty

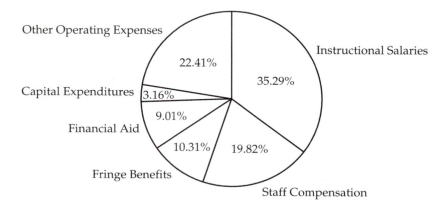

FIGURE D.2   Excellence University's Expenditures

and students; and becoming more professional in its administrative structure and function.

Weaknesses and Challenges

Increased Competition and Tuition Costs

There is growing competition in the area market for adult, part-time graduate education. By and large, EU cannot compete successfully for the adult students with limited financial resources and without tuition support from employers. Regardless of EU's reputation for academic excellence and the attractiveness of its off-campus programs, the University will face serious difficulties retaining or increasing its share of the continuing education market. EU's tuition costs prohibit access for students with limited resources or for whom tuition remission benefits from employers are increasingly restricted, capped, or taxed as income. Moreover, EU is not well positioned to compete for adults who want to enroll for only one or, at most, a few courses and when comparing per course tuition charges.

However, EU can successfully compete for a sizable share of the market of adults who have relatively high incomes or access to employee tuition remission benefits and who intend to earn a degree. For such students the academic reputation of the degree-granting institution is often decisive in the selection process. In this regard, EU has real and perceived advantages in attracting highly qualified students.

Institutional Ambivalence

One of the most common concerns in higher education administration in recent years has been defining the appropriate role of continuing education.

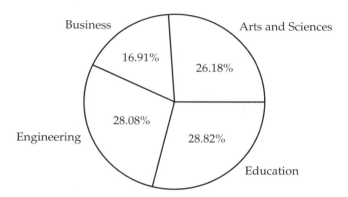

FIGURE D.3   Excellence University's Instructional Expenditures by School

Most U.S. colleges and universities acknowledge the importance of lifelong learning and they recognize that there is a vast and lucrative, albeit competitive, market for part-time degree programs for working adults with neither time nor inclination to attend classes on a downtown campus or on a full-time basis. What is less clear is the manner in which universities should structure opportunities for "off campus" continuing education to ensure that programs are academically credible and financially profitable.

Fundamental questions often remain unaddressed:

- Should continuing education be a "transparent" service unit integrated into the larger university so that prospective students are presented with a seamless portfolio of graduate programs distinguished only by their classroom site? Or should continuing education be a separate, clearly identifiable academic unit that purposefully differentiates "on" and "off" campus programs?

- Should the principal responsibility of continuing education be to extend, preserve, and promote the academic reputation of the university regardless of the location where classes are held? Or should maximum profitability be the primary mission of continuing education?
  Do the principles of good practice in teaching apply to teaching students of any age and at any place? Or is there a pedagogy specific to adult education?

- Should credit and noncredit programs be administratively separate, as they respond to different markets and require different recruitment and support? Or is the distinction between credit and noncredit merely an administrative convenience inviting redundant marketing efforts for adults interested in continuing education and training?

- Should continuing education be a part of an office of external affairs? Or, should it report to an office of academic affairs?

- More basically, is the university a place with a necessary distinction between the "mother campus" and its remote outposts? Or is the university a resource that distributes programs to locations and times that best match the needs and interests of qualified students?

Notwithstanding some notable exceptions around the country, to the extent that universities address these issues, the answers are typically ambivalent, ambiguous, or indifferent.

The _____ academic year has been turbulent for EP, filled with rapid changes in leadership, reporting lines, and expectations. Perhaps change is endemic to continuing education units. A review of Annual Reports from most recent years would, no doubt, refer to efforts at reorganization. Also, the claim of constant flux is not unique to universities, nor within universities is change unique to continuing education. But, no matter how familiar the claim may be, this year's experience with institutional turbulence surrounding continuing education at EU has been unusually distracting. Under these recent circumstances, the Division of Evening Programs takes special pride in its many significant accomplishments this year, summarized in the report that follows.

TECHNICAL CAPACITY

Beginning summer 19__, new emphasis was placed on technical improvements in EP offices. With help from a contracted agency, EP offices installed in a local area network (LAN) modeled after VPTCOMP's new LAN. The new LAN runs approximately fifty PCs including five Macs for administrative and marketing functions. The offices have six shared LAN printers, one label printer, a variety of application software, a dial-in PC with remote control software, and University backbone and World Wide Web connectivity, including interoffice and Internet electronic mail.

After installation of the LAN the prospect database was cleaned, reorganized, and reinvented into a new "system" to take inquiries for all programs offered through EP. This new database was designed for more ergonomic data entry including automatic fill for city and state fields based on zip codes and automatic retrieval of existing records. Information Session dates and locations for each program "pop up" on-screen so that the Public Relations Representative can inform the potential student of the event while the student is on the phone. A menu drives all reports for labels, callback reports, Information Sessions, marketing statistics, and personalized letters.

FACULTY AND STUDENT SERVICES

Academic Staffing

Approximately 415 courses across 21 departments were held this year at off-campus sites. This load was carried by nearly 200 adjunct faculty members. (See Figure D.4.)

EP's academic staffing office provides support to adjunct faculty teaching in EU's off-campus degree programs. Primary duties include collecting and sorting data from the various teaching departments, generating Employee Hire Forms and appointment confirmation letters, and creating necessary reports for the Division's senior education associates. This office also acts as an immediate contact for faculty with any administrative concerns. All of these processes were improved this spring through creation of a new database system that allows for greater flexibility in data collection and report generation.

Student Services

The office of Student Services had many successes during the year, processing registrations, resolving problems in a timely manner, establishing excel-

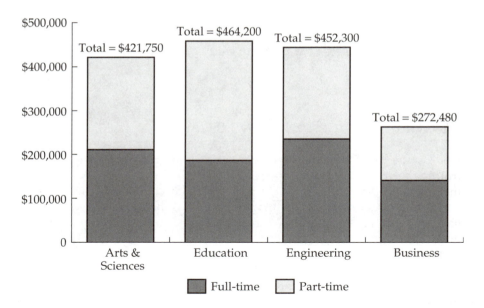

FIGURE D.4 **Excellence University's Instructional Salary Expenditures by School, Full-Time vs. Part-Time**

lent working relationships throughout the entire university community, and, in general, providing a level of service second to none at the University.

Demand for Degrees

Students overwhelmingly demand career fields (89%) over liberal arts fields (11%). Of the former the most popular are business (19%), computers (16%), public affairs (11%), and education (10%). As shown in the earlier program listing, EU meets these demands.

Scheduling Preferences

Graduate students in the University's metropolitan market show little preference for time of year–over 40% expressed a willingness to study during each month except during the summer. The preferred time of day is weekday evenings (60%), with the largest aggregate preferring classes that start between 6:00 and 7:00 p.m. (42%). Classes that meet one to two times per week for 2–3 hours each session are the most popular. These preferences match EU's current scheduling patterns (typically, a class that meets once per week from 6:00–8:30 p.m. for 14 weeks).

Location Preferences

Students surveyed generally prefer to study in an area that is 40 minutes or less from home.

CONTRACT PROGRAMS OR AGREEMENTS

The Division of Evening Programs administered nine contract programs during the year and made proposals for four more to begin in the next academic year. This year's contract programs represent a significant increase based to a large extent on company and government agency educational needs for employees in specified fields. Contract programs are delineated on a cohort basis, usually at the customer site, to a specified number of employee students. All contracts are graduate credit programs and students are encouraged to participate in the degree, if eligible, even though the contract may be for a limited number of courses. Students must meet the degree admission requirements in order to participate as degree candidates. Certificates are awarded for successful completion of most contract programs.

PROMOTIONS

Direct Mail, Advertising, Publications

The Division set its advertising and promotions efforts on a new course this year by formulating a thorough promotions plan to serve as a blueprint for all major promotional efforts. The plan described the nature and scope of each major effort and detailed the procedures to be followed in developing, producing, and evaluating those efforts. As a result, the Division can now present numerical analyses of its direct mail and advertising campaigns and can provide plans for future development and improvement.

The foundation of these plans and analyses is a vastly improved, customized database of prospective students. This database system has given the Division an ability to prevent most data entry errors; automate searches and reports; collect and examine a wide assortment of data about students, programs, and promotional efforts; and create fully personalized mailings to hundreds of people in minutes. Further applications are still being explored.

These two developments have been the dominant factors driving this year's surge of new inquiries and have provided the Division an opportunity to not only judge the success of its promotions efforts, but also to make format revisions, process improvements, and strategic marketing decisions on the basis of empirical data.

Inquiries

During the year the Division received 9,176 new inquiries about off-campus graduate programs, or 54% of the current total of 16,873 prospective students. These include 4,595 direct response inquiries (i.e., requests pertaining to a particular program and/or event) plus an additional 2,168 inquiries attributed to other promotions such as radio advertisements, long-term magazine advertisements, brochures, and flyers. This figure represents 73.7% of all inquiries made during the fiscal year to date.

Program Brochures

During the academic year four brochures were significantly revised, and a fifth remains in production The goal of the Division has been to develop brochures that are more attractive and more sensibly organized without raising the cost of production. To meet these objectives, a standardized outline was created so that all brochures contained roughly the same information, in the same order. Brochures were produced in this fashion for five programs.

Appendix E

Private University: On-Campus and Off-Campus School of Engineering Report (Excerpts)*

In an era of burgeoning technology and increasing international economic competition, many universities are reexamining the principles that guided their engineering education programs for decades. In 199_ a council established by the American Society for Engineering Education produced "Engineering Education for a Changing World," a report that addressed the role of engineering in our society and how education programs should grow to reflect the technology-dependent world in which we live.

The report concluded that engineering education should be "relevant, attractive, and connected" for students to be adequately prepared for the challenges of the twenty-first century. It cited sixteen recommendations for action, among them identifying individual missions for engineering schools, reshaping the curriculum, sharing research/resources, and broadening educational responsibility to include outreach to elementary schools.

STATUS OF THE SCHOOL

In reviewing the report's action items and comparing them with the Engineering School's current efforts, it was noted that the school is well ahead in most areas to educate students for fulfilling careers in engineering. The School has not achieved all of its goals, by any means, but the hard work of faculty, students, staff, alumni, and friends has begun to reap rewards. In

*Names have been changed to protect the privacy of the writer and the institution.

this message a recurrent theme seemed to be one of intense activity of many fronts, coupled with a year of satisfying results. Noteworthy accomplishments of the past year:

- New student programs
- New initiatives in departments
- The fund campaign for the Engineering School begins . . .

(See Figure E.1 for funding sources for the total budget.)

BUILDING THE ROAD TO THE 21ST CENTURY

It's called the "Private University Initiative." What it means to the University is an important campaign to raise $800 million over the next 5 years. What it means to the Engineering School is a giant step into the twenty-first century.

The School's goal is to raise $50 million during the campaign, which officially began September 1. Given the theme "Designing for Technological Leadership," the campaign will oversee improvements and investments to benefit students, faculty, and the entire engineering community for years to come. The money raised through the engineering campaign will fund five priorities:

- Hiring new faculty and creating more endowed chairs
- Adding and modernizing classrooms, laboratories, and offices
- Providing scholarships and fellowships for graduate students and increased research opportunities for undergraduates
- Supporting special academic programs
- Funding endeavors into the twenty-first century . . .

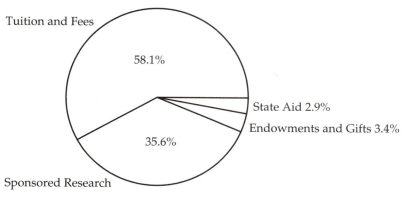

FIGURE E.1   Total Budget: Sources of Funds

Appendix F

State University Annual Report (Excerpts)*

Teamwork was the State University watchword for the Fiscal Year. New collaborative programs, adoption of a systemwide academic calendar, and the emergence of a shared agenda of service to our students are three accomplishments of which we are particularly proud. This report details many more achievements that reflect our strength as a system. . . .

Throughout institutions of higher education today there is a great deal of discussion about the "university of the future." At State University our discussions about the university of the future have centered around three major goals: addressing rapidly changing needs for education when and where students need it, improving access to an increasingly diverse student body, and increasing effectiveness and efficiency. . . .

As a student at commencement said,

Education as I know it . . . is coupled with the pressure of earning a living and tending to our families. For us, finding quiet time and a place to study is a challenge. Getting to class after a long, hard day is an even bigger challenge. Many of us who are in our 30s and 40s have written our own tuition checks, and when we purchased our class rings we used our own credit cards—not our parents'. For those reasons, today's commencement holds a special meaning for each one of us.

*Names have been changed to protect the privacy of the writer and the institution involved.

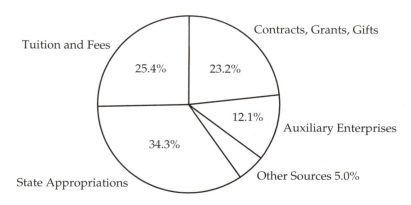

FIGURE F.1   State University's Annual Financial Report—Revenues

HARNESSING TECHNOLOGY TO FACILITATE LEARNING

The popularity of distance learning at State University attests to its value to students. In the past 5 years the percentage of State U. students in distance education courses has increased from 22.9% to 29.8%. There were 6,300 students enrolled in courses at a distance during the last Fiscal Year.

REVENUES

The sources of revenues for the last Fiscal Year are diagrammed in Figure F.1.

Appendix G

Distance Education Organizations—Worldwide

Distance education facilities around the world demonstrate great variability in terms of shape, size, and relationships with government and business. They use a great many interesting methods to deliver educational materials and have different relationships with the learners themselves. The following categories are listed in this appendix:

- Distance education departments within conventional institutions
- Open and distance learning institutions
- Virtual campuses
- Distance learning networks

(The entries in the listings were accessed through http://ccism.pc.athabascau.ca in 1997.)

DISTANCE EDUCATION DEPARTMENTS WITHIN CONVENTIONAL INSTITUTIONS

Assiniboine College: Distance Education & Extension: Assiniboine offers distance education–related services through the DENIM Centre, including curriculum design, professional development, program planning expertise, and access to technology.

Centre for Distance Education: The centre is headquartered at Simon Fraser University. Internationally, under the auspices of a number of agencies—the Canadian International Development Agency, The Commonwealth of Learning, CREAD (a pan-American consortium network for distance education with the Inter-American Organization for Higher Education)—the Centre for Distance as a whole or its staff individually have participated in several international outreach projects, most of which are of an ongoing nature.

University of Waterloo Distance and Continuing Education: Through its extensive distance education offerings, UW extends access to degree studies to students from coast to coast. A provider of distance education for over 27 years, the University of Waterloo runs one of the largest distance education operations in North America. Students are able to complete degree programs in Arts, Science, and Environmental Studies entirely through distance study. Over 250 courses in fifty disciplines are offered via print, audio, and video. Many professional organizations utilize UWís distance courses in their training programs.

Acadia's Continuing Education Home Page

Mohawk College: Mohawk College's Faculty of Continuing Education delivers credit and general interest courses to 62,000 adults annually and currently offers seventy-seven credit and professional development courses in a distance education (home study) format.

Distance Education at Algonquin College: Six complete, approved certificate programs and more than sixty courses are available via print-base, videotape or e-mail/Internet.

Cambrian College Distance Education: The Distance Education Department of Cambrian College offers a wide variety of programs via Independent Learning, teleconferencing, and Internet technology.

Penn State Continuing and Distance Education (C & DE)

University of Wisconsin—Extension

University of Louisville Distance Education

University of Idaho: As part of the College of Engineering, the Engineering Outreach program uses videotape, microwave, satellite, and video-conferencing technology to deliver graduate-level courses to distant students. Established in 1975, the program has grown into one of the top providers of graduate off-campus engineering programs, delivering seventy courses per semester to over 400 students in 300 locations.

Indiana University Distance Learning

Center for Distance Education

University of Phoenix: Online Degree Program: The University of Phoenix Online Campus offers working adults wishing to earn a graduate or undergraduate degree in business, management, or technology the unparalleled convenience and flexibility of commuting to class by modem.

The Home Education Network (THEN): THEN offers distance learning on-line education through Internet courses in business management, organizational behavior, risk management, accounting, screenwriting, fiction writing, test preparation, and teacher certification. THEN on-line courseware is offered in conjunction with the UCLA Extension University. At-home study courses can be completed on-line or through employers and an affiliated Intranet training and distance education network.

Deakin University: The mission of Deakin University is to offer innovative and flexible high-quality courses that are informed by current scholarship, research, and professional practice to all of its students, whether studying on campus, in the workplace, or at home.

Monash Distance Education Centre: Monash University offers by distance education sixty fully accredited award courses, ranging from Associate Diplomas to Master Degrees. It also offers over 50 semester units for the Open Learning Agency of Australia (OLAA).

University of Southern Queensland—Distance Education Centre

Université Sains Malaysia (USM): The USM was established in 1969 to offer courses tailored to suit the demands of the home-based adult learner. It is a mixed-mode institution offering both face-to-face instruction and distance education. The USM is unique among the Distance Teaching Institutions of the Association of South East Asian Nations region in that it is one of the very few conventional dual-mode universities having such a program.

OPEN AND DISTANCE LEARNING INSTITUTIONS

Athabasca University: Canada's open university, Athabasca University is dedicated to the removal of barriers that traditionally restrict access to and success in university-level studies and to increasing equality of educational opportunity for all adult Canadians regardless of their geographical location or prior academic credentials.

Commonwealth of Learning (COL): COL is an international organization established by Commonwealth Governments in September 1988. Headquartered in Vancouver, it serves to create and widen access to education and to improve its quality, utilizing distance education techniques and associated communications technologies to meet the particular requirements of member countries.

The Open Learning Agency (OLA): OLA is based in Burnaby, British Columbia. OLA is a fully accredited, publicly funded educational organization and provides a wide range of formal and informal educational and training opportunities for learners around the world. Through its Open University it has established collaborative bachelor programs in British Columbia. OLA also maintains a list of distance education resources.

Fern Universität: This is an autonomous institution and an integral part of the existing and recognized university system, with equal rights and functions in teaching and research and offering high-quality university study programs.

The Consorzio per l'Università a Distanza (CUD): The CUD was founded in 1984 to set up a distance teaching university system in Italy. The CUD is a consortium of Italian multinational companies, universities, and semi-governmental organizations. It is one of the newest members of EADTU developing a distinctive, distance education model. The CUD was established to create a new model for a distance teaching university, which would cater to the special needs of the Italian education system. In Italy, university education is free and prestigious and universities are scattered throughout the country.

Open University UK (OU): OU is Britain's largest and most innovative university. Founded by Royal Charter in 1969, it has grown rapidly both in student numbers and range of courses. There are professional development programs in management, education, health and social welfare, manufacturing, and computer applications, as well as self-contained study packs.

National Extension College (NEC): NEC has been offering home study courses with tutor support and learning resources for colleges and training organizations for over 30 years. Their mission statement is to "provide learning resources and opportunities to enable individuals to meet their vocational and personal goals."

Commonwealth Open University (COU): Commonwealth Open University, Ltd. is an international institution registered and established in the British Virgin Islands (U.K.). COU provides adult continuing education. It was developed to meet the needs of adults by offering nonresident degree and other programs on an international basis.

The Open University of Israel: The Open University is a distance education university designed to offer academic studies to students throughout Israel. Its home study method allows students all over the country to pursue a higher education, whenever and wherever convenient, without interfering with their other personal and vocational obligations.

Open Learning Foundation: The Foundation was set up in 1990 by a group of universities. It now has twenty-nine members, including twenty-five British universities, which together enroll about 400,000 students. The Foundation provides practical support and advice to its member institutions on new approaches to teaching and learning. It acts as a development agency for open learning in higher education.

Open University of the Netherlands

Flander's EuroStudy Centre Open University

East-Hungarian Regional Centre of Distance Education

Open Learning Australia (OLA): OLA is an innovative education venture offering all Australians, regardless of age, location, or educational qualifications, the opportunity to study university and TAFE units leading to diplomas, degrees, and other qualifications.

American Center for the Study of Distance Education (ACSDE): ACSDE seeks to promote distance education research, study, scholarship, and teaching and to serve as a clearinghouse for the dissemination of knowledge about distance education.

City University: City University is a private, nonprofit institution of higher education based in Bellevue, Washington. Founded more than two decades ago, the University operates with the mission of making education available to all who desire it.

Heritage OnLine: "Heritage OnLine Courses for K–12 Educators" offer 400/500-level continuing education courses from the Heritage Institute that integrate use of the Internet into the K–12 curriculum. Course credit is granted by Antioch University.

Rochester Institute of Technology (RIT)—Distance Learning: Rochester Institute of Technology is a leader in education offering interactive distance learning programs based on flexible and affordable technology. Today, more than 3,000 students across the United States and overseas enroll each year in RIT's distance learning programs.

IMLearn: IMLearn (Interactive Multimedia Learning Technologies, Inc.) is a company that develops, markets, and manages a unique and highly effective form of distance education for organizations and teaching institutions that need to educate people over a wide geographic area. Students learn from their homes or offices using a combination of network-TV-quality videotaped presentations, interactive CD-ROM exercises, and a very intensive Internet on-line component.

Universidad Estatal a Distancia (UNED)

Universidad Nacional de Educación a Distancia, Costa Rica

Universidad Nacional Abierta, Venezuela

Universidad Abierta y a Distancia, Columbia

Sukhothai Thammathirat Open University (STOU), Nonthaburi, Thailand: As an open university, STOU adheres to the principle of lifelong education, aims at improving the quality of life of the public in general, seeks to increase the educational qualifications of working people, and strives to expand educational opportunities for secondary school graduates in response to the needs of individuals and society. To fulfill these goals, the University has established a distance teaching system that employs correspondence media, radio and television programs, and other methods that enable students to study on their own without having to enter a conventional classroom.

Allama Iqbal Open University (AIOU) Pakistan: AIOU is the oldest distance teaching institution in South Asia. Adhering to national educational objectives and local needs, AIOU provides a variety of teacher education programs, programs of particular interest to women, as well as vocational and agricultural education.

Open Learning Institute of Hong Kong: The Institute was established by the Hong Kong government in 1989. Two characteristics set it apart from other conventional tertiary institutions: It is "open," and it is the first institution in Hong Kong to provide higher education mainly through distance learning.

University of South Africa: This is one of the largest distance teaching universities in the world. It affords equal education and employment opportunities to qualified persons regardless of race, color, religion, gender, national origin, age, handicap, ancestry, place of birth, marital status, political affiliation, or domicile.

University of Cape Town

VIRTUAL CAMPUSES

Virtual-U: Virtual-U at Simon Fraser University is a framework for providing on-line educational resources by developing intelligent software tools that enable the instructor to organize learning where student interaction is via computers in the students' business, educational, or home environments.

Virtual Online University: Virtual Online University, Inc., is a nonprofit corporation offering a novel and effective approach to academic excellence, professional development, and lifelong learning.

University Online (UOL): University Online, Inc. is in the business of serving the needs of educational institutions and corporate campuses that wish to put their programs on-line with seamless integration into the World Wide Web. Meeting the needs of the institutions, UOL will provide access to vast library of interactive on-line courses in business, technology, sciences, language arts, and basic skills.

The Internet University: This site has almost 1,000 individual pages of information. It is the most comprehensive source of information about on-line college courses available on the Internet today. This is the companion site for the book The Internet University published by Cape Software and is provided by the publisher as a service to the educational and Internet communities.

Louisiana College Virtual Campus: LC Online is a Louisiana College program that offers courses for college credit via the Internet. Through a combination of taped lectures and on-line resources, Louisiana College gives qualified nontraditional students an opportunity to obtain a college education while they pursue their normal work and family responsibilities.

University of Maryland University College (UMUC): UMUC offers a bachelor's degree at a distance in eight career-related specializations including computer and information science and management. Selected graduate courses are also available. Enrollment is open to U.S. citizens worldwide.

Spectrum Virtual University: Spectrum was one of the first to develop and offer interactive courses by modem. In the mid-1980s the nonprofit organization pioneered virtual workshops on creative writing, drug education, and prevention of child abuse. Today Spectrum is reaching a global audience through the World Wide Web and by electronic mail.

The Virtual Global College: The Virtual Global College was started in 1995 to offer information, education, and training programs to people around the world who have access to the Internet.

CyberCampus Ontario: CyberCampus is a computer-based virtual campus existing on the Internet with the primary purpose of supporting the education system in learning about information technology, in helping teachers and students use information technology for education, and ultimately in enhancing Ontario's global competitiveness in the educational technology field.

Christopher Newport University Online: Christopher Newport University is a comprehensive, coeducational, state-supported institution within Virginia's public university system. The University is organized and instruction is provided to take into consideration the lifelong learning interests and needs of a largely part-time and mobile student body.

CyberEd University: CyberEd offers a selection of standard, full-credit University courses to the global audience of the WWW through the UMass Dartmouth Division of Continuing Education. Their objective is to create a distance learning environment that rivals the traditional classroom environment in the quality and content of the learning experience.

Edith Cowan University Virtual Campus Australia (ECU)

DISTANCE LEARNING NETWORKS

TéléÉducation NB TeleEducation: This is a network of community learning centers in the province of New Brunswick, Canada. These "electronic classrooms," established in partnership with local communities, educational institutions, and industry, are outfitted with specialized equipment both for receiving and delivering courses. TéléÉducation NB TeleEducation is also home to an extensive list of distance learning resources.

Canada's SchoolNet: This is a cooperative initiative of Canada's provincial, territorial, and federal governments, educators, universities and colleges, and industry. It aims to link all of Canada's 16,000-plus schools to the electronic highway.

Northern Finland Learning Network (NOFNET): NOFNET aims mainly in every way to support the development of the teaching environment in northern Finland by cooperation across the boundaries of various institutes of education and by offering more efficient, more versatile, and better-quality education.

EuroStudy Centres: The EuroStudy Centre network was launched by the European Union on November 30, 1994, with thirty-six Centres. Each Centre provides information and services about higher education courses available through flexible learning packages.

NetLinkS: Based in the Department of Information Studies at the University of Sheffield, the NetLinkS project aims to encourage the development of networked learner support (NLS) by providing awareness-raising and professional development activities and resources. NetLinkS is a Training and Awareness project supported by the Joint Information Systems Committee of the Higher Education Funding Council of England, as part of its Electronic Libraries program.

C-Net: C-Net is a comprehensive communications network that links Canadians to each other and to the world. C-Net is maintained by Community Access Canada, an Industry Canada initiative to Support Public Access to Connectivity through Education (Cspace).

CANARIE INC. WWW: This is a nonprofit corporation established on March 5, 1993. It has evolved out of the efforts of more than 200 people from fifty-six organizations representing Canada's research, university, business, and government communities. Their efforts, over a 4-year period, developed the 7-year multiphase Business Plan, which defined a program to improve Canada's overall competitiveness in the Information Age.

The Community Learning Network (CLN): The CLN is a province-wide K–12 educational network that is operated and maintained by the Ministry of Education in British Columbia, Canada.

Contact North/Contact Nord: This is a distance education network that provides students access to a wide range of courses in their own communities. High school, college, university, and general interest courses are offered at more than 150 Contact North/Contact Nord sites throughout northern Ontario, Canada.

Mind Extension University (ME/U): ME/U is a cable TV network dedicated to distance education that is available to over 25 million households in more than 8,500 communities. The network connects people to courses and degree programs offered by over thirty regionally accredited universities and education providers plus education-related services. (Appendix H describes a program on ME/U.)

The Wisconsin Overlay Network for Distance Education Resources (WONDER): WONDER is a digital, fiber optic–based, two-way interactive television system connecting nine higher education sites in central Wisconsin.

Distance Learning Resource Network (DLRN): The Distance Learning Resource Network is a Far West Laboratory for Educational Research and Development (FWL) project, established through the Star Schools Dissemination Project Funding. DLRN disseminates information from and for educators, administrators, policy makers, and parents interested in the effective implementation of distance education.

Georgia Statewide Academic and Medical System: This is the largest and most comprehensive distance learning and healthcare network in the world. Through advanced telecommunications technology, people in up to eight locations can see and speak with each other regardless of geographic distance.

Mid-Atlantic Network for Teaching Learning Enterprises (MANTLE): The purpose of MANTLE is to create a forum for sharing and disseminating knowledge about distance education with a particular focus on the professional development of educators engaged in this type of instruction. MANTLE's objective is to promote the development and implementation of distance education in the mid-Atlantic region of the United States.

Queensland Open Learning Network (QOLN): QOLN empowers individuals and organizations to access and provide education and training opportunities. The Network consists of over forty Open Learning Centres throughout Queensland, Australia.

Africa Growth Network: The Africa Growth Network is a distance learning organization delivering training and education programs via satellite.

Appendix H

Teaching with Technology at One Institution of Higher Education

ABOUT THE EDUCATIONAL TECHNOLOGY LEADERSHIP (ETL) PROGRAM

Welcome Message from Bill Lynch, Ph.D., Program Director (Note to Students–italics show links to other "pages")

The Educational Technology Leadership (ETL) program is a full Master's degree offered through Jones Education Communications (JEC) College Connection. All courses in the program are taught off-campus and involve instructional television and online computer networks. You can choose to take individual courses or enroll as a degree student. In the latter case, you must satisfy the graduate admission standards of George Washington University.

All courses are taught by the full and part-time faculty of the George Washington University. Even though JEC administers the program, your course credits and degree are awarded by GWU and are no different than those awarded to on-campus students.

There are hundreds of students across the country who have taken ETL courses or are enrolled in the program (see the web *sites* they have created). Most of these students have full-time jobs as teachers, educational administrators, media coordinators, instructional developers, active duty military, or training specialists. (At the time of this writing, 340 students are enrolled.) One of the strengths of the program is that you will have an opportunity for extensive interaction with your fellow students via computer email and a chance to share your learning experiences with other educational professionals around the country.

REQUIREMENTS

As of Fall, 1997, students should have at minimum:

- An IBM-type 386, or better (be sure to see the IBM Note below), or a comparable Macintosh computer running system software version 7.1, or higher.
- 30 megabytes available storage space, or more (this need may vary greatly from student to student and will depend upon a number of individual factors).
- A modern of 28.8 baud rate, or higher.
- A printer.
- A color monitor (with appropriate graphics card).
- A CD-ROM D drive.

Required

- A word processing package.
- E-mail software that supports file attachments (Eudora Lite shareware is adequate for current ETL program needs).
- WWW browser that is configured to recognize PDF format (Netscape 3.0 is probably the most commonly used by our students—configuration instructions are available). To get the maximum benefit from program materials, your browser also should have "plug-ins" to run audio and video clips, but these are not presently a requirement.
- Adobe Acrobat Exchange version 3.0—Note that the free Acrobat Reader, alone, is not sufficient/ Read the PDF Note, below, carefully.
- Other software may be required by the Instructor of Record for a specific course.

(PDF Note: The list price for this software is far higher than the educational discount price-which is about the same as a typical graduate-level textbook. While you may purchase this software wherever you wish, we recommend that you check with ETL Tech Support soon after classes have begun to see if they can direct you to a vendor that offers the educational discount. Students who register through JEC will be given information about purchasing Adobe Acrobat Exchange at the educational discount price. It can also be downloaded free of charge, but this version is not quite sufficient.)

Suggested, But Not Required for All Courses:

- Graphics utilities software
- File Transfer Protocol (FTP) software (e.g., Fetch)
- Telnet capability

Distance Learning in the ETL Program

Learning at a distance is a difficult undertaking that requires considerable self-discipline and determination. You will need to create your own learning schedule and environment. Most students find it desirable to set aside a regular block of time to study (e.g., a few hours in the morning, after dinner, or weekends) which is relatively free of distractions.

Many students find it helpful to make notes while watching the television programs and videotapes to summarize the key ideas. While most students prefer to study alone, some individuals watch the program with their families or colleagues in order to create opportunities for discussion of the content.

There is no one approach to distance learning that works for everyone. We suggest that you experiment with different approaches to distance learning to discover what works best for you.

Locating Resources

Another way in which distance education is different from traditional on-campus study is that you must take more responsibility for finding the resources needed for learning. You will need to identify local libraries, individuals, and facilities which are good sources for the literature, materials or equipment needed for courses. It is strongly recommended that you join at least one professional organization relevant to your specific interests since it will provide you with periodicals and regional/national conferences where you can get up-to-date information. This will not only help you be more successful in your ETL classes, but will also contribute to your long- term career development. Course syllabi, videotape segments, and the ETL web site provide you with more details on relevant organizations.

Do not overlook the opportunities for acquiring information and assistance from your classmates via the internet. In every class you will have a chance to interact electronically with individuals from all over the country who represent a diverse range of educational professionals and institutions/organizations. This represents a tremendous resource that you should take advantage of as much as possible. In addition, you may be able to find useful information online by accessing databases through the internet. The ETL website in particular provides access to many types of online resources.

One of the most important leadership skills that we hope you will obtain from the ETL program is the ability to seek out and find information or resources you need on a local, regional, or national basis.

Keeping Up

The ETL program provides you with a lot of flexibility in terms of when and where you learn. However, you do need to keep up with the course materials (whether delivered via the Internet, television, or videotape) and online assignments. While students have a great deal of flexibility for scheduling when they work and study, they are expected to meet all scheduled assignment deadlines. In addition to keeping up with the weekly course materials, regular online participation is *required* for all ETL courses. This means that you must sign on at least every 2-3 days. If you will be away for an extensive period, you will need to make arrangements to receive the course materials and to have online access. This may mean having videotapes forwarded to you and/or taking along a laptop computer (or using a local computer).

Due dates for assignments are specified in the course syllabus or via online messages. Be sure that you know these due dates at the beginning of a course. If there is a problem that prevents you from submitting an assignment on time, send a message to your section leader or instructor explaining the situation and asking for a time extension. Failure to hand in assignments by their due dates without having asked for and been granted an extension of the due date may result in a grade of zero on the assignment.

Guidelines for Completing and Submitting Assignments

Graded assignments for the ETL Program generally take one of three forms:

- Online Assignments
- Special Projects
- Papers

Online Assignments:

Online assignments are the most common of the three. They are usually based on specific topics that are scheduled (see the syllabus) throughout the semester. Online assignments are submitted in the same manner as class discussion contributions. In other words, they are posted to NetForum, where others in the class may see them. One of the key features of submitting online assignments is that the subject line of that message should contain the coded identity of the student and the assignment. This special format is almost identical to the one discussed-later in this document—in the section on PDF files. The one exception is that online assignments should be labeled OL* (where * = the assignment number) Example: John Smith's fourth online assignment would be labeled SMITJOL4

Special Projects:
Some ETL courses require special projects in which materials, such as a video tape or a software application, are required (usually as the final project). In cases where such a special project is a course requirement, students will be told how and where to ship the completed project materials.

Papers:
Most courses in the ETL program require major written assignments and project reports which are sent electronically to the section leader (if there is one) or instructor (if it is a single-section class) for grading and feedback. Unless otherwise stated, formal papers will be submitted in Acrobat PDF format. This format is discussed in detail below.

Here are some general guidelines to follow in completing and submitting your work:

Focus:
Before starting work on the assignment, read the instructions carefully to be sure that you understand what is expected. Unless instructed otherwise, always try to relate your answer to your own educational setting and experience. Try to be critical in your response; analyze the strengths and weaknesses of whatever you are writing about.

Organization & Writing:
Divide your answer into sections with a heading corresponding to each major idea or element. Put a blank line between each section. Be concise in your answers. There are never extra points for being long-winded and in fact you may lose points for rambling answers.

Literature Reviews:
Most major assignments require that you find and read articles about specific aspects of educational technology and leadership. When reviewing literature, try to read journals or technical magazines rather than general publications. You can locate suitable literature in libraries, from colleagues, and via online sources (e.g., WWW). Note that the *Educational Technology* magazine CD-ROM is available to all ETL students, as well.

Submitting work:
Formal Papers (not online assignments)
Beginning with the Spring, 1997, semester, the standard method for submit-

ting formal written assignments for the ETL Program is by sending it as an Adobe Acrobat PDF file attached to a mail message to your SL or Instructor. (A professor may always supercede these standards with specific directions for a given assignment).

Why use PDF?

PDF files begin as documents created with your word processor or other software application and then are converted to Programmable-Document-Format (PDF) by using Adobe's Acrobat software. The PDF file is then ATTACHED TO an e-mail message and sent to the Instructor or SL (as specified). Because PDF files can be created using Adobe Acrobat installed to most Mac or Windows software, and because it can include enriched text formatting, illustrations, graphics, and because it can be read by anyone with the appropriate Acrobat software, this is an exciting step forward for our program. It allows students to prepare graduate-level materials using a wide variety of application software packages, convert them to a format that can be viewed by all as if it were the original document, submitted electronically, and returned via the same means to the student, who can read attached comments in "post-it" form that were placed there by the Instructor or SL.

More information about obtaining (at substantial educational discount) and using Acrobat software will be provided to our students on a semester-to-semester basis.

Problems:

If you are having a problem completing an assignment or project on time, or having difficulty transferring it as a PDF document, let your section leader or instructor know. They can grant you a short extension of the due date while you are getting technical assistance.

Please do not ask your SL to help you with technical problems or questions (they can only pass them on to tech support). Refer problems and questions directly, and immediately, to *etltech@www. gwu. edu*. This will assure that you get the fastest response. Additional information about the use of NetForum and Acrobat can also be found on the *ETLTECH* web pages. Check it out!

Some Misconceptions about Online Education

Some Notes from Greg Kearsley

People who have little or no experience with online learning or teaching tend to harbor some misconceptions (which are quickly cleared up after actual participation in online classes). The most common misconception is that online classes will be fairly sterile and impersonal. But once a person starts to interact with other group members, they quickly discover that an online learning environment can be a wonderful learning experience and highly personal.

Another common misconception is that online classes will be easy—easier than conventional classes. But almost all participants report that they find online classes much more work—and much more rewarding—than traditional courses they have taken. Again, this has to do with the amount of thought about the subject matter that results from online discussions. Such classes also require the self-discipline to do the preparation required for online participation and activities—homework is homework, whether online or offline!

Finally it should be mentioned that almost any form of assessment or evaluation is possible with online classes. You can do traditional quizzes or tests with multiple choice questions or problems to be solved if you want; they can even be done with time limits. However, it seems that assignments and projects that involve critical thinking, creativity, problem-solving and group discussion/interaction are more appropriate for online education. Portfolio methods that involve journals or work samples are also ideal for computer mediated communication (CMC) especially when the web is used since they can include multimedia components.

A Guide to Online Education

The changes in the social dynamic of the classroom brought about by online education are pretty profound. Online classes emphasize social interaction among the participants and nullify the authoritarian role of the teacher or subject matter expert. People need to get used to working in online teams/groups. Teachers must get used to fulfilling the role of facilitator/moderator in which they have to cultivate both personal and group participation. And assessment techniques need to move away from testing to projects, assignments, and case studies.

Everyone who experiences online education realizes that this is the beginning of a new paradigm for learning and teaching. Welcome to the 21st century! And enjoy your journeys along the information highway.

BIBLIOGRAPHY (STUDENTS MAY CLICK ON EACH LISTING FOR ACCESS at http://www.gwu.edu/~etL)

Anderson, T. (1996). The virtual conference: Extending professional education in cyberspace. Intl J. Educ. Telecommunications, 2(2/3), 121–135. See *ICDE 95 Online Conference.*

Angell, D. & Heslop, B. (1994). The Elements or E-mail Style. Reading, MA: Addison-Wesley.

Berge, Z. (1996). *Example case studies in Post-secondary Online Teaching.*

Berge, Z. (1995). *The Role of the Online Instructor/Facilitator*

Berge, Z. & Collins, M. (1995). Computer Mediated Communication and the Online Classroom (Vols I-III). Cresskill, NJ: Hampton Press.

Berge, Z. & Collins, M. (1996). Wired Together: The Online K-12 Classroom. Cresskill, NJ: Hampton Press.

Campbell, D. & Campbell, M. (1995). The Student's Guide to Doing Research on the Internet. Reading, MA: Addison-Wesley.

Collis, B. et al. (1995). *Online Learning & Distance Ed papers* (Univ Twente).

Collis, B. (1996). Tele-Learning in a Digital World. International Thomson Computer Press. Duchastel, P. (1996). *Web-Based Learning* (numerous articles)

Eastmond, D.V. (1995). Alone But Together. Adult Distance Study Through Computer Conferencing. Cresskill, NJ: Hampton Press.

Harasim, L. (1990). Online Education: Perspectives on a New Environment. NY: Praeger.

Harasim, L. (1993). Global Networks: Computers and International Communication. Cambridge: MIT Press.

Harasim, L., Hiltz, S.R., Teles, L. & Turoff, M. (1995). Learning Networks: A Field Guide to Teaching and Learning Online. Cambridge, MA: MIT Press.

Hiltz, S.R. (1995). *Impacts of College-Level Courses Via Asynchronous Learning Networks: Focus on the Learner.*

Hiltz, S.R. (1994). The Virtual Classroom: Learning Without Limits via Computer Networks. Norwood, NJ: Ablex.

Hiltz, S.R. (1993). The Network Nation: Human Communication via Computer. (Revised Edition). Cambridge, MA: MIT Press.

Jones, S.6. (1995). Cybersociety. Newbury Park, CA: Sage.

Kaye, A. (1992). Collaborative Learning Through Computer Conferencing. NY: Springer-Verlag.

Kearsley, G., Lynch, B. & Wizer, D. (1995). *The Effectiveness and Impact of Computer Conferencing in Graduate Education*

Khan, B. (1997). *Web-based Instruction.* Englewood Cliffs, NJ: Ed Tech Publications.

Kilian, C. (1996) *"Why teach online?"* (Community College Online conference presentation)

McManus, T. (1995) *"Delivering instruction on the web"* Miller, S. (1996). Civilizing Cyberspace. Reading, MA: Addison-Wesley.

Rheingold, H. (1993). The Virtual Community. Reading, MA: Addison-Wesley.

Riel, M. & Levin, J. (1990). Building electronic communities: Success and failure in computer networking. Instructional Science, 19, 145-169.

Sproul, L. & Kiesler, S. (1991). Connections: New Ways of Working in the Networked Organization. Cambridge, MA: MIT Press.

Waggonner, M.D. (1992). Empowering Networks: Computer Conferencing in Education. Englewood Cliffs, NJ: Educational Technology Press.

Index